RECORDS OF CHRISTIANITY

Volume II

D0914217

RECORDS OF
CHRISTIANITY

VOLUME II
Christendom

David Ayerst & A. S. T. Fisher

BASIL BLACKWELL

OXFORD

Set by the
Northumberland Press Ltd, Gateshead
Made and printed in Great Britain
by Billings Ltd, Guildford

CONTENTS

483878

CHAPTER THREE
THE CHRISTIAN EAST:
HOLY WISDOM, HUMAN FOLLY

CHAPTER FOUR
ISLAM AND CHRISTIANITY

CHAPTER FIVE
PILGRIMS AND CRUSADERS

CHAPTER SIX
CLUNY AND CITEAUX

Contents

Contents

PLATES

To be found between pp. 158–159

1 The monastery on the Skellig, off the coast of Kerry, Republic of Ireland.
2 Opening words of St. John's Gospel from the Lindisfarne Gospels with Anglo-Saxon translation of the Latin between the lines. A page from the M.S. of *c*.700 in the British Museum.
3 Constantine and Justinian presenting models of their city and church to Christ. The mosaic cn the south door of St. Sophia, consecrated in 538.
4 The Crusader castle of Krak des Chevaliers, Syria.
5 The Cistercian Fountains Abbey, Yorkshire. Compare the plan on p. 152.
6 'Here is Hell and the angel who shuts the door.' The mouth of Hell from the Winchester Psalter, *c*.1160.
7 Mary as the Queen of Heaven with the infant Christ over the 13th-century west front of Notre Dame Cathedral, Paris.
8 Bishop Adalbert receives his crozier from the Emperor Otto, Bronze door of Gnesen, Germany.

MAPS

DRAWINGS

INTRODUCTION

The first volume ended with the death of Augustine; this starts with the baptism of Clovis in 496 and carries on the story of Christianity in the words of contemporary writers to the collapse of the medieval synthesis eight centuries later. In the field of significant events we end with the captivity of Pope Boniface VIII in 1302, but we have drawn freely on the fourteenth century for illustrative material because it was many years before men realized that the world would never be the same again.

We still worship in churches built by men whose writings we have used. We are often architecturally knowledgeable about their churches, but more often than not their minds are a closed book to us. What were they really like? The purpose of this anthology is to give them a chance to tell us this. We shall find that in spite of the vast difference between their material circumstances and ours and between their knowledge of the universe and ours, their faith is our faith. If in these pages there is much evidence of ignorance, superstition, and brutality, there is also abundance of heroic devotion and a spiritual sensitivity often beyond our reach. Francis Thompson wrote of Shelley, 'He is gold-dusty from tumbling among the stars. The universe is his box of toys.' Readers will find here men of whom also this praise is true. We have tried to keep a balance.

We have drawn on many great men—Dante and Thomas Aquinas, Bede and Alfred the Great, Francis of Assisi and Peter Abelard to name only a few whose names are still household words. But there is also a general's letter to his wife written from the front in the First Crusade and a private soldier's account of how, in spite of the defeat of the Third Crusade, he was able to visit Jerusalem before he came home. Readers will hear much nonsense and more good sense as Caesarius of Heisterbach instructs his novices. They can listen to a debate in the Althing about whether Iceland should adopt Christianity and, if so, on what terms. They can trace in the Koran Islam's blood-relationship with Christianity and its distance from it.

They may travel to China at a time when it seemed possible that a Christian Asia would be called into existence to redress the balance of the lost heartland of the Christian Middle East.

This wide variety shows that this is not a book for the specialist. There is theology in it, but it is not a theological source book. There is politics in it because of course there had to be—Christendom is a political as well as a religious conception. But it is not a political history. Like the first volume, 'The Church in the Roman Empire', this book is intended for the general reader with an interest in religion, for the man in the pew, the parson in his study, the teacher in his classroom.

The separate indexes of persons and subjects will enable readers with a general knowledge of the eight centuries to find easily the passage that meets their need or takes their fancy. But those who start without this advantage may find it useful to use the book in the order in which it is printed with the help of the introductions and notes to the various chapters. This is especially true because eight centuries is a long time and five thousand miles a great distance. When for Christians it was high noon in Constantinople it was hardly dawn in Sweden. To understand any particular extract it is necessary to fix its position in time and place. This is the purpose of the editorial matter. The illustrations are an important and integral part of the evidence—as much so as the extracts. We intend no disrespect to holy men and women by refusing them the title 'Saint', a status decided after death, when we are writing of them in their life-time.

A word is needed about the translations. Some medieval Latin writing is exquisite. We have tried to match this fineness in English by using the translations of writers such as William Crashaw, Swinburne, and Helen Waddell. We have included some passages from English vernacular writers of the middle ages, simplified only enough to make them intelligible to modern readers. Some of these passages are original compositions—the Dream of the Rood, for instance, and Chaucer's Good Parson. Others are translations from other languages, such as Alfred the Great's version of Gregory the Great's 'Pastoral Care', and Caxton's of Boethius and of Ramon Lull. Why use a translation separated by several centuries from the original and by even more from us? We have done this because, although not contemporary in date, they are, we feel, nearer in spirit to the originals than we can be. And they are themselves fine English.

But undeniably much medieval Latin is dog Latin, even mongrel dog Latin. A literal translation often makes hard, sometimes even almost unintelligible reading. This is partly because of the style and partly because of technicalities which are understood only by specialist readers. We have therefore felt ourselves free to produce versions which we hope will be easy reading while conveying the sense of the original writer, though not always in all his own exact words.

We are very grateful to those writers, living and dead, on whose work we have drawn. We have tried, as the Acknowledgements show, to secure the permission of all copyright holders, and we apologize to any whom we have overlooked or been unable to trace.

ACKNOWLEDGEMENTS

The compilers and publishers thank the following for permission to reproduce copyright and other material (the numbers refer to the extracts):

Prof. James Carney (Séamus O'Ceithearnaigh) for extracts from *Early Irish Poetry*, Cork, 1965, 2.7, 2.12: Chatto and Windus and the Literary Estate of Isaac Gollancz for passages from A. J. Grant, *Einhard's Life of Charlemagne*, 14.1: Columbia University for extracts from F. J. Tschan, *Halmod's Chronicle of the Slavs*, 2.32, P. K. Hatti, *Usamah ibn-Munqidh's Memoirs*, 5.15, and M. J. Hubert, *The Crusade of Richard Lionheart*, 5.19: Constable for passages from Helen Waddell, *Beasts and Saints*, 2.8, *Mediaeval Latin Lyrics*, 1.7, 8.8, *Peter Abelard*, 8.7, *Wandering Scholars*, 1.5: Cornell University for extracts from Ari Thorgilsson, *Book of the Icelanders*, 2.31: Dr. Joan Evans for extracts from *Monastic Life at Cluny*, 5.1, 2, 6.1, 6, 7: T. Gilby, *St. Thomas Aquinas: Theological Texts*, 8.15: Manchester University Press for a passage from J. R. H. Moorman, *Sources for the Life of St. Francis of Assisi*, 7.1: Penguin Books for an extract from Barbara Reynolds, *Dante's La Vita Nuova*, 5.4: Routledge and Kegan Paul for a passage from F. A. Wright's translation of Liutptand of Cremona's *Historia Ottonis*, 1930, 14.5, and to the same publishers and Rabbi David Goldstein for two excerpts from *Littman Library of Jewish Civilisation*, 12.11: Sheed and Ward for extracts from G. P. Fedotov, *A Treasury of Russian Spirituality*, 13.5, 6: The S.C.M. for extracts from Wilson Cash, *Christendom and Islam*, 4.17, 18, 19, 21, 22: Thomist Press for a passage from C. M. Hoinacki, *Dominicana*, 7.22: Collins and Eleanor Duckett for a passage from *Wandering Saints*, 2.11.

CHAPTER ONE

DARKNESS LIGHTENED

1.1 The Baptism of Clovis

The first volume of *Records of Christianity* ended with a death-bed. This begins with a baptism. When Augustine died, the great creative period of early Christian history ended. Everything in the political scene pointed also to such a complete collapse of secular civilized society as would make the annihilation of the Christian church probable. The baptism with which this volume begins was of a cruel, calculating, brave and ferocious barbarian kinglet who was little changed by his Christian profession. As Gibbon put it: 'The savage conqueror of Gaul was incapable of examining the proofs of a religion which depends on ... historical evidence and speculative theology. He was still more incapable of feeling the mild influence of the gospel... As soon as Clovis had dismissed a synod of the Gallican church, he calmly assassinated all the princes of the Merovingian race ' Yet the baptism of Clovis most improbably turned out to be the christening of a new world. This volume records how the Dark Ages grew up into and were, so to speak, confirmed as Christendom.

Most of the earlier barbarians who had overthrown settled Roman government in the West were already Christians before they seized power. But they were Arians, who refused to accept the doctrine of the Trinity with the full godhead of Christ. Their new and more civilized subjects were orthodox Catholics. There was estrangement and friction between rulers and ruled. Clovis and his Franks on the other hand were still pagan when they crossed the Rhine and conquered what is now northern France. But in 496 Clovis was baptized by a Catholic bishop into the Catholic faith. Unity of belief between rulers of Church and State was established. This unity was to be the distinguishing mark of the Christian Middle Ages.

There is no contemporary account of the baptism. The best is that given here from the History of the Franks by Gregory of Tours. Gregory belonged to a noble senatorial family; he was descended from one of the second-century martyrs of Lyons (see Volume I. pp. 73–84); an uncle was bishop of Clermont, a great-uncle had been bishop of Lyons. Gregory was not born until a generation and a half after the baptism of Clovis and he did not write about it until towards the end of his life—between eighty and ninety years after the event. But his account carries conviction partly because he was well placed to know what happened and partly because it is free of later embroideries.

Note how the Christian God is to Clovis a god of battles. He evoked a warrior's response. A writer of the next generation tells a story which is at least in character. When Clovis was told the story of the Passion he burst out 'If I and my Franks had been there I would have avenged him.'

Also note the mass baptism of the troops. A soldier naturally followed his lord in religion as in war.

THE BAPTISM OF CLOVIS 496

Clotild had previously made several efforts to convert her husband Clovis, king of the Franks, who was a pagan. He had agreed to allow their child to be baptized, but when the boy died he would have nothing more to do with Christianity.

Queen Clotild did not stop urging the king to accept the true God and give up his idols. But she had no success until he was engaged in a war with the Alemanni. In the battle the army of Clovis suffered heavy casualties and was on the point of being utterly routed. The king saw what was happening and felt his conscience prick him. He looked up to heaven with tears in his eyes and said, 'Jesus Christ, Clotild says you are the son of the living God. You are said to help those in distress and to grant victory to those who pin their hope on you. I appeal in all sincerity to you for your splendid help. If you grant me victory over these enemies of mine and the result confirms the power that your worshippers claim to have experienced, I will believe in you and be baptized in your name. I now call on you; I am eager to believe in you, if only I may be rescued from the hands of my adversaries. I have called on my own gods, but it is clear that they have given up helping me; and so I think they have no power since they do not come to rescue their servants.' As Clovis spoke the Alemanni turned tail and began to flee. Their king was killed and they surrendered.

[Clovis went home and told Clotild what had happened. She sent for Remigius, bishop of Reims, who instructed Clovis in the Christian faith. The day of Clovis's baptism came.]

The streets were gay beneath coloured banners. The churches were decked in white. The baptistery was made ready. There the air was thick with clouds of smoke from the incense while scented candles glittered. From around the font the whole church was filled with a holy sweetness. The king began by asking the bishop for baptism. Like a new Constantine he stepped forward to the water to wash away the foul stains from his past. As he went into the water to be baptized the saintly bishop addressed him in words full of eloquence: 'Meekly bow your proud head, adore what you have burned, burn what you adored.' So the king, professing faith in Almighty God, three in one, was baptized in the name of the Father, the Son, and the Holy Spirit, and annointed with the consecrated chrism with the Cross of Christ. More than 3,000 of his soldiers were baptized, and his sister Albofled was also baptized.... Another of his sisters, Lanthechild, was converted. She had been an Arian heretic. She also received the consecrated chrism, having confessed that the Son and the Holy Spirit are equal to the Father.

1.2–1.4 The dark world of Gregory of Tours

These three extracts all come from Gregory of Tours and relate events which happened in his own life-time either in Clermont Ferrand, where he had been born about 540, or near Tours of which he became the nineteenth bishop in 573. They give a reasonably accurate picture of the state of the church as Gregory saw it. One may hope that few bishops were as bad as Cautinus (1.2), but Chilperic, grandson of Clovis, was no worse than many other kings (1.3), even though few were as theologically minded. It is clear that, although the Franks were Catholics, Arianism still had its attractions for them (1.4).

1.2   A BISHOP 'WORSE THAN HEROD'   *c.* 565
Now Cautinus, after he became bishop (of Clermont) behaved so badly that all hated him. He was often so drunk that it took four men to carry him away from the dinner table. His excesses, which brought on epilepsy later, often occurred in public.

He was also so avaricious that he thought life not worth living unless he could get hold of some part of any property bordering his own. If the owner was someone of importance, he robbed him after a quarrel and abuse; if one of less account, he merely took what he wanted by force...

At that time a certain priest of Clermont, Anastasius, of free birth, held property by deed of Queen Clotilda of glorious memory. At several encounters the bishop had pressed him to give up the deeds and cede the land. Anastasius was slow in yielding to the will of the bishop, who would now coax him with kind words and then terrify him with threats. At last the bishop shamelessly ordered him to be brought to the city by force, detained, and, unless he surrendered the deeds, beaten up and starved to death. Anastasius resisted manfully and refused to surrender the deeds, saying he would rather waste away with hunger than leave his children destitute....

In the church of St. Cassius the Martyr was an ancient and obscure crypt which contained a great sarcophagus of Parian marble wherein the body of someone long dead had been placed. In this tomb on the dead body the living priest was laid and the cover stone replaced; guards were then posted at the door of the crypt. These men, satisfied that he was safe under the weight of stone, lit a fire—for it was winter—warmed some wine and fell asleep from its effect.

Then the priest like a new Jonah prayed unceasingly to the Lord from the inside of the sarcophagus as from the belly of hell. Now the tomb was spacious, as I have said, and though he could not turn his whole body he could move his hands freely. There came from the corpse, he would say, a deadly stench, which made not only his body shudder but his very vitals. By stopping his nose with his cloak he escaped the worst, but when, half-stifled, he moved it a little way off, the deathly smell invaded not only mouth and nose but, so to speak, the ears as well. . . .

To be brief, he stretched out his right hand and found a crowbar which at the closing of the sarcophagus had been left between the lid and the edge of the trough. Moving this little by little, by God's help, he found the stone could be shifted and when he had prized it open far enough to get his head through he was able more easily to widen the opening to let his body through. The shades of night were falling but had not yet overspread the sky. Anastasius found another door to the crypt, which was secured by the strongest bars and bolts but so ill-made that he could see between the planks. Bending his head to the gaps he saw a man passing by. He called to him in a low voice. The man heard, and immediately seized an axe and cut the planks to which the bolts were fixed, and opened a way for the prisoner, who went off in the darkness and hurried home after urging the man to say nothing of the affair to any one.

Anastasius entered his house, found the deeds Queen Clotilda had given him and took them to King Lothar and told him how he had been buried alive by the bishop. All present were astounded; they said not even Nero or Herod had committed such a crime as bury a man alive.

While they still spoke bishop Cautinus appeared before the king, but on the accusation of Anastasius he retreated, defeated and confounded. . . .

In Cautinus there was no holiness, nothing to admire. He was completely ignorant of books, whether sacred or secular. He was on friendly terms with the Jews and subservient to them, not for their conversion as a good shepherd should have been, but to buy their goods, which they sold to him at exorbitant prices while grossly flattering him.

1.3 SECOND GENERATION 'CHRISTIANS' *c.* 575

Chilperic was angered and sent his eldest son Theodobert (who, when he was once a prisoner of Sigibert, had sworn fealty to him), to invade Sigibert's cities, Tours, Poitiers, and the other places south of the Loire. Theodobert came to Poitiers and fought against Gundovald, whose army fled from the field; many of the people of the city were then massacred. He also burnt most of the places round Tours whose citizens, by a timely submission, saved the complete territory from devastation....

He burnt the churches, looted the sacred vessels, slaughtered the clergy, destroyed the monasteries, desecrated the nunneries and spread havoc everywhere. At that time there was a greater outcry in the churches than in the days of Diocletian's persecution.

And today we are still amazed. Why did such disasters fall upon them? Remember what their fathers did and consider what they themselves are doing now. After the preaching of the bishops, their fathers discarded their temples for churches: their sons daily plunder the churches. Fathers reverenced the bishops of the Lord and listened to their word: their sons not only refuse to listen to them, but even persecute them. The fathers enriched the monasteries and churches: the sons obliterate them.

1.4 KING CHILPERIC'S CHRISTOLOGY *c.* 578

About the same time, King Chilperic wrote a treatise on the holy Trinity, which, he said, should signify only God, not three distinct persons; it was unseemly that God should be called a person like a man of flesh. The Father, he affirmed, is the same as the Son, and the Holy Spirit is the same as the Father and the Son. This was the view of the prophets and patriarchs and the teaching of the law itself. He ordered his views to be read to me.

'It is my will that such shall be your faith and that of the other doctors of the Church.'

'Good king, abandon this belief,' I said, 'and follow what the apostles and later fathers of the Church have handed down to us, the doctrine of Hilary and Eusebius which you professed at your baptism.'

'It is clear that Hilary and Eusebius [Bishop of Vercelli, d. 371] are my bitter enemies,' said the king in anger.

'Neither God nor his saints are against you, as you should know.... But it was not the Father who was made man, nor the Holy Spirit, but the Son.... What you say about persons must be understood not in a bodily sense, but a spiritual. In these three persons is one glory, one eternity, one power.'

The king was furious and retorted, 'I will explain these matters to wiser men than you and they will agree with me.'

I answered, 'Any one who follows your proposals would not be a wise man, but a fool.'

At this he gnashed his teeth, but said no more.

The Poetry of Venantius Fortunatus

In this more than half savage world of the sixth century there lived a competent maker of well-turned occasional verse who became in the end one of the greatest of Christian Latin poets, the first still audible voice of the Middle Ages. Venantius Fortunatus was an almost precise contemporary of Gregory of Tours. He was born near Treviso and brought up in Ravenna which had long replaced Rome as the seat of secular government in Italy. There he contracted a disease of the eyes which was healed, so he believed, by a drop of oil from a lamp burning before the shrine of St. Martin in the church of St. Paul and St. John in that city.

He determined to express his gratitude by a pilgrimage to the parent shrine of St. Martin at Tours. He crossed the Alps, but for two years he lingered at the court of Sigebert, grandson of Clovis, at Metz. There he became a kind of poet laureate, but he shook himself free of the court, travelled on westwards, completed his pilgrimage, and finally decided to settle at Poitiers, some 75 miles south of Tours. There he celebrated his devotion to St. Martin by a long, ecstatic life of the saint in verse. Helen Waddell, paraphrasing, has caught its spirit in a paragraph of admiration:

> If St. Martin is going to heal a leper, never a leper so foul: the kiss that heals him has the waters of Jordan in it. The scene at the Emperor's Banquet spurs him to terrific efforts at upholstering; but at the vision of the Bridegroom the verse marches in a kind of carapace of precious stones. The doors of Zion set him off again: no renaissance tyrant, no Jew of Malta, gloried in jewels, their colour and sound, as Fortunatus did. In the fields, his thumb breaks off lilies and his nail snaps off roses, and he walks on violets and finally goes to sleep among all odours at once. At the last, the coat he has made for Martin is poor rough stuff, camelskin: it ought to be silk and gold thread, amethyst and white, with a crown of roses and lilies and precious stones. But anyhow, go, little book, and ask your pardon at Tours, and trot through Italy, with greetings from Fortunatus to his friends and genuflexions at the tombs of the saints,

till you come to Ravenna, to the church of St. Paul and St. John and the shrine of the Blessed Martin: and there abide. (Waddell: The Wandering Scholars p. 25.)

What kept Fortunatus at Poitiers, what changed the versifier into the poet was the friendship of Queen Radegunda and her adopted daughter, Agnes, the abbess of the convent which the queen had founded there. In their company something happened to the pleasant worldly man who enjoyed good living and good company, 'le poète épicurien, l'abbé gastronome,' (he never lost the taste for either). His imagination was kindled to a religious intensity which found expression in the two great Passiontide hymns still sung by millions year by year (1.5; 1.6; sample verses only). The occasion which gave rise to these hymns was the gift by the emperor at Constantinople to the church at Poitiers of a fragment of the True Cross. (For the earlier history of the cross as a Christian symbol see Vol. I, p. 131.) The second hymn is in the rhythm of the marching songs of the Roman army. Both were favourites of the Crusaders. Their spiritual insight and imagination are a devout man's counterpart to the aggressive outburst with which Clovis greeted the Passion story.

Queen Radegunda, to whom Fortunatus sent a poem with a bunch of flowers (1.7), was a German princess whom Lothair, son of Clovis, had carried off in a raid after killing her brother and her kinsmen. He married her, but before long she could stand him no longer and retired to Poitiers to her convent of the Holy Cross. Fortunatus was ordained priest at Poitiers and for the last ten years of his life or so he was its bishop.

1.5   VEXILLA REGIS PRODEUNT
The royal banners forward go;
The Cross shines forth in mystic glow;
Where he in flesh, our flesh who made,
Our sentence bore, our ransom paid...

Fulfilled is all that David told
In true prophetic song of old;
Amidst the nations, God, saith he,
Hath reigned and triumphed from the tree.

O Tree of beauty, Tree of light!
O Tree with royal purple dight!
Elect on whose triumphal breast
Those holy limbs should find their rest:

On whose dear arms, so widely flung,
The weight of this world's ransom hung:
The price of humankind to pay,
And spoil the spoiler of his prey.

1.6   PANGE LINGUA
          Sing, my tongue, the glorious battle,
            Sing the ending of the fray;
          High above the Cross, the trophy,
            Sound the loud triumphant lay;
          Tell how pains of death enduring
            Earth's redeemer won the day.

          Faithful Cross, above all other
            One and only noble tree!
          None in foliage, none in blossom,
            None in fruit thy peer may be;
          Sweetest wood and sweetest iron!
            Sweetest weight is hung on thee.

1.7   TO THE LADY RADEGUND, WITH A BUNCH OF FLOWERS *c.* 570
            O Queen, that art so high
            Purple and gold thou passest by,
          With these poor flowers thy lover worships thee.
          Though all thy wealth thou hast flung far from thee,
                Wilt thou not hold
            The violet's purple and the crocus' gold?

            Take this poor offering,
            For it thy thoughts shall bring
          To that blest light that is to dawn for thee,
                Fields bright as these,
            And richer fragrances.

            And when thou comest there,
            Hear, O my saint, my prayer,
          And may thy kind hand draw me after thee.
                Yet, though thine eyes
            Already look on flowers of Paradise,

            These thine own flowers
            Would have thee out of doors.
          Yea, though the flowers of Paradise are sweet,
                These fain would lie
            Where thou wert passing by.

Source: The Poems of Venantius Fortunatus, translated by Helen
Waddell.

1.8 Boethius in the Condemned Cell 524

In 1885 the Quaker historian, Thomas Hodgkin, remarked that fifty pages of the British Museum catalogue were devoted to editions and translations of the works of Boethius, a contemporary of Clovis but a citizen of quite another world, almost of another planet. Boethius was a Roman senator of an old family, rich, civilized, scholarly. He translated much of Aristotle into Latin and, thanks to him, although Greek was forgotten, Aristotle became 'the philosopher' to all medieval thinkers, their all but inspired textbook. Boethius was a good mechanic, perfecting, for instance, a water-clock or 'orrery' to show the movements of the sun and the stars. He translated Euclid; he wrote exhaustively on music. He wrote also on theology. He was a poet, and not a bad one.

He was also, fortunately for us, a politician. It was his undoing. Theodoric, the Ostrogothic King of Italy, whose friend and servant he was, suspected him of treachery. He was imprisoned, tortured, executed. Later he was regarded, wrongly, as a Christian martyr put to death by an Arian king for his Catholic faith. The trouble was plainly political. While awaiting execution he wrote *The Consolation of Philosophy*, which Gibbon called 'a golden volume not unworthy of the leisure of Plato or Tully' (Cicero). This is the book which occupies most of those fifty pages in the British Museum catalogue. It was translated into English by, among others, Alfred the Great, Chaucer, and Queen Elizabeth. It was one of the first books that Caxton printed.

For a thousand years, all through the ages of faith, it was a specially loved part of the cultural heritage of almost every great mind. This is strange, stranger than Gibbon's praise, since, although Boethius was an orthodox Catholic, there is nothing specifically Christian in the book. It is the Consolation of Philosophy, not of religion. It is more akin to Plato's *Apology* than to the Gospels. But it is in no sense anti-Christian or inconsistent with Christianity. Perhaps in an over-theological age there was relief in a book which was on the side of the angels, but not obsessed with them. At any rate the first passage given—the translation is from Chaucer—must surely have been present in Dante's mind when he wrote the last words of the *Divine Comedy*—'the love which moves the sun and the other stars'.

The last extract shows Boethius wrestling with the problem of time and eternity, of free will and determinism. On this note the book comes abruptly to a close, not working up, as one would expect to a set ending. Is it fanciful to think with Hodgkin that for Boethius time had run out and at this point he was roughly called to eternity?

ALL THINGS BOUND BY LOVE

That the world with stable faith varies concordantly, that the contrary qualities of elements hold among themselves perpetual alliance, that Phoebus the sun with his golden chariot brings forth the roseate day, that the moon has command over the nights, which nights Hesperus the evening star has brought, that the sea, greedy to flow, constrains his floods within certain limits so that it is not lawful to stretch his broad borders over the land—all this concord of things is bound with Love, that governs earth and sea and has also commandments to the heavens. And if this Love slacked the bridles, all things that are now loving together would make battle continually and strive to undo the fashion of this world in which we now live in accordant faith by fair motions. This Love holds together people joined with a holy bond and knits the sacrament of marriage of chaste loves; and Love indites laws to true fellows. O joyful were mankind, if that Love which governs heaven governed your spirits!

CONCORD IN NATURE

If thou wilt deem in thy pure thought the rights or the laws of the high Thunderer, that is to say, of God, look thou and behold the heights of sovereign heaven. There the stars keep by rightful alliance of things their old peace. The sun, moved by his ruddy fire, disturbs not the cold circle of the moon. Nor the star called the Bear, that inclines his ravishing courses about the sovereign height of the world is never washed in the deep western sea, nor covets to dip his flames in the ocean, although he sees other stars plunged into the sea. And Hesperus the star bodes and tells always the late nights; and Lucifer the star brings again the clear day.

And thus interchangeable Love makes the courses perpetual and thus is discordant battle put out of the country of the stars. This accord tempers in equal measures the elements, that the moist things striving with the dry things, give place at times; and the cold things join themselves by faith to the hot things; and the light fire arises to the height, and the heavy earths fall down by their weights. By these same courses the flowery year yields sweet smells in the first warming of the summer-season; and the hot summer dries the corn, and autumn comes again, heavy with apples; and the flowing rain bedews the winter. This tempering nourishes and brings forth everything that breathes life in this world; and this same tempering, ravishing, hides and takes away and drenches all things born under the last death.

Among these things sits the high Maker, King and Lord, Source and Beginning, Law and wise Judge. And those things he sets moving he withdraws and arrests, and he makes firm the moveable or wandering things. For if he did not recall things to their right course, and constrain them forthwith to their orbits, the things that are now maintained by stable ordinance would depart from their source and fail, come to naught.

This is the Love common to all things; and all things ask to be held by goodness at the end; for otherwise they might not last if they failed to come quickly again, returned by Love, to the cause that had given them being, that is to say, to God.

FREE WILL AND DETERMINISM

Boethius:

The fact that God foreknows everything denies us any freedom of will, for all things must happen which his providence has foreseen to happen.... We ought to condemn what we now consider right and proper, that evil men are punished and the good rewarded, since it was not their own will which directed their actions, but a fatal necessity. And why should man hope in God or pray to God since everything is immovably fixed by the law of destiny? This does away with the only links between God and man: hope and prayer.

Philosophy:

This is the old objection to the Prescience of God, urged strongly by Cicero in his *Book of Divination*. The cause of the difficulty is that man cannot understand the simplicity of the divine prescience.... Prescience is not the necessary cause of events, and freedom of will is not shaken or prevented by prescience ... [Fourteen pages of argument follow].

A future event is inevitable when it is referred to the divine knowledge, but considered in its own nature we see that is absolutely free from all compulsion. For there are two kinds of necessity. The simple necessity is such as this: that all men must die. The other necessity is a conditional one: if you know a man walks, he must necessarily walk ... but no necessity compels a man to walk. He goes by his own freewill, but if he goes he must necessarily walk ...

Boethius:

So actions are not necessary, considered by their own nature; but they seem to be necessary when considered by divine knowledge.

Philosophy:

... God, who sees and foreknows everything, dwells on high and his ever-present knowledge always keeps pace with our various deeds, dispensing rewards to good men and punishment to the wicked. Nor is our hope in God an idle one, nor are our prayers in vain; if they are rightful, they cannot be unsuccessful or ineffective.

Then resist and refrain from vice; honour and love virtue. Lift up your hearts to righteous hopes, offer your humble prayers to heaven. Great need of courage and virtue is imposed upon you and commanded, if you would not act falsely, as all your actions are done before the eyes of an all-discerning Judge.

[And here the MS ends.]

1.9   The Old Age of Cassiodorus   *c.* 480–575

Cassiodorus was born in or about the same year as Boethius. He out-lived him by fifty years. Like Boethius he belonged to a well-known family which had been distinguished for several generations in public life. But he came from farther south—Calabria, not Rome. He had a passionate love for his home town of Squillace in the toe of Italy, 'so bathed in the brightness of the sun that it, rather than Rhodes, might be thought to be its native land. Its winters were sunny, its summers cool so that life there was spent without sorrow and man found himself freer of soul than else-where.'

Cassiodorus rose to be what we should call head of the civil service in Italy under King Theodoric (see 12.1). Then after a life-time of public service he retired at the age of sixty.

If Cassiodorus had gone peacefully into retirement at this point his name would today only be known to a few specialists in sixth-century Italian history. But at sixty Cassiodorus started a new career with the result that for a thousand years learned men throughout Europe honoured his reputa-tion and used his books. Cassiodorus returned to his beloved Squillace and founded two monasteries there. One at Vivarium (Fishponds) was on the collegiate plan; the other at Castellum was more austere and intended for those who were called to the solitary life. We do not know whether Cassiodorus himself ever became a monk, let alone an abbot. But certainly the remaining 35 years of his life—he lived to be 95—were completely devoted to these two monasteries. He provided for them one of the great libraries of the early Middle Ages. For them he wrote numerous books—lengthy commentaries on the Psalms, for instance, and a new revision of Jerome's Latin Bible. Extract 1.9 comes from his *Introduction to Divine and Human Letters*, a complete plan of education for his monks, not only for their own good but so that they might be fit for the great work for which he was specially training them. His scheme was felt to be so important that manuscripts of this long work were widely distributed in monasteries throughout western Europe. Part Two of his book, which deals with the basic secular subjects such as arithmetic, geometry, logic, and music was to be found in the libraries of at least nineteen English monasteries 700 years after it was written.

Without the help of monastic foundations such as Vivarium devoted to preserving the literature of the Bible and of Greece and Rome it is likely that western Europe would have reverted completely to barbarism.

The copying of manuscripts and their illumination and binding were exacting tasks beautifully executed but Cassiodorus did not expect all his monks to be capable of it, nor did he undervalue those who were not. 'We know,' he wrote, 'that intelligence does not reside in formal education alone; God gives perfect wisdom "to everyone as he will" (1 Cor. 12.11). For if knowledge of God were in books alone, unlettered men would lack suitable wisdom.' A monk who could not follow the standard curriculum devised by Cassiodorus might be encouraged to work in the gardens, the orchards or on the farm. But even so a certain literacy was expected of him, and Cassiodorus points out that he has put a number of horticultural books in the library.

1.9   LIFE AT VIVARIUM AND CASTELLUM   *c.* 555

Monks at Vivarium

The site on which the monastery is built simply invites you to provide generously for travellers and those in need.... Nearby is the river Pellena which is neither unduly turbulent nor sluggish, but rich in fish. You have trained it to irrigate your gardens and turn your mill-wheels.... There is sea fishing as well. With God's help you have constructed pleasant tanks below the monastery which are so like the natural caves of this hilly landscape that the fish do not realize that they have been caught! The water is limpid. Its taste is delicious. It is a pleasure to bathe in it, and we have provided baths for the sick. No wonder your monastery attracts visitors, while there is no temptation for you to leave it. But of course you realize that these are pleasures of the here and now, not those joys to which the faithful look forward. These pass; those are endless. Let us who are monks set our minds to desire those heavenly things that make us reign with Christ.

Hermits at Castellum

There is the sweetness of solitude at Castellum-on-the-Hill for those of you who through God's grace and the training of the monastery come to wish for a still higher way of life. Up there, through the Lord's loving-kindness, you can live the happy life of hermits. There, shut off from others by the ancient walls, you can contrive to be as lonely as in the desert. Those of you who have already been trained as monks and your vocation tested are right to choose this life—if in your heart you are ready for the journey upwards. It is through study that you learn what you can aspire to and what you can endure. A man who is useless as a master in a schoolroom can be a wonderful teacher by the goodness of his life.

Cleaning a skin & stitching parchments together.
From a MS, c. 1125, at Bamberg Staatsbibliothek, Par.f.iv.

The Scriptorium

I admit that to my mind the work of a careful scribe is the most attractive physical task which monks undertake. I hope that I am justified in this preference because as a monk reads the Bible he teaches himself and as he writes it out he spreads the Lord's teaching far and wide. Each one of the Lord's words that he copies is a wound on Satan's body. The copyist stays in one place, but his work travels far and takes him on long journeys.... Man multiplies the heavenly word. What the Holy Trinity says is written, if I may use the expression, by a trinity of fingers (the three that hold the pen)— a glorious thing to see for those with observant eyes.

But there is a risk that copyists may make spelling mistakes and

13 Cent. monastic scribe
Trin. Coll. Camb. MS 0.9.34.

that untrained sub-editors may not know how to put these and others right. They should read the books of the standard writers on Handwriting. . . . I have collected as many of them as possible to satisfy my own eager curiosity. Some passages in them are hard to understand, mainly because of copyists' mistakes in case-endings. I have therefore taken a great deal of trouble to draw up for you a handbook of selected rules which should clear up your doubts and enable you to make better corrections.

We have provided skilled book-binders so that the beauty of the sacred manuscript may be handsomely clothed—in rather the same way that in the parable those wedding guests were dressed whom the Lord found worthy to attend the heavenly feast. Unless I am mistaken we have prepared for the binders a style book from which each may choose the type of binding he prefers.

Doctors
You doctors who are sad when others suffer, full of sorrow for those in danger, and upset by the misfortunes of others—we know from experience how devotedly you help the sick. You will receive your reward from him who is able to give a reward in eternity for an act in time. Learn therefore the properties of various herbs and mix your drugs carefully; but do not pin all your hope of good health on herbs and human knowledge. Medical science indeed is god-given, but it is God himself, the life-giver, who makes men well. For it is written, 'And whatever you do, in word or deed, do everything in the name of the Lord Jesus, giving thanks to God the Father through him.' (Col. 3. 17.)

Peasants
Give the peasants on your monastic lands sound moral teaching, and do not overburden them with taxes. For it is written, 'My yoke is easy and my burden is light.' (Matt. 11. 30). Peasants generally are known to be familiar with the worship (of the old gods) carried on in sacred groves. May yours be free of that knowledge and live in innocence and happy simplicity. . . . Encourage them to come frequently to the monasteries so that the shame of your peasants not knowing you personally may be avoided. May they also realize that God in his goodness will make their fields fertile if they regularly and faithfully pray to him.

Benedict and his Rule   . *c.* 480–*c.* 543

Monasteries were the means by which the Christian religion and Roman civilization were preserved through the Dark Ages. They were not of course invented by Benedict or even in Europe (see, for instance, volume I pp. 158–174). But Benedictine monasteries had something which others lacked—the power to endure. About 250 years after Benedict's death Charles the Great (Charlemagne) ordered an enquiry to find out whether there were any monasteries in his empire which did not follow the rule which Benedict had written about the year 528. Nobody had ordered that all monasteries were to adopt this rule; it was the proved excellence of its working which quickly made it universal. Each Benedictine monastery was a self-contained independent unit.

The extracts which follow illustrate some aspects of the life which his monks lived. All took life-long vows of poverty—the monk could have no private property of his own—chastity—the monk could have no sexual intercourse of any kind—and obedience—monks must obey their abbot (whom they had elected and who, like them, must himself obey the Rule). In a monastery the abbot is considered to take the place of Christ, 'since he is called by his name ... Abba, Father,' but he is bound to consult his brother monks. The monastery was the monk's home for life, and he must not leave it. There he must work as well as pray. It was this balanced, measured life with its mixture of absolute obedience and full discussion which gave Benedictine monasteries the stability and strength which others often lacked.

Benedict's own autograph copy of his Rule was preserved at Monte Cassino until the Moslem invasion of southern Italy. It was then taken for safety to the monastery at Teano where it was burned in a disastrous fire. The oldest surviving manuscript of the Rule was written in England in the seventh or eighth century.

Benedict's life was written by Pope Gregory the Great, himself a Benedictine monk, who was born about the time that Benedict died. He took very great care with the necessary research, drawing on the recollections of four of Benedict's own younger monks. It is a satisfying book to the extent that it provides convincing evidence that Benedict's contemporaries recognized him as a man of quite exceptional sanctity and spiritual power. It thus explains the initial impetus which gave authority to a Rule, 'conspicuous for its discretion' (i.e. humanity) as Gregory put it.

It is unsatisfying because in almost every chapter it leaves us quite unable to determine what actually happened in spite of the first-rate oral evidence on which it is based. The devil, man's 'ancient enemy', runs in and out of its pages, a powerful figure but one which the Christian can defy. He sits on a stone so that the builders of the church at Monte Cassino cannot move it until Benedict drives him off with his prayers. He disguises himself as a vet to paralyse a monk drawing water at a well, but Benedict sends him packing by slapping the monk.

There was, of course, nothing new about miracles. The novelty is their thickness on the ground and one might say their triviality. It recalls the wonders of the apochryphal gospels which the Church wisely refused to accept. For the next thousand years men seem determined to see the miraculous wherever possible. There were, of course, plenty of fools and knaves in the Dark and Middle Ages as there are today, but Gregory and Benedict were neither. This is precisely the difficulty.

The Benedictine rule provided for regular worship as the monk's work. Rules 8 and 16 below show how it was distributed round the clock. The whole of the Psalter was repeated each week so that its poetry became so familiar that monastic writers could not avoid recalling it in everything they wrote. This stands out clearly in the extracts in this book. The detailed biblical references have been provided by the editors. The monks would not have needed them.

1.10   RULE OF SAINT BENEDICT

From the Prologue
If we would flee from the pains of hell and attain everlasting life, we must hurry to do now what will profit us for all eternity. So we are now going to found a school for the service of God. Nothing harsh or oppressive will be ordered, we hope, but if we are rather severe in certain matters sound reason recommends it, to correct vice and preserve charity. Let it not frighten you away from the path of salvation which is always narrow at first (Matt. 7, 14). For by living our life and by the increase of faith as the heart grows larger you will run the path of God's commandments with inexpressible sweetness and love. So stay in his school and persevere in the monastery in his teaching until death, and by sharing in the sufferings of Christ by our patience we win a share in his kingdom.

Rule 3. Whenever important matters must be dealt with, let the abbot summon the whole community and himself introduce the business. After hearing the brethren's advice let him think it over by himself and do what he judges to be right. And all must be called to the council, because the Lord often reveals what is best to the young.

8. The night Office. In winter from November 1 to Easter, within reason, they must get up at the eighth hour of the night after sleeping for a little more than half the night. Let the time that remains after Matins be spent in study by those who have yet to learn psalter or lessons. From Easter to November 1 let the time for Matins be so arranged that (allowing a short break for the necessities of nature) it is closely followed by Lauds which are always to be said at daybreak.

16. The day Offices. The prophet says 'Seven times a day I praise thee' (Psa. 119, 164). Therefore we keep this sacred number of seven if we do our duties of service at Lauds, Prime, Terce, Sext, Nones, Evensong and Compline.

22. Sleeping arrangements. . . . If possible let all sleep in one room. . . . Let a candle be kept burning there until morning. Let them sleep in their clothes, girt with belts or cords, but without knives by their sides lest they harm themselves in their sleep. . . .

23. Punishments. If a brother is found to be stubborn, disobedient, proud, or a grumbler, acting in any way against the holy Rule and despising the orders of his seniors, let him, according to our Lord's command (Matt. 18, 15), be privately warned by those seniors once or twice. If he does not amend, let him be publicly rebuked before everyone. But if even then he does not correct his faults let him be excommunicated, if he understands the meaning of that punishment, and if quite incorrigible he is to undergo corporal punishment.

27. Care of the Excommunicated. The abbot must take all possible care of brothers who offend, for 'those who are well have no need of a physician, but they that are sick' (Matt. 9, 12). Therefore like a wise doctor he should use every remedy, sending older and wiser brothers like playmates to console their wayward brother in secret and win him to humble atonement; and they should comfort him lest he be overwhelmed by too much sorrow. . . .

33. Ownership. Above all else cut out from the monastery the vice of property, root and branch. No one without leave of the abbot should give, receive, or keep as his own anything at all. Have nothing, neither a book nor tablets, nor a pen: nothing at all. For monks are not allowed to have power even over their own bodies or wills. They can expect to receive the necessary things from the father of the monastery, and anything not given or permitted by the abbot is forbidden. All things are to be common to all, as it is written, 'None said that anything he possessed was his own' (Acts 4, 32).

36. Care of the sick. First and foremost, you must take care of the sick, tending them as though they were Christ himself. For he said, 'I was sick and you visited me' and 'as you did it to one of the least of my brethren you did it to me' (Matt. 25, 36:40) . . . Let a cell be set apart for them, with an attendant who is God-fearing, diligent and careful. They shall be allowed baths as often as necessary, though the healthy and especially the young should be seldom indulged. Meat may also be given to the sick and those in delicate health to give them strength, but as soon as they recover they must all abstain from flesh according to the normal custom.

38. Reading at meals. During meals there should always be reading . . .

39. Food. In the daily meals at the sixth and ninth hours . . . let two dishes of cooked food suffice for the brethren, so he who cannot eat of one may eat of the other. Fruit or fresh vegetables when obtainable may be added as a third dish. 1 lb of bread shall be the daily ration, whether there is one main meal or both dinner and supper. If there is a supper the cellarer must keep back a third of the pound for that meal. But when very heavy labour has been done the abbot may increase the allowance at his discretion, always avoiding excess.... All must abstain from the flesh of four-footed beasts, except the delicate and the sick.

[Rule 40 suggests that a pint of wine a day should be the normal allowance of drink. Rule 42 enjoins absolute silence after Compline. Rule 48 gives the daily time-table, complicated by the fact that day and night were always counted as 12 hours each. This meant that in winter each hour of the night could be 80 minutes, and each hour of the day 40 minutes. From Easter to October they worked from about 6.30 a.m. until 9.30 a.m., then read until noon, and rested on their beds after dinner until 3.30 p.m., when they worked again until evening. There was only one work period in winter of four hours, with an extra half hour in Lent (i.e. 10 a.m.–2.30 p.m.).]

53. Receiving Guests. All guests are to be received as Christ himself, for he will say, 'I was a stranger and you took me in' (Matt. 25, 35). Show due honour to all, but especially to those of the household of faith and pilgrims. When a guest is announced therefore, the prior or the brothers shall hurry to meet him with all the marks of loving kindness. And first they shall pray together, establishing the bond of peace. The kiss of peace must not be given until after prayer, on account of the wiles of the devil.... The abbot as well as all the community shall wash the feet of all guests (John 13, 14)...

55. Clothing. Clothing must be appropriate to the locality or the climate.... It is for the abbot to decide. But ordinarily we think it is enough for each monk to have a cowl and tunic, of thicker stuff in winter, of finer or worn cloth in summer. He should have a scapular [a kind of cape] for working in, and shoes and stockings for the feet....

Gregory the Great *c.* 540–604

Gregory belonged to an old and rich Roman family. When he was in his early thirties he was appointed Prefect of the City, the senior civilian official in Rome. Some two years later he threw up his career, turned his family palace on the Caelian Hill into St. Andrew's monastery and entered it as a simple monk. He founded six monasteries in Sicily and distributed the rest of his possessions to the poor. Three or four years later he was sent to represent the Pope at Constantinople. He returned to Rome and became abbot of St. Andrew's.

In 589 there were great floods followed next year by a terrible plague. The Pope died. Gregory was chosen to succeed him by popular acclaim very much against his will. The first extract, from a sermon on the plague, led to measures against the plague which must in fact unintentionally have helped to spread it.

1.11   GREGORY AND THE PLAGUE   590

The judgments of God are upon us, dearest brethren. Let grief and fear open the way to penitence in our hearts for our condition is indeed that which the prophet Jeremiah described of old: 'The sword has reached the life itself.' (Jer. 4. 10). The whole people is hit by the sword of the divine anger and sudden death lays waste the city.... Each one who is struck down is hurried off before he has had time to turn to repentance. The citizens are not cut off one by one, but hurry to the grave in whole companies. Houses are left empty; parents see their sons' funerals, and their own heirs die before them.

Let us then turn to him who has said that he wills not the death of a sinner.

Let us imitate the three days' penitence of the men of Nineveh and beseech our merciful God to turn away his anger from us. Therefore, dearest brethren let us come with contrite hearts and pure hands and minds prepared for tears to the Sevenfold Litany to which I now invite you beginning at dawn on the fourth day of the week. *Source:* Gregory of Tours, *History of the Franks* 10.1.

[Accordingly seven processions—clergy, monks, nuns, children, laymen, widows and wives—set out each day from Wednesday to Friday from seven different churches to march to St. Maria Maggiore singing *Kyrie, eleison.* A deacon of Tours who was present told his bishop, the other Gregory, that in one hour while the procession was passing eighty men fell down dead.]

1.12   THE PATRIMONY OF ST. PETER   591

By Gregory's time the Pope had become the owner of vast estates in Italy, France, Jugo-Slavia, Sardinia, Corsica and especially in Sicily. The extent of this Patrimony of St. Peter as it was called was approximately 1,800 square miles. The Pope was one of the greatest of landowners. Gregory found that many abuses had grown up. He replaced the laymen who had run the estates by clerics. He bombarded them with detailed orders. These two extracts from letters to the sub-deacon Peter in Sicily show the kind of abuses that had grown up. Note that slavery still continues and is accepted.

It has come to my ears that during the past ten years ... many complain of the loss of slaves, saying that any runaway slave who claims
to be under ecclesiastical law is at once claimed and kept by the
Church's bailiffs who, without a court order in their favour, back
up the slave's assertions by force. All this displeases me as much
as it is abhorrent to the spirit of justice and truth. Wherefore I desire
that your Experience should shake off all sloth [Gregory's letters
to Peter are full of mock serious rebukes to his Laziness] and correct
all misdeeds of this kind which you may discover. Let any slaves
now in the Church's hands, who were taken without a court order,
be restored before any proceedings are taken; and if any do lawfully
belong to Holy Church, let the title be proved in a regular action.
Amend all these abuses with firmness. You will prove yourself a
true soldier of the blessed apostle Peter if in causes where he is
concerned you anxiously maintain truth without suspicion of
partiality even towards Peter himself.
Source: Letters of Gregory, 1.36.

1.13   SOLDIERS AND MONKS   593

Gregory became involved in a controversy with the Emperor Maurice about
soldiers who wished to leave the army and become monks ('Conversion,
convert' are technical terms for becoming a monk). They were not con-
scientious objectors in the modern sense but men who recognized a higher
call, even in time of war, than that of military duty. The practice had
become common and Maurice had decided to put an end to it. Gregory
wrote to him:

... Christ answers you, the master of all things, through me, the
lowest of his and your servants: 'From a lawyer I made you Captain
of the Guard; from Captain of the Guard, Caesar; from Caesar,
Emperor—and not only that but father of future emperors. I have
committed my priests to your keeping; would you withdraw your
soldiers from my service?' Most religious Lord, please tell your
servant what answer you will make to *your* Lord when he comes
and says these things to you at the Judgment?
    But perhaps you think that there is no such thing as the honest
conversion of a soldier to the monastic life? I, your unworthy servant,
know how many converted soldiers have in my time worked miracles
in the monasteries they have entered. But under this law not even
one soldier is to be allowed the privilege of conversion.... Consider
too that men are by this law forbidden to renounce the world at
the very time when the end of the world is drawing near. There will

certainly be no delay. The time is at hand when, while the earth and the sky burn and the elements flash fire, the terrible Judge shall come with angels and archangels, with thrones and dominations with principalities and powers. If he has forgiven you all your other sins, what excuse can you make if he charges you with issuing this one law?

1.14   'SERVANT OF THE SERVANTS OF GOD'   595

Gregory was even firmer in the line he took with John the Faster, Patriarch of Constantinople, who in a letter to Gregory referred to himself in almost every line as Ecumenical Patriarch, that 'wicked word' (sceleste vocabulum) as Gregory called it. There were precedents for the usage, but Gregory was determined to uphold the primacy of Rome against the court bishop of Constantinople. He hurried off two letters from which extracts are given below. The gap between East and West is widening over a matter, not of doctrine, but of jurisdiction for that is the reality which lies behind the dispute over titles. Gregory himself took over a phrase which had occasionally been used in the past and regularly described himself in his letters as 'servant of the servants of God', which became and has remained a papal title. Gregory was consistent. In the third extract he declined to accept for Rome what he had refused to Constantinople.

Gregory to John the Faster. In the days of my predecessor a letter was sent to you in which the acts of a synod ... were disallowed because of the proud title attributed to you in them, and the Archdeacon sent (as my representative) to the Emperor was forbidden to celebrate mass with you on account of it. That prohibition I now repeat.... The apostle Paul rebuked the spirit which would shout 'I am of Paul and I of Apollos' (1 Cor. 1.12). You are reviving that spirit and rending the body of Christ.... Our Lord humbled himself for our sakes, and he who was inconceivably great wore the lowly form of manhood, yet we bishops are imitating, not his humility, but the pride of his great foe. Remember that he said to his disciples, 'Be not called Rabbi, for one is your master, even Christ, and all you are brethren'.... I have by my representative once and twice told you your fault and am now writing to you myself. If I am despised in this endeavour to correct you, it will only remain to call in the Church....

Gregory to the Emperor Maurice. This is not my cause, but the cause of God himself. It was to Peter, the Prince of the Apostles, that the Lord said, 'Thou art Peter, and on this rock I will build my Church'. He who received the keys of the kingdom of heaven, he to whom the power of binding and loosing was entrusted, was never called the Universal Apostle; and yet that most holy man, my fellow bishop John, tries to get himself called Universal Bishop. When I see this I have to cry out *O tempora O mores*.... We are all suffering from the scandal of this thing. My most religious Lord, you must coerce this proud man, who is destroying the canons of the Church, and is even setting himself up against the honour of your imperial dignity by this proud private word.... I am myself the servant of priests so long as they live priest-like lives. But as for this man, who in his swelling vain glory raises his neck against Almighty God and against the statutes of the fathers, I trust in God that he shall never bend *my* neck, no, not with swords.

Gregory to Eulogius, patriarch of Alexandria. I have said that neither to me nor to anyone else ought you to write anything of the kind, yet lo! in the preface of your letter you apply to me who prohibited it the proud title of Universal Pope. I beg your sweet Holiness to do so no more, because what is given to others beyond what reason requires is subtracted from you. I do not esteem that an honour by which I know my brethren lose their honour. My honour is that of the universal Church. I am then truly honoured when all and each are allowed the honour that is due to them. For, if your Holiness calls me Universal Pope you deny yourself to be that which you call me universally. But no more of this! Away with words which inflate pride and wound charity!

Source: Letters of Gregory, 5.18, 5.20, 8.20.

1.15   GREGORY AS STATESMAN AND PEACEMAKER

In Gregory's time the Lombard invaders had over-run three-quarters of Italy. Gregory found himself undertaking the duties of a temporal sovereign —waging war and making a separate peace with the Lombards in 592 much to the annoyance of the emperor when he heard of it. It marks a great step towards the emergence of the Papacy as a secular as well as a religious power. Gregory worked hard to bring about a peace between the Lombard king and the emperor. It took seven years of hard diplomacy. In his efforts he was greatly helped by the Catholic wife of the Arian Lombard king. The abbot Probus of this letter was Gregory's representative at the Lombard court.

598

Gregory to Theodelinda, Queen of the Lombards. We have learnt from the report of our son, the abbot Probus, how your Excellency has laboured earnestly and kindly, in your usual manner, for the conclusion of peace. Indeed it was only to be expected that you would show such perseverance and goodness in the cause of peace. Therefore we thank Almighty God, who rules your heart with his loving kindness, so that he has given you a right faith and also grants that you should do always what is pleasing in his sight. For you may be assured that you have gained no small reward for saving so much bloodshed on both sides. So, returning thanks for your goodwill, we implore the mercy of our God to repay you with good, in body and soul, here and in the world to come.

Moreover, in fatherly affection, we exhort you so to deal with your most excellent consort that he may not reject the alliance of the Christian republic. For, as we believe you also know, if he could bring himself to embrace its friendship, it would be profitable in many ways. Do, then, in your own way, strive for whatever tends to goodwill and conciliation between the parties, labouring wherever there is a prospect of reward and commending your good deeds the more to the eyes of Almighty God.

Source: Letters of Gregory, 9.43.

1.16   GREGORY'S CASE FOR PURGATORY

Heaven or hell was the ultimate fate of every human soul. This had always been clear to Christians from their reading of the New Testament, especially the parables of Dives and Lazarus (Luke 16, 19–31) and of the sheep and the goats (Matt. 25, 31–46). The great volcanoes of southern Italy, pictured as the mouth of hell, made its torments real and vivid.

Charity refused to consign any but the most abandoned to hell; holiness stumbled at the idea of plainly sinful men passing straight after death to heaven, to the presence of God. Equity seemed to demand some intermediate stage. Gregory was by no means the first Christian theologian to teach the doctrine of what from the eleventh century came to be called Purgatory. But he preached it more insistently and his great authority endorsed what the conscience of those days felt to be fitting. Because in the sixth century, and indeed for many centuries to come, physical punishment was accepted as a necessary part of any system of discipline or education, Gregory naturally incorporated it in his vision of the process of purification after death. How he derived his teaching from Scripture can be seen in the curious piece of argument in the following extract from his *Dialogues*: 4.26, 41.

Peter: Are souls of the righteous received in heaven before they are finally reunited with their bodies?

Gregory: We can neither assert nor deny this of all the elect, because some righteous souls are delayed somewhere outside heaven. This check seems to show that they are still lacking in perfect righteousness.

Peter: I should like to know if we must believe in a purging fire after death.

Gregory: Clearly everyone will be brought to the Judge in his exact state at death, but there must be a purging fire before judgment because some little faults may remain to be purged. Christ, the Truth, says that if any one blasphemes against the Holy Spirit he shall not be forgiven, 'neither in this world nor in the world to come' (Matt. 12, 32). From this we learn that some sins can be forgiven in this world and some in the world to come, because if forgiveness is refused for a particular sin it is logical to conclude that it is given for some others. As I said, this can be only for minor faults, such as idle chatter, too hearty laughter, mistakes in the care of property (which can scarcely be avoided even by those who know the mistakes to avoid), or errors due to ignorance in trivial concerns. All these faults mean trouble for the soul after death if they are not forgiven while you are alive.

Paul, when he says Christ is the foundation, adds that on this foundation 'men will build gold, silver, precious stones, wood, hay, stubble ... and the fire will test what sort of work each one has done. If the work which any man has built thereon survives, he will receive a reward. If any man's work is burnt he will suffer loss, though he himself will be saved, but only as through fire' (1 Cor. 3, 12 15). Though this may be taken to mean the fire of suffering which we experience in this life, it may also refer to the purging fire of the world to come.

If we accept it in this sense, we must examine Paul's words carefully. When he says that men are saved by passing through fire, he is not referring to those who build on this foundation in iron, bronze or lead, that is to say in mortal sins, which cannot be destroyed by fire. He denotes those who build in wood, grass and straw, that is venial or trivial sins which fire easily consumes. And in this case we must remember that no one will be purged in the world to come, even of the slightest faults, unless he has deserved it through the good deeds done in this life.

1.17   GREGORY ON THE WORK OF BISHOPS

Gregory's most lasting and valuable contribution to religion, as distinct from church organization, was his great work 'On Pastoral Care', in which he discussed the work of bishops and others to whom the spiritual care of people was committed. The following extracts show both how closely he stuck to Scripture as the ground of his thinking and with what understanding he approached the great diversity of character and temperament not only of bishops but also of their people. Almost at once it became a classic. This translation comes from chapters 7, 15, 16 of the Anglo-Saxon version which Alfred the Great made nearly three hundred years after Gregory wrote. The name he gave it was 'Herdbook'.

GREGORY'S PASTORAL CARE

If a man understands that it is God's will that he be put over others and then refuses it, that is not true meekness, which is to submit to God's will and decree, and forsake the sin of obstinacy.... However, many desire rule and supremacy very blamelessly, and many are compelled to undertake it very blamelessly. This we may easily understand if we think of the two prophets God wished to send to teach. One of his own will undertook the teaching and the journey. The other, for fear of not doing it so well, refused. This was Jeremiah. When God wished to send him, he humbly begged him not to send him, and said, 'Alas, alas, Lord, I am a boy! What can I say?' But Isaiah, when the Lord asked him whom he might send, said, 'I am ready; send me.' See now what different speeches came from the mouth of these two men. But they arose from a very similar desire, for they flowed from the same spring; although they flowed in different directions, the source was true love.

Of this we have two behests: the one is that we love God, the other that we love our neighbour. From love Isaiah wished to be the most helpful to his neighbours in this earthly life, and so he desired the office of teaching. Jeremiah craved only to abide in the love of his Creator, and therefore he refused, and did not wish to be sent to teach. What he blamelessly dreaded to undertake, the other very praiseworthily desired. The one feared losing what he had gained in silence and meditation; the other feared that he may be concealing some harm in his silence, that he might have spoken helpfully if he had laboured zealously. But we should consider both cases very closely, for he that refused did not fully refuse, and he who wished to be sent saw that he was first cleansed by the coals of the altar....

Let a teacher be moderate and discreet and helpful in his words, lest he keep unsaid what is helpful to speak, or speak what should be kept silent.... Moses was bidden that priests should be hung about with bells (Exodus 28, 33–4). What else does the robe of the priest signify but good works? The prophet David showed it when he said, 'Let thy priests be clothed with righteousness' (Psa. 132, 9). On the priest's robes were bells hanging; that means that the works of the priest and his tongue are to proclaim the way of life... It was said by the divine voice that among the bells were to hang red apples [pomegranates in A.V.] ... As the apple is covered with a single skin and yet has many pips inside it, so the holy Church encloses many folk of a single faith; yet they who dwell therein have very different merits. ... The teacher must therefore consider beforehand with careful meditation not only how he is to avoid preaching bad doctrine, but also how he is not to preach what is right too lengthily, too immoderately, or too severely.

The teacher must be the nearest to all men, sympathizing with all men in their troubles, yet lifted above all with the divine foresight of his mind. ... So Paul, though he was taken to Paradise and surveyed the mysteries of the third heaven, though he was exalted in the sharpness of his mind by the revelation of unseen things, yet he condescended to direct his mind to carnal bedrooms and instruct men how they should behave therein. He said, 'Let each man have his wife and each wife her husband, and let the wife do what is lawful with the man and he with her in the same way lest they commit fornication.' And soon after he said, 'Deprive not one another, unless ye abstain for some time before the time of your prayers and offerings and then return forthwith to your lawful intercourse' (1 Cor. 7, 2–5).

Look now, how the holy man who was so familiar with the mysteries of heaven had the kindheartedness to consider how carnal man should behave in their bedrooms and on their beds. ... For he connected through the love of God and men both the highest and the lowest of things. In himself he was greatly exalted through the might of the Holy Ghost and yet for earthly men in their need his piety equally humbled him. Therefore he said, 'Who is weak and I am not weak? Who is shamed and I am not shamed?' (2 Cor. 11, 29.)

For Truth itself, that is Christ, when he was on earth, prayed on mountains and in desert places, but he worked his miracles in towns, thus preparing the path of imitation for good teachers, lest they despise the fellowship of weak and sinful men, though they themselves aspire to the highest. Because when love descends to kindliness and is occupied with the need of his neighbours then it rises marvellously; and the more cheerfully love descends, the easier it rises.

1.18 Prayers and Praises

The fifth and sixth centuries saw first a multiplication and complication of forms of worship and then something of a codification and simplification.

The result was the structure for the Mass which has lasted to the present day, and which almost everywhere in the West replaced local usages. It is still with minor modifications the universal form in the Roman Catholic Church in every country, and in its main outlines is followed, for example, by the various Anglican churches. Prayers (collects) for use at various times are found in three successive, cumulative Sacramentaries linked, but without firm evidence, with the name of three Popes—Leo the Great (d. 461), Gelasius (d. 496) and Gregory the Great (d. 604). Certainly they belong to this period. Many of the collects are familiar in English through the translation made by Archbishop Cranmer for the First Book of Common Prayer in 1549. Some are given here in his original words from which the disciplined form of the Latin original can be appreciated. The sacramentaries also fixed the order of the Christian year with its succession of feasts and fasts in the form which it has kept in the Roman Catholic and Anglican churches.

Gregory's name is associated also with the development of church music. The first great name in western church music is Ambrose (d. 397 see Vol. I, pp. 241–3). Rome developed its own style to which the name Plainsong or Gregorian is given, though it is not clear how much Gregory himself had to do with it—probably a little more than Victoria, for instance, had to do with the Victorian novel. In his time two schools of church music were established in Rome and the Antiphonary set out the way of singing the psalms and other musical parts of the services. Extract 2.19 in the next chapter refers to its introduction into England.

PRAYERS FROM THE GELASIAN SACRAMENTARY
I

Grant to us Lord we beseech thee, the spirit to think and do always such things as be rightful; that we, which cannot be without thee, may by thee be able to live according to thy will; through Jesus Christ our Lord.

II

Let thy merciful ears, O Lord, be open to the prayers of thy humble servants, and that they may obtain their petitions, make them to ask such things as shall please thee; through Jesus Christ our Lord.

III

Almighty and everlasting God, give unto us the increase of faith, hope, and charity; and that we may obtain that which thou dost promise, make us to love that which thou dost command, through Jesus Christ our Lord.

PRAYERS FROM THE GREGORIAN SACRAMENTARY
I

Lighten our darkness, we beseech thee, O Lord, and by thy great mercy defend us from all perils and dangers of this night, for the love of thy only Son, our saviour Jesus Christ.

II

O Lord our heavenly Father, almighty and everliving God, who hast safely brought us to the beginning of this day, defend us in the same with thy mighty power, and grant that this day we fall into no sin, neither run into any kind of danger, but that all our doings may be ordered by thy governance to do always that is righteous in thy sight: through Jesus Christ our Lord.

III

God, which hast prepared for them that love thee such good things as pass man's understanding, pour into our hearts such love toward thee, that we, loving thee above all things, may obtain thy promises, which exceed all that we can desire; through Jesus Christ our Lord.

IV

O God, forasmuch as without thee we are not able to please thee, grant that the working of thy mercy may in all things direct and rule our hearts; through Jesus Christ our Lord.

V

Grant, we beseech thee, merciful Lord, to thy faithful people pardon and peace, that they may be cleansed from all their sins, and serve thee with a quiet mind; through Jesus Christ our Lord.

CHAPTER TWO

NORTH-WEST FRONTIERSMEN

Roman Britain had been Christian. When the legions left in the fifth-century pagan barbarians—Angles and Saxons—poured in. The Christian British were defeated, enslaved or forced to retreat into the hills of Wales and other outlying parts. Those who remained usually gave up Christianity. Christian Ireland, which had never been part of the Roman Empire, was cut off from the rest of the Christian world. For a time it was content to go its own solitary way, developing in the middle of a primitive society a high level of artistic achievement in great monastic settlements. Then in the middle of the sixth century there came a sudden breaking out of bounds, a spectacular outburst of missionary activity which took Gaelic speaking monks from Ireland and Scotland on great journeys over much of pagan northern Europe.

This spontaneous, unplanned eastward thrust met a disciplined, planned northern thrust from Rome. The meeting was not without difficulty. Not only was the Celtic church of Ireland out of touch with Roman developments, but it was not anxious to be put right. The matters in dispute seem trivial, looking backwards, but they had all the emotive power of symbols. How to calculate the date of Easter, the respective roles of abbots and bishops, even the style of a monk's haircut were bitterly debated, but the real problem was how Celtic exuberance could come to terms with Roman organizing power.

The extracts in this chapter give glimpses of this great pincer movement which eventually after many setbacks brought all Northern Europe into Christendom. Map 1 shows the chief places mentioned in this chapter.

Gregory and England

Even before Gregory became Pope he had interested himself in England. According to the story it was in the slave market of Rome that he saw fair-haired Anglian boys from what is now Yorkshire exposed for sale. Either Gregory or his eighth-century biographer had a taste for puns. Not Angles but angels, he thought them. Where did they come from? Who was their king? They came from Deira whose king was Aelle, he was told. Let them then flee from the wrath of God (de ira Dei) and Alleluia be sung in the land of Aelle. Gregory went further than pious good wishes. He set out himself for England but was recalled by the pope when he was only three days out. He was needed for administrative work in Rome. Some twenty years later Gregory himself became pope and at once began to lay plans for the conversion of England. He arranged for his manager to buy pagan English slaves in the markets of France so that they might be brought up as Christians. When they became monks they would of course become free men equally with all the other monks.

2.1   BUYING ENGLISH SLAVES   595
Gregory to the priest Candidus. When you go with the aid of our Lord Jesus Christ to manage the patrimony [papal possessions] in Gaul, we wish you to buy clothes for the poor with the money you will receive, and also English boys who are 17 or 18 years old, that they may be dedicated to God and educated in the monasteries. By this means the money of the Gauls, which cannot be spent here in our country, will be usefully spent in the land where it belongs ... and the boys will advance in the service of God. But since those you get will be pagans, I wish you to send a priest with them lest any should fall sick by the way; then he may duly baptise those who are dying.

2.2   GREGORY ENCOURAGES AUGUSTINE   596
Next year Gregory decided to send a mission to England. The king of Kent had married a Christian wife. The opening was there. Gregory sent Augustine to lead the party. In France they heard such frightening reports of English savagery that they persuaded Augustine to go back to Rome and ask for leave to give up the task. Gregory refused and sent Augustine back to them with this letter:

July 23, 596
My beloved sons, because it is better never to begin a good work than to think of abandoning it when once begun, you are bound to complete this holy task which, with the Lord's help, you have undertaken. Therefore do not allow the hardships of the journey or the evil tongues of men to stop you, but with all possible sincerity and zeal fulfil what, with God's guidance, you have already begun. Be assured that such great labour earns an eternal reward.

With the return of your leader Augustine, whom we have appointed your Abbot, obey him humbly in all things, knowing that whatever he directs you to do will always be to the good of your souls.

Almighty God protect you with his grace and grant that I may see the fruits of your labours in our heavenly home. And though I cannot labour beside you, yet because I long to do so I shall enter

into the joy of your reward. God keep you safe, most beloved sons.
Source: Bede, *History of the English Church and People,* 1.23.

2.3   ·GREGORY APPROVES LITURGICAL EXPERIMENT   601

Augustine's mission prospered. Kent became Christian and Augustine first
Archbishop of Canterbury. Various problems arose on which he thought
he ought to get a ruling from Rome. One point which had to be settled
was how Mass ought to be said in England. Augustine had noticed the
differences between the Roman rite and what was done in the French
(Gallican) churches. Gregory sent him this answer:

601

You know, my brother, the rite of the Roman Church, remembering
it from your upbringing. But if you find anything in the customs
of the Gallican, or any other Church that may be more acceptable
to Almighty God, I shall be pleased if you would make a careful
selection from them and teach the Church of the English, which is
still young in the faith, the best you can gather from the various
churches. For things are not to be loved for the sake of places, but
places for the sake of good things.

Choose, therefore, from every Church those things that are
devout, religious, and worthy, and when you have, as it were, incorporated them, let the minds of the English grow accustomed thereto.
Source: Bede, *History of the English Church and People,* 1.27.

2.4   FROM DEVIL'S TEMPLE TO GOD'S CHURCH   601

Before long Gregory had to send reinforcements to Augustine. Mellitus took
with him a letter telling Augustine how to make things easy for the new
converts by turning their temples into churches and taking over in a changed
form old religious practices. This left plenty of room for misunderstanding.
Old religious beliefs and practices long continued underground.

June 17, 601

I have decided that the temples of the idols of the English nation
should not be destroyed. Let the idols in them be destroyed, but
let the temples be washed with holy waters, and altars built with
relics deposited in them. For if those temples are well built, they
should be converted from devil-worship to the service of the true
God, so that the people, seeing that their temples are not destroyed,
may the more readily resort to such familiar places and, removing
error from their hearts, come to know and adore the true God.

And since they have been accustomed to the slaughtering of many
oxen in sacrifices to devils, let some other ceremony be substituted

on such occasions as the day of Dedication or the Nativities of those holy martyrs whose relics are deposited there. Then they may build themselves huts of branches of trees around those churches converted from temples, and celebrate the holy day with religious feasting. No longer shall they offer beasts to the devil, but kill cattle for eating to the glory of God, returning thanks to the Giver of all gifts for their provisions. Because if they are allowed some outward indulgences, they may more easily accept the inward comforts of the grace of God. For it is surely impossible to erase everything from their obstinate minds at one stroke, because he who strives to reach a summit rises gradually by steps and not by leaps.

Source: Bede, op. cit., 1.29.

2.5   FALSE DAWN IN YORK   625

Edwin, king of Northumbria, married the king of Kent's daughter, Ethelberga. He was a pagan, she a Christian. She took with her Paulinus who became the first Archbishop of York. Pope Boniface V sent her the following encouraging letter. The king became a Christian and, as things then usually happened, his people with him. But seven years later he was killed in battle. The queen and Paulinus fled to Kent. Northumbria for a short time reverted to paganism though a Christian remnant remained. Such see-saws were common. Note once again the influence of women, especially queens.

To the renowned lady, his daughter, Queen Ethelberga, from Bishop Boniface, servant of the servants of God. ... We have been informed by those who came to report the praiseworthy conversion of our illustrious son King Eadbald, that your majesty, who has also received the wonderful sacraments of the Christian faith, continually excels in the performance of holy works, pleasing to God. We learn that you also carefully refrain from the worship of idols, and the temptations of temples and auguries, and that, having changed your allegiance, you are wholly devoted to the love of your Redeemer, labouring unceasingly for the propagation of the Christian faith.

But in fatherly affection we earnestly enquired about your illustrious husband and were informed that he still serves abominable idols and will not follow or even listen to the words of the preachers. It grieved us greatly that the half of you should remain a stranger to the knowledge of the supreme and undivided Trinity. In fatherly concern we hasten to urge your Christian majesty that, God helping you, you will not delay to do the duty required of us, both in season and out of season, that with the help and strength of our Lord and Saviour Jesus Christ, your husband may also be numbered among the Christians, and that you may thereby enjoy the rights of marriage in the bond of a pure and holy union. For the Scripture says, 'The two shall become one flesh'. But how can it be called a true union, so long as he remains alienated from the brightness of your faith by the barrier of a dark and hateful error?

Wherefore, pray without ceasing that God of his mercy will send enlightenment....

Source: Bede, op. cit., 2.11.

Saints, Scholars, Irishmen

'Go forth from your country and your kindred and your father's house to the land that I will show you' (Gen. 12, 1), God's command to Abraham, caught the attention, one might almost say took the fancy, of many Irishmen from the 6th to the 9th century. They took to the monasteries; they forsook them for hermit's cells; they applied the words literally and went into exile from Ireland yet never lost their love of home. There was a great restlessness in them which made them eagerly obedient to the call. The following extracts give some faint idea of what they took with them and gave to the peoples they settled among. Four strands are specially important. They would probably have put first the penitential system which provided moral guidance and discipline for priests and laymen alike. (Extract 2.6.) But though they were harsh with themselves they were imaginative and tender in their feeling for nature and for the beauty of the natural world (2.7, 8). This overflowed into the exquisite designs with which they decorated their precious books (Plate 2). The skill and beauty of their artistry underline the value they attached to learning. The lands through which they wandered had either never been civilized or were rapidly sinking back into deepest savagery. The Irish monks kept alive the humane values and intellectual curiosity of the ancient world. Some classical learning they brought with them; some they hungrily picked up on their travels. The important thing is their appetite for it and their good digestion (2.13B).

2.6   PENANCE FOR SINS

'It was in Ireland that the ancient Christian system of public penance was first replaced by private confession and private penance, consisting of prayers and works of mortification enjoined on the penitent by the confessor. Starting with the monasteries, this new penance soon found its way also to the laity. The confessor (Irish *anmchara*, "soul-friend") begins to assume the role of spiritual director and counsellor.' (L. Bieler: *Ireland, Harbinger of the Middle Ages* p. 49.) The earliest Irish penitential dates from the 6th century and was the work of one Vinnianus, possibly St. Finnian of Clonard, the teacher of Comgall. It is a manual for confessors rather than a book for self-examination. These extracts show something of the task which confronted the Church in moral education.

6, 7. Should a cleric plan to assault or kill his neighbour, he shall do penance by an allowance of only bread and water for half a year and no wine or meat for a year. Then he will be reconciled to the altar. A layman shall do this penance for seven days; since he is a man of the world his guilt is less in this world as his reward is less in the world to come.

10. If a cleric falls sadly into fornication and loses his crown, if it only happened once and though known to God is hidden from men, he shall do penance of bread and water for a year and abstain from meat and wine for two years, but shall not lose his clerical office. For sins can be absolved secretly by penance, by great devotion of heart and body.

12. If a cleric sinks so low as to have a child and kill him the crime of fornication with murder is a grievous one but can be absolved by penance and God's mercy. He shall do penance on bread and water for three years, abstain from meat and wine for a further three years ... and be deprived of his clerical office and exiled from his country for seven years. Then a bishop or priest can decide to restore him to his office.

18, 19. If a cleric or woman leads another astray by magic the monstrous sin can be absolved by penance for six years ... and if he has led none astray but given a love-potion to someone, he shall do a penance of bread and water for a year.

20. If a woman kills a child she has conceived, by magic, she shall do penance for half a year...

36. If a layman defiles his neighbour's wife or virgin daughter, for a whole year he shall do penance on bread and water and not have intercourse with his own wife; then he shall be admitted to holy communion and give alms.

39, 40. If a married layman has intercourse with his female slave, the slave is to be sold and he himself forbidden intercourse with his wife for a whole year, but if he has one, two, or three children by this slave he must set her free and is not allowed to sell her.

2.7 HERMIT AND KING

Irish monks lived in buildings and under conditions quite unlike those of monasteries of the middle ages. A circular wall shut in an enclosure in which were many bee-hive huts for two or three monks. They were made of wood as were the communal buildings and the small chapel or chapels. As a monastery grew, additional small chapels were usually added instead of building a large church. At first only in the west, where timber was scarce, did the monks build in stone as on the Skellig (see Plate 1).

A hermit describes his cell in this ninth-century poem:

> I have a bothy in the wood—
> none knows it save the Lord, my God;
> one wall an ash, the other hazel,
> and a great fern makes the door.
>
> The doorposts are made of heather,
> the lintel of honeysuckle;
> and wild forest all around
> yields mast for well-fed swine...

Then come dear white ones,	herons, sea-gulls
sea chant hearing;	
no harsh music	when grouse is calling
from russet heather.	
The sound of wind	in branching trees,
day grey and cloudy;	
stream in torrent,	swans a-singing,
sweet the music.	
I hear the soughing	of the pine-trees
and pay no money;	
I am richer far	through Christ, my Lord,
than ever you were...	

Source: Anon, trans. by James Carney.

2.8　　　　　　COLUMBA ON IONA: THE CRANE　　　　563–597

Columba belonged to the noble family of O'Neill. He founded two famous monasteries at Durrow and Derry (not yet by a thousand years Londonderry). Then about the year 563, when he was in his middle thirties, he left Ireland and settled on the island of Iona off the coast of Mull, 'not great either,' said Bede, 'but as though it were of five households by estimation of the English.' Columba soon became accepted as the leading Christian figure in that part of the world and the local ruler came to him to be blessed as king—the Scots and the Irish were then one in race, language and religion. But beyond the Scots were the Picts. It fell to Columba, as Bede put it, 'by word and example' to convert their nation to the faith of Christ.

Iona thus became the centre of Christianity in the north of Britain. It was also the centre of a great network of monasteries founded by Columba or his disciples and following his Rule. Bede noticed that a hundred years later, 'Iona is always ruled by an abbot in priest's orders, to whose authority the whole province, including the bishops, is subject, contrary to the usual custom. This practice was established by its first abbot Columba (it was

in fact the usual Irish pattern) who was not a bishop himself but a priest
and a monk.

His life was written by Adamnan, a Donegal man who came to Iona
as a novice in 650. He became its abbot in 679 and died in 704. He was
responsible at the synod of Tara for forbidding the practice of making
women and children prisoners of war. The following story, one of many,
shows Columba as a man who loved and understood birds and beasts and
was understood by them. The name he took as a monk, Columba or Dove,
and in its full form Columcille or Church-dove, typifies this side of the man
who was also statesman, missionary, scholar, artist and poet—he was a
member of the 'filid', the order of bards, which he saved from suppression.

And another time it befell, while the Saint was living on Iona, that
he called one of the brethren to him, to speak to him. 'Go thou,'
he said, 'three days from now to the west of this island at dawn,
and sit above the shore and wait: for when the third hour before
sunset is past, there shall come flying from the northern coasts of
Ireland a stranger guest, a crane, wind-tossed and driven far from
her course in the high air: tired out and weary she will fall on the
beach at thy feet and lie there, her strength nigh gone: tenderly lift
her and carry her to the steading near by: make her welcome there
and cherish her with all care for three days and nights; and when
the three days are ended, refreshed and loath to tarry longer with
us in our exile, she shall take flight again towards that sweet land
of Ireland whence she came, in pride of strength once more: and
if I commend her so earnestly to thy charge, it is that in that countryside where thou and I were reared, she too was nested.'

The brother obeyed: and on the third day, when the third hour
before sunset was past, stood as he was bidden, in wait for the coming
of the promised guest: and when she had come and lay fallen on
the beach, he lifted her and carried her ailing to the steading, and
fed her, famished as she was. And on his return that evening to the
monastery the Saint spoke to him, not as one questioning but as
one speaks of a thing past. 'May God bless thee, my son,' said he,
'for thy kind tending of this pilgrim guest: that shall make no long
stay in her exile, but when three suns have set shall turn back to
her own land.'

And the thing fell out even as the Saint had foretold. For when
her three days housing was ended, and as her host stood by, she
rose in first flight from the earth into high heaven, and after a while
at gaze to spy out her aerial way, took her straight flight above the
quiet sea, and so to Ireland through the tranquil weather.

Source: Adamnan, *Life of Columba.*

2.9   AIDAN AT LINDISFARNE

The lasting conversion of north-east England, after a temporary set-back, was the result of a mission from Iona. Lindisfarne, or Holy Island, which is now joined to the mainland even at high tide by a causeway, lies just off the Northumbrian coast and looks across an inlet to Bamburgh where Oswald's palace was. The Scottish tongue which Aidan spoke was Gaelic.

When Oswald became king, he desired that all his nation should receive the Christian faith, which he had proved to be so helpful in resisting the heathen. So he sent to the Scottish chiefs among whom he and his followers had received the sacrament of Baptism during his exile, and asked them to send him a bishop to confer the blessings of the Christian faith upon the English nation and administer the sacraments. They granted his request immediately and sent him bishop Aidan, a man of rare humility, holiness, and moderation, and zealous in the cause of God. ...

On his arrival the king gave him the island of Lindisfarne to be his see as he asked. This place, as the tide ebbs and flows, is enclosed twice a day by the waves of the sea like an island, and twice a day when the shore is left dry it is joined to the mainland. The king always listened humbly and willingly to Aidan's advice and busily strove to build and extend the Church of Christ in his kingdom, and when the bishop, who knew little of the English language, preached the Gospel, it was most delightful to see the king himself interpreting the word of God for his thanes and ministers. For he had learned the Scottish tongue perfectly during his long exile.

From that time many Scots came daily into Britain and preached the word with great devotion in all the English provinces ruled by Oswald, while those in priest's orders administered the grace of Baptism to those who believed. Churches were built in many places and the people flocked gladly to hear the word. By the king's bounty money and lands were given to build monasteries, and the English, great and small, were instructed by their Scottish masters in the rules of the disciplined life; for most of those who came to preach were monks.

Aidan himself was a monk of the island of Hii (Iona), whose monastery was for long the chief of all those of the northern Scots and Picts, exercising control over them. That island belongs to Britain, separated from the mainland by a narrow strait; but the Picts of that part of Britain had given it to the Scottish monks long ago, because they had received the faith of Christ through their preaching.

Source: Bede, op. cit., 3.3.

At Lindisfarne Aidan trained a number of Northumbrian boys who became prominent in the Church, among them Chad, later bishop of Lichfield, and Wilfrid who became bishop of York. Wilfrid travelled south to Canterbury, went on to Rome and decided that the customs of his own church were wrong and that Rome was right. He was a quarrelsome man and an enthusiastic convert to the Roman view. Back in Northumbria he led a party against his own bishop, Colman who, like Aidan, had come from Iona. The king supported Colman; the queen, a Kentish princess, backed Wilfrid. The king decided that this must stop. The controversy was not only unseemly but awkward. The king, for instance, found himself keeping Easter while the queen had got no further than Palm Sunday. He called a synod at Whitby which Bede described. As a result Colman returned to his native Ireland. The Northumbrian church became fully integrated in the Western Church, but it long retained, especially in the field of art, the marks of its Celtic origin.

King Oswy began by saying that all who served one God ought to follow one rule of life, and as all expected the same kingdom in heaven, so they ought not to differ in the way they celebrated the sacraments of heaven. They should discover which was the truest tradition, and then this should be accepted by all. He then directed his own bishop, Colman, to speak first, to explain the customs he followed and how they had originated.

Then Colman said, 'My way of keeping Easter was taught me by my elders who sent me here as bishop, and all our forefathers, men beloved of God, are known to have kept it in the same manner...'

When Wilfrid was ordered by the king to speak, he said, 'The Easter we celebrate is the one we saw universally celebrated in Rome, where the blessed Apostles Peter and Paul lived, taught, suffered, and were buried. We saw the same done in Italy and Gaul when we travelled through those countries for pilgrimage and prayer; we found that the same custom was followed in Africa, Asia, Egypt, Greece, and throughout the world, wherever the church of Christ has spread, in many different countries and languages, yet at the same time. The only ones who foolishly oppose the rest of the world are these, and their accomplices in obstinacy, the Picts and Britons, living in these furthest isles, and only in a portion even of them'...

'As for your Father Columba and his followers, whose sanctity you say you imitate and whose rules and regulations you claim have been confirmed by signs from heaven ... I do not deny that they were servants of God, beloved by Him and, with a devout but rude

simplicity, loving Him in return. Nor do I think that their way of
keeping Easter was particularly harmful as long as no one came to
show them a more perfect way; in fact I am sure that, if any Catholic
adviser had come among them, they would have accepted his advice
as readily as they are known to observe those commandments of
God already learnt by them.

'But you certainly sin, you and your companions, if, having heard
the decrees of the Apostolic See and of the universal Church, which
are confirmed by these letters, you refuse to follow them. For although your Fathers were holy, do you think that those few, in a
corner of the remotest island, are to be preferred before the universal
Church of Christ throughout the world? And even if your Columba
—and also *our* Columba, if he was the servant of Christ—was a
saint of miraculous power, can he take precedence of the most blessed
prince of the Apostles, to whom our Lord said, "Thou art Peter,
and upon this rock I will build my church, and the gates of hell
shall not prevail against it, and to thee I will give the keys of the
kingdom of heaven"?'

When Wilfrid had finished, the king asked, 'Is it true, Colman,
that these words were spoken to Peter by our Lord?'

'It is true, O king.'

'Can you show that any such authority was given to your
Columba?'

'None.'

'Do you both agree that these words were particularly addressed
to Peter, and that the keys of heaven were given to him by our
Lord?'

'We do.'

'Then,' concluded the king, 'I also say to you, I will not contend
with this guardian of the gates, but obey his decrees to the best of
my knowledge and ability, lest when I come to the gates of heaven
there should be none to open them, since he who is proved to hold
the keys may prove to be my enemy.'

At this, all present, both high and low, gave their assent, renounced
their imperfect customs, and resolved to conform to those they had
found to be better.

Source: Bede, op. cit., 3.25.

2.11   COLUMBAN ON THE LOIRE

A second missionary drive went from Bangor in County Down to the Vosges,
the upper Rhine, and north Italy. About 590 Columban left Bangor with

twelve companions for what is now France. It was then the land of the Franks, split into three petty kingdoms, nominally Christian but with a massive sub-structure of paganism. Columban established a Celtic-type monastery at Luxeuil in the foot-hills of the Vosges. Eventually he was deported. From Nantes Columban wrote a farewell letter to the Frankish monks who had remained at Luxeuil. He named Athala as his successor and urged them all to follow him and be of one mind or cease to live in one community. We give here a few passages from the letter, in a version by Eleanor Duckett.

Athala, you must resist those who oppose you, but do it with charity and in the peace of our Rule. I have tried to help all, to trust in all, but the burden has been too great for me. It has broken my strength and made me look almost a fool. Be wiser than I, and do not take upon yourself my load. You know now how little I understood; you have learned the lesson that all cannot be taught alike because men are different in character, in spirit and in mind. Treat as individuals the men who obey and love you, and remember that love, too, has its danger.... A messenger has just come; the ship is ready. But my guards seem to understand how I feel. Perhaps if I ran for liberty they would look the other way. I haven't told you all that is in my mind for you think so differently among yourselves. That monk is my brother who loves peace and unity.
Source: Columban's Works, Scriptores Latini Hiberniae; Vol 2. Dublin.

2.12 COLUMBAN ON THE RHINE

Columban and his Irish twelve moved up the Rhine. They put in two strenuous and partly successful years of missionary work on the lake of Zurich and at the south of the Bodensee. Gall, who had quickly mastered the German speech of the district, stayed behind to Columban's displeasure when the rest moved on to Lombardy. A poem, very likely by Columban himself, recalls their voyage up the Rhine (translated by James Carney).

See, cut in woods, through flood of twin-horned Rhine
passes the keel, and greased slips over seas—
    Heave, men! And let resounding echo sound our 'heave'...

Endure and keep yourselves for happy things;
ye suffered worse, and these too God shall end—
    Heave, men! And let resounding echo sound our 'heave'...

2.13 COLUMBAN AT BOBBIO 614–5

In Lombardy Columban found himself at the court of the Arian king whose wife was Catholic. He was well received, but longed for the solitude of a monastery. In 614 he had his wish as this passage from his *Life* shows. It was written by Jonas, a monk of Bobbio, within about thirty years of Columban's death.

A.

When Columban saw that Theudebert had been conquered by Theodoric, he left Gaul and Germany and went to Italy. There he was received with honour by Agilulf, king of the Lombards, who granted him the privilege of settling in Italy wherever he pleased; and he did so by God's direction. During his stay in Milan, he resolved to attack the errors of the heretics, that is, the Arian perfidy, which he wanted to cut out and exterminate with the cauterizing knife of the Scriptures. And he composed an excellent and learned work against them.

At that time a man named Jocundus appeared before the king and announced that he knew of a church of the holy apostle Peter in a lonely spot in the Apennines. The place had many advantages, it was unusually fertile, the water was full of fishes. It had long been called Bobium (Bobbio) from the brook that flowed by it.... Thither Columban now went and with all diligence restored to its old beauty the church which was half in ruins.

In this restoration the wonderful power of the Lord was visible. When the beams of fir were cut amid the precipitous cliffs or in the dense woods, and fell into places that the beasts of burden could not approach, the man of God, going with two or three companions (all that the steep paths furnished footing for), would place the immensely heavy beams on his own and companions' shoulders, beams which 30 or 40 men could scarcely carry on level ground. And where they had hardly been able to walk before, on account of the steepness of the paths, they now walked easily and joyfully.... Therefore he restored the roof of the church and the ruined walls, and provided whatever else was necessary for a monastery.

After a single year in his monastery of Bobbio, Columban, the man of God, ended his devout life on November 1st [615?].

B.

When Columban came to Bobbio he was already in his seventies, but he retained his zest for life as he shows in sprightly verses written to a friend, given here in a translation by Thomas Hodgkin. Bobbio itself became one of the greatest centres of learning in the West with an outstanding library. Books from it are now the greatest treasures of the Ambrosian Library in Milan.

Haply the metre
May to you seem strange.
Yet 'tis the same which
She, the renowned bard
Sappho, the Greek, once
Used for her verses...
Now then, my loved one,
Brother Fedolis,
Who when you choose are
Sweeter than nectar,
Leave the more pompous
Songs of the sages,
And with a meek mind
Bear with my trifling.
So may the World-King,
Christ, the alone Son
Of the Eternal,
Crown you with Life's joys.

2.14   TAILPIECE: AN IRISHMAN AND HIS CAT

Irishmen continued to find their way to Europe. In the ninth century an unknown Irish monk of the great abbey of Reichenau wrote in his native Gaelic this poem about his white (Bán) cat, Pangur. Reichenau, one of the great northern centres of learning is a small island on the upper Rhine just after the river leaves the Bodensee. The translation is by Robin Flower.

I and Pangur Bán, my cat,
'Tis a like task we are at;
Hunting mice is his delight,
Hunting words I sit all night.

Better far than praise of men
'Tis to sit with book and pen;
Pangur bears me no ill will,
He too plies his simple skill.

'Tis a merry thing to see
At our tasks how glad are we,
When at home we sit and find
Entertainment to our mind

Oftentimes a mouse will stray
In the hero Pangur's way;
Oftentimes my keen thought set
Takes a meaning in its net.

'Gainst the wall he sets his eye
Full and fierce and sharp and sly;
'Gainst the wall of knowledge I
All my little wisdom try.

When a mouse darts from its den,
O how glad is Pangur then!
O what gladness do I prove
When I solve the doubts I love.

So in peace our tasks we ply,
Pangur Bán, my cat, and I;
In our arts we find our bliss,
I have mine and he has his.

Practice every day has made
Pangur perfect in his trade;
I get wisdom day and night,
Turning darkness into light.

Source: MS of Reichenau now at St. Paul, Carinthia.

Two English Poets

In spite of the sadness of Colman's withdrawal to an Irish monastery, the
Synod of Whitby marked the beginning of a golden age of Christianity in
England. A sign of this was the birth of poetry.

2.15   CAEDMON AND HILDA   *c.* 680

Caedmon, first of English poets, was a lay brother of the great double
monastery for monks and nuns at Whitby. The founder and head of this
monastery was Hilda, a Northumbrian princess, who became a nun when
she was in her thirties and in 649 was made abbess of Hartlepool by Aidan,
moving to Whitby ten years later. She took the Celtic side at the synod
of Whitby but accepted the synod's ruling.

Double monasteries for monks and nuns, separate establishments under
a common head and worshipping in the same chapel, were not peculiar
to Northumbria. In the fifth century in Ireland Bridget had founded the
famous double establishment at Kildare.

In the monastery of this abbess [Hilda], there was a certain brother
who was made remarkable by the grace of God. He used to compose
religious and devotional verses, and whatever passages of Scripture
were explained to him, these he could quickly turn into sweet and
moving poetry in his own English tongue. By these verses of his

he often stirred the minds of many to despise the world and to aspire to heaven. Other Englishmen after him tried to compose religious poems, but none could ever compare with him, for he learnt the art of poetry not from men but from God. For this reason he could never compose any trivial or vain verses, for only those on a religious subject suited his religious tongue; and although he followed a secular occupation until late in life, he had never learnt anything about versifying, so that when, at a feast, all the guests agreed to entertain the company with a song in turn, he would rise from the table and go home when he saw the harp coming near.

Once, when he had done this and left the feast-hall for the stable, where he had to take care of the horses that night, he lay down to sleep in due course, and one appeared to him in a dream and greeted him by name.

'Caedmon, sing me a song!'

'I cannot sing. That was why I forsook the feast and took refuge here: because I could not sing.'

'But sing you shall.'

'What shall I sing?'

'Sing the beginning of the Creation.'

And Caedmon immediately began to sing verses to the praise of God upon this theme:

> Praise now the Keeper of the heavenly kingdom.
> The power and the purpose of our Creator,
> The acts of the Author of glory. The eternal God,
> Maker of marvels, almighty Preserver,
> First raised the sky as a roof for the races of men
> And then spread the earth beneath them.

This is the meaning, but not the actual words, of the song which he sang in his sleep; for poetry, however well composed cannot be translated from one language into another [in this case from Old English into Latin] without losing much of its grace and dignity.

When Caedmon awoke he remembered all that he had sung in his dream, and soon added many more words in the same strain, worthy of the majesty of God.

In the morning he went to the steward, his superior, and told him about this gift which he had received. He was led to the abbess, who ordered him to tell his dream and repeat the verses in the presence of many learned men, so that they might judge the quality of the poem and the source of his inspiration. They all agreed that heavenly grace had been given to Caedmon by the Lord. They then explained to him a passage of sacred history or doctrine and asked him to put it into poetry, if he could. He agreed and departed. In the morning he returned with the set piece rendered into excellent poetry. The abbess, delighted that the grace of God was made manifest in the man, advised him to abandon secular life and take the vows of a monk; and when she had admitted him into the community of the brethren, she ordered that he should be taught the whole course of sacred history.

So Caedmon, storing up in his memory everything he heard and, as it were, chewing upon it as a cud, transformed it into such musical verse that when he repeated it, like a sweet echo, he turned his teachers into his listeners. He sang of the creation of the world, the origin of man, and all the story of Genesis. He sang of Israel's exodus from Egypt, their entry into the promised land, with many other histories from holy writ. He sang of the incarnation of our Lord, his passion, resurrection, and ascension into heaven: the coming of the Holy Spirit and the teaching of the Apostles.... For he was a deeply religious man, humbly submissive to the monastic rule but full of zeal against those who would do otherwise.
Source: Bede, op. cit., 4.24.

2.16   THE DREAM OF THE ROOD   *c.* 780
This famous Old English poem has been ascribed to Cynewulf, a Northumbrian poet who lived nearly a hundred years after Caedmon. It is certain that it belongs to this golden age of Northumbrian Christianity before the Viking invasions. Its survival only in a manuscript in the Italian monastery at Vercelli is a good illustration of the Celtic Christian penetration of Europe. A few lines from it are also found on the Ruthwell Cross near Dumfries. This extract is about a third of the original. Rood was the Old English word for the Cross of Christ, now used chiefly in the compound 'roodscreen' between nave and choir.

> Hear me! I tell of a marvellous dream
> At midnight when men were all sleeping.
> I dreamed I saw a tree most strange,
> Lifted aloft and girded with light;
> For bathed in gold was all that beacon.
> At the foot of the cross gems flamed in beauty:
> Five shone on the shoulder-beam.
> Angels of the Lord, eternally lovely,

Watched over it; that was no wicked tree...
A long time I lay there and I looked
At the cross of our Saviour in sadness,
Till that wood of wonder spoke these words:—

'In the years of yore, that I yet remember,
On the forest's fringe they felled me.
Struck from my stem, the stern foes took me
And shaped me for a shameful show.
Bad men then bade me bear their felons.
So on their shoulders they shifted me,
Hoisted me on a hill and held me fast.
Then I beheld the Master of mankind
Coming with courage as if to climb me.
Since God forbad, I could not bend or break.
Earth trembled. Might was mine
To fell all his foes, but I stood fast.
The almighty God laid his garments by
And climbed the cross, constant in courage,
Fearless before folk, all souls to free...
I, the rood upreared, raised the royal One,
Lifted the Lord of heaven and dared not bow.'

The Wonderful Ways of God

Miracles were expected of saints (see 10, 6–8). The two incidents which follow were recorded by Bede. The first is a story of Cuthbert who, coming from the abbey of Melrose, spent many years in Northumbria, first at Lindisfarne and then as a solitary hermit on Farne island nine miles offshore. His last two years were spent as bishop of Lindisfarne. He died when Bede was fourteen. Bede did not know him, but took the trouble to check his facts with the monks of Lindisfarne when he wrote his biography. The second story, the healing of Herebald, was told Bede by Herebald himself. The bishop who healed him, John of Beverley, was the man who ordained Bede deacon and priest. Both stories are described by Bede as miracles.

John of Beverley was a monk of Hilda's monastery at Whitby, became successively bishop of Hexham and York, but retired to Beverley where he had founded a monastery and died there in 721. His fame was great for at least 700 years: Henry V ascribed his victory at Agincourt to his intercession and ordered his feast to be kept throughout England.

2.17   SAINT CUTHBERT AND THE RAVENS

Here I can tell of another one of the blessed Cuthbert's miracles
... in which the pride and stubbornness of man are openly shamed
by the humble obedience of birds.

One day ravens, which had long inhabited the island, were seen to tear the straw from the roof of the guest-house and carry it off to build nests. The saint raised his right hand a little in rebuke and ordered them to leave the monks' property alone. The birds simply flouted his order.

'In the Name of Jesus Christ, go at once!' he shouted. 'Do not dare to stay and do more damage!'

Almost before he had finished speaking, the ravens flew off in shame. Three days later one of a pair returned and stood before Cuthbert as he was digging, spread out its feathers and bowed its head to its feet in sign of grief. It made such signs as it could to show repentance and ask forgiveness. When Cuthbert understood its purpose he gave permission for all the birds to return, and back they came with a suitable present—a lump of pig's lard. Cuthbert often showed it to his visitors and invited them to grease their shoes with it.

'How careful men should be,' he would say, 'to cultivate obedience and humility, when even birds hasten to wash away the stains of pride by prayers, sorrow, and gifts.'

Source: Bede, *Life and Miracles of St. Cuthbert,* 20.

2.18   JOHN OF BEVERLEY SAVES A DISOBEDIENT HORSEMAN

In the prime of my youth I (Herebald) lived among the bishop's clergy, giving my mind to reading and singing; but I had not entirely closed my heart to youthful pleasures. One day, as we were travelling with him, we happened to come to a stretch of a level open road suitable for galloping our horses. The young men with him, mostly laymen, began to beg the bishop to allow them to gallop and test the quality of their horses. At first he refused, saying it was a foolish request, but at last he gave way to the unanimous desire of so many.

'Do so if you wish, but let Herebald stay out of the race.'

I pressed him to let me ride with the rest, for I had every confidence in the excellence of my horse—which he had given me—but I could not get my way.

When they had galloped to and fro several times, the bishop and I looking on, my reckless mood prevailed and I could not restrain myself, and despite his prohibition I dashed in among them and began to gallop at full speed.

'Alas! how you grieve me by riding like that,' I heard him call after me. But though I heard him, I went on, against his command. Immediately my fiery steed made a great leap over a hollow place and I fell, and lay as if I were dead, stunned and motionless; for at that spot was a stone, level with the ground and barely covered by the turf, the only stone to be found in all that plain. And it happened, either by chance or divine providence, as a punishment for my disobedience, that my head and a hand I clapped to it as I fell struck upon that stone, so that my thumb was broken, my skull cracked, and I lay, as I said, like one dead.

Because I could not move, they stretched a canopy over me, and from the seventh hour of the day until evening I lay as still as a corpse. Then I revived a little, and was carried home by my companions, but lay speechless all that night, vomiting blood because something was broken inside me by the fall. The bishop, expecting me to die, was much distressed by my accident, for he was particularly fond of me; nor would he stay with his clergy that night, as he usually did, but spent it all in vigil and prayer, imploring God of his goodness, I believe, to restore me to health. Early next morning he came and said a prayer over me, calling me by my name and waking me as if from a heavy sleep.

'Do you know who is speaking to you?' he asked.

I opened my eyes and said, 'I do. You are my beloved bishop.'

'Can you live?'

'I can, through your prayers, if it shall please our Lord.'

He then laid his hand on my head, blessed me, and returned to prayer. When, a little later, he visited me again, he found me sitting up and able to talk. Then, divinely inspired, as was soon shown, he asked me if I knew for certain that I had been properly baptized. I answered that I was quite sure that I had been washed in the waters of salvation for the remission of sins, and I named the priest who had baptized me.

'If you were baptized by that priest,' he answered, 'your baptism is not valid; for I know him, and when he was ordained priest he was so dull of understanding that he could not learn how to catechize and baptize, for which reason I ordered him to cease presumptuously to exercise a ministry he was incapable of performing.'

He there and then took pains to catechize me, and when he chanced to breathe on my face I began to feel better immediately. He called the surgeon and told him to close up and bandage my skull where it was cracked; and, after receiving his blessing, I was so much better next day that I mounted my horse and travelled with him to another town.

I was soon completely recovered and received life-giving baptism.

Source: Bede, *History of the English Church and People*, 5.5.

The Age of Bede   673–735

This title may seem to give undue prominence to a man who spent all his life in one monastery, travelling no further north, as far as we know, than Lindisfarne nor south than York. But the hundred years between the coming of Aidan to England and Bede's death are known to us largely through his writings; known to us with remarkable accuracy thanks to his scrupulous care; and vividly known to us because of the skill with which he told his story.

Bede was placed by his parents at the age of eight in the care of abbot Benedict Biscop in the new monastery he had founded at Monkwearmouth. Two years later a branch monastery was established at Jarrow on the river Tyne. Benedict Biscop remained abbot of both houses with Ceolfrid in charge at Jarrow to which Bede was transferred. Benedict Biscop was a man of great learning with a European reputation. He paid five visits to Rome.

2.19   GREGORIAN CHANTS

Bede here describes how English monks were taught, by the arch-cantor of St. Peter's, Rome, abbot John, the chanting skills of Rome.

Church music was composed in a variety of 'modes'. These dominated European music for 1100 years and still influence musical composition. Modes are not keys. All our major keys are exactly the same except for pitch. The difference between one mode and another is the sort of difference between C major and C minor, a different arrangement of tones and semitones. There were at first four 'Ambrosian Modes'. These can be heard by using only the white notes of a piano and running from D to D, E to E, F to F, and G to G. They were called the Dorian, Phrygian, Lydian and Mixolydian modes. If the Dorian mode was being used in the liturgy, the reciting note was at the important interval of a fifth, i.e. the note A, called the 'dominant', the voice dropping to the 'final' D. Gregory added four further modes, one of which from C to C is our present key of C major; it became very popular with the troubadours of the 11th to 13th centuries and was nicknamed the 'wanton mode', *modus lascivius*. See also the note to 1.18.

Benedict [Biscop] received abbot John and conducted him to Britain where he was to teach his monks the chant for the liturgical year as it was sung at St. Peter's, Rome. In accordance with the Pope's instructions, abbot John taught to cantors of the monastery the theory and practice of singing aloud, and he put into writing all that was necessary for the proper observance of festivals throughout the year. His teachings are still followed in this monastery and many copies have been made for other places. John's instructions were not limited to the brethren of this monastery alone for all who were proficient singers came from nearly all the monasteries of the pro-

vince to hear him, and he received many invitations to teach elsewhere.
Source: Bede, op. cit., 4.10.

2.20 THE LIBRARY AT JARROW

Ceolfrid became abbot in 690 on the death of Benedict Biscop. This extract comes from an anonymous writer. Among the books brought back from Rome were copies of Gregory the Great's letters to Augustine, which enabled Bede to tell with accuracy the story of the Roman mission to Kent.

When Benedict was carried from death into life, Ceolfrid took care of both monasteries, or rather the single monastery situated in two places, and he sustained it with care and ability for 27 years. For he was a man both quick in understanding and energetic in action, burning with zeal for righteousness, glowing equally with love and fear of God, sternly rebuking sinners, gently encouraging penitents, diligently supporting and teaching the monastic rules, kind to the poor and generous with alms.... And he saw that the recital of prayers and singing of psalms were performed regularly and reverently.

Thus the monasteries in his care gained both temporal and spiritual riches.... He endowed them most plentifully with vessels for the service of the church and altar, and greatly enlarged the library which either he or Benedict had brought from Rome. One of his actions was to have three bibles transcribed, two for the churches of his twin monasteries, so that any one who wished to read a chapter of either testament could find it with ease. The third bible he resolved to carry to Rome as a gift to Peter, Prince of the Apostles.

[Ceolfrid died on this journey at Langres, September 25, 715.]

Some of the Brothers completed the journey to deliver the gifts he had sent. Among these was the bible translated from the old Hebrew and Greek versions by the blessed priest Jerome, inscribed at the beginning with these lines:

'To the body of Peter, supremely exalted, rightly reverenced, whom ancient faith proclaims the head of the Church, I, Ceolfrid, abbot from the furthest ends of England, send tokens of my deep love, praying that I and mine may have a place for ever among the joys of our great father, a memorial in heaven.'
Source: The Life of Ceolfrid, 19, 20, 27 (B. Mus. Harley MS 3020).

2.21 BEDE ON CHURCH ABUSES November 5, 734

Although Bede was only a simple monk, his reputation was enormous and important men turned to him for advice. Among them was Egbert, a member of the Northumbrian royal house, who had been made deacon in Rome and appointed bishop of York about 732. Next year Bede went to stay with him there. By 734 Bede was too ill to travel south again as had been arranged but sent Egbert a long letter of advice. Egbert was a considerable liturgical scholar and founded the cathedral school at York where Alcuin (see Extract 2.27) was educated. He died in 766.

Above all, holy father, I urge you to refrain with episcopal dignity from idle talk, scandal, and the other harms of a clacking tongue and to occupy your mouth and your mind with the sacred words of the Scriptures and meditations thereon, especially the epistles of the apostle Paul to Timothy and Titus, and also those words of the most holy Pope Gregory where he discusses very skilfully the life and vices of rulers both in the *Book of Pastoral Care* and in sermons on the gospels....

There are rumours abroad that certain bishops serve Christ by associating with men of no religion or chastity, but with those addicted to laughter, jests, tales, feasts, drunkenness and other lures of a dissolute life; instead of feeding the soul on the heavenly sacrifice they daily stuff their stomachs at banquets. I would have you correct them by your holy authority....

Above all make sure that you try to impress firmly on the memory of all under your jurisdiction the Catholic faith contained in the Apostles' Creed and in the Lord's Prayer as it is taught us in the holy gospel. It is of course quite certain that all who have studied Latin have learnt these well, but make the unlearned who know no language but their own say them in their own tongue and repeat them diligently. This should be done not only in the case of laymen still leading a secular life but also by clergy or monks who know no Latin....

We have heard that many villages and hamlets of our people are situated among inaccessible mountains and thick woods, where for years together they never see a bishop ... to confirm the baptized by the laying on of hands. Nor is there even a teacher to impart the truth of the faith and the difference between good and evil....

You have, however, a very willing helper in this good work, King Ceolwulf, who through his inborn love of religion will diligently help forward all that makes for godliness, and he will give you special help because you are his dearest kinsman....

So I think it best to hold a great council and obtain a site among the monasteries where a bishop's see may be established. And if the abbot or monks try to oppose this order, give them permission to elect one from among themselves who may be consecrated bishop, with episcopal charge of all the neighbouring places within that same diocese together with that monastery.

If it seems necessary that more lands and possessions should be bestowed on such a monastery because it is receiving a bishop, we all know that there are countless places given the name of monasteries in a silly manner of speaking. I would like you to take over some of these to help maintain the new bishopric that ought to be established.

It is also necessary to care for those who continue in the secular life, to employ for them suitable teachers of the way of salvation, to make them learn the kind of deeds that will be most pleasing to God, the kind of sins to shun if they want to please God, with what sincerity of heart they ought to believe in God, and how devoutly to pray for the mercy of God. Teach them to strengthen themselves and fortify their possessions by repeatedly making the sign of the Lord's Cross against the continual snares of the unclean spirits. Teach them what a saving power for all kinds of Christians is the daily partaking of the body and blood of our Lord, as you know is the wise custom of the Church of Christ throughout Italy, Gaul, Africa, Greece and the whole East.

Source: B. Mus. Harley MS 4688.

2.22   THE DEATH OF BEDE   May 25, 735

Bede's friend and pupil, Cuthbert, wrote this account of his last days in a letter to another of his pupils, Cuthwin. Previous extracts have shown Bede as historian and ecclesiastical statesman; this shows him as biblical scholar. The English Church still found Latin difficult. Bede's letter to Egbert showed that there were priests and monks who knew no Latin. Here he is helping them by translating John's gospel. The Lindisfarne gospels (Plate 2) written about this time have an English translation interlined some 200 years later.

... For about two weeks before Easter he was troubled by weakness and had difficulty in breathing although with little pain. After that he remained cheerful until Ascension Day, rejoicing and giving thanks to God every hour of the day and night. Daily he gave lessons to us his students and spent the rest of the day, as far as his strength allowed, in singing the Psalms. He passed the whole night cheerfully too, in prayer and thanksgiving to God, except when a light sleep overtook him. But the moment he awoke he would go over the melodies of the Bible, never ceasing to stretch out his hand in thanksgiving to God. In truth I can declare that I have never seen or heard of anyone who so unceasingly gave thanks to the living God. O truly blessed man!

He would repeat the words of the holy apostle Paul, 'It is a fearful thing to fall into the hands of the living God' (Heb. 10, 31) and many other scriptural texts, to rouse our sleeping souls and make us think of our last hour.... To comfort us and himself he would sing antiphons. This is one:

'O king of glory, Lord of might, who on this day ascended in triumph far above the heavens, leave us not comfortless we beseech thee, but send us the Father's promise, even the Spirit of truth. Alleluia.'

And when he came to the words 'Leave us not comfortless' he burst into tears and wept much....

During these days, besides the lessons which he gave us and the chanting of the psalms, he was working to complete two notable works. He was translating the Gospel of St. John into our own language for the benefit of the Church of God and had reached the words, 'But what are these among so many?' (John 6, 9). He was also making extracts from the works of Bishop Isidore [of Seville], for he said:

'I do not want my children to read what is untrue and labour unprofitably after I am gone.'

On the Tuesday before Ascension his breathing became more laboured and his feet began to swell, but he continued to teach and dictate all day, saying from time to time:

'Learn quickly. I do not know how long I shall be with you, how soon my Lord will take me'...

When dawn broke on Wednesday he told us to write diligently what we had begun until Terce, when we walked in procession with the relics of the saints as custom requires. The lad who stayed with him said:

'There is still one chapter missing in 'he book you have been dictating, but it seems hard that you should be questioned further.'

'Nay, it is easy. Take your pen and sharpen it and write quickly.'

At the ninth hour he said to me, 'I have a few treasures in my casket: pepper, napkins, and incense. Run and fetch the priests of our monastery that I may distribute among them the gifts God has given me.'

And in great agitation I ran. He spoke to them all and each in turn, beseeching them to offer masses and prayers for him which they gladly promised. All wept, sorrowing most of all because of the word he had spoken that they should see his face no more (Acts 20, 38). But they were heartened when he said:

'It is time, if it be his will, to return to my maker who formed me out of nothing. I have lived a long life and my merciful Judge has disposed of it well. The time for my departure is at hand (2 Tim. 4, 6), for my soul desires to see Christ my king in his beauty (Isa. 33, 17).'

Many such things he said and passed the day in gladness until evening. Then that same lad named Wilbert said:

'There is still one sentence, dear Master, not written down.'

'Well then, write it.'

'Now it is finished,' the boy said a moment later.

'You have spoken truly: it is finished. Raise my head in your hands, for it would give me great joy to sit facing the holy place where I used to pray. I shall sit and call on my Father.'

So upon the floor of his cell he chanted, 'Glory be to the Father and to the Son and to the Holy Ghost,' and breathed his last.

The Age of Boniface

To the age of Bede there succeeded the age of Boniface, when the most distinctive contribution of Englishmen to the Christian faith was the evangelization of Germany. Wynfrith, a Devon man from Crediton, was a scholarly monk in his late thirties who was being groomed for the abbacy of a Hampshire monastery. He was reluctantly allowed to go to Holland as a missionary in 716, but met with little success. Two years later he tried again. He went first to Rome and secured the full support of the pope. Then he set up a regular mission in the lands between the Rhine and the Elbe. At this time he took the name of Boniface. He kept close links with England, recruiting priests and nuns from there. He kept a watchful eye on what was going on at home, intervening when he thought it necessary. What gave Boniface's work lasting success, compared with that of some Irish monks who had preceded him, was his care for organization and his realization that it was necessary to enlist the support of the state as well as the Church.

Boniface became bishop and then archbishop of Mainz, but when Holland again ran into difficulties he returned there and was murdered while quietly sitting in his tent.

2.23   BONIFACE FELLS THOR'S OAK   *c.* 725

This, his best known exploit, the felling of the sacred oak at Goslar and the building of a chapel with its timbers was a symbolic act. The account comes from his *Life* by Willibald, an English recruit to his mission.

Then many Hessians, converted to the catholic faith, were confirmed by the grace of the sevenfold Spirit through the laying on of hands. Others, not yet made strong in soul, would not accept the teaching of the pure faith in its entirety. Some secretly, some openly, sacrificed to trees and springs. Some secretly, some openly made inspections of the bodies of victims, used fortune-telling, legerdemain and spells. Some gave heed to prophecies and omens and various sacrificial ceremonies, others, more sensibly, gave up all heathen practices and did none of these things.

With the encouragement of these last and the servants of God by his side, the saint, at a place called Gaesmere, tried to fell a certain giant oak called by the ancient pagan name, the Oak of Thor. When in the strength of his determination he had cut the lower notch, the great crowd of the heathen were inwardly cursing the enemy of their gods; but the fore side of the tree had been notched only a little when the vast bulk of the oak was smitten by a divine blast from heaven and crashed to the ground, shattering its crown of branches as it fell. Then, as though by the gracious command of the Highest, it also split into four parts, four trunks of equal length, wrought by no hand of those present.

At this sight the heathen, who had formerly cursed, reviled no more, but now believed and blessed the Lord. Finally the most holy bishop, after consulting with the brethren, built an oratory from the wood of the tree and dedicated it to St. Peter the Apostle.

2.24   MISSIONARY WOMEN

English women played a considerable part in the conversion of Germany, as the next two extracts show. Eadburh, abbess of Minster in Thanet, was clearly a good scholar and artist. Her pupil Leoba, Boniface's young kinswoman, took to Germany the skills she had learned in England, where she was a nun in the double monastery at Wimborne under abbess Tette.

A. Boniface to Eadburh   735

May Almighty God, who rewards all good works, give you an eternal reward for all the kindnesses which you have shown me, because you have comforted me with books and helped me with clothing. So now I pray you to add to what you have begun by transcribing for me in gold the Epistles of my lord St. Peter the Apostle, to gain honour and reverence for the Holy Scriptures when they are preached before the eyes of the heathen and because I have a particular desire always to have beside me the words of him who guided me to this undertaking. And by the priest Eofa I send [the materials] for the writing.

B. *Leoba in Germany* 736

At the time when the blessed maiden Leoba pursued the heavenly life in this monastery, the holy martyr Boniface was ordained bishop by Gregory, bishop of Rome, and was sent to preach the word of God to the German people. Finding the harvest great there and the people inclined to the faith, but that the labourers working with him in the Lord's field were few (cf. Luke 10, 2), he sent to the abbess Tette for the maiden Leoba, to solace his exile and support his mission, for the fame of her sanctity and holy teaching had been spread abroad to distant lands and filled the mouths of many with repeated praise. The mother of the community felt her departure grievously, but as she could not oppose the divine orders, she sent her with honour to the blessed man....

Boniface put Sturmi as abbot over the monks (of Fulda) and decided that Leoba should be the mother of virgins, establishing a monastery for her at Bischofsheim. Many handmaids of God were gathered there, who were set to the study of heavenly lore, following the example of their blessed mistress, and they profited so much by her teaching that many of them were later made mistresses over others, so that there were few or no monasteries of women in those districts which did not desire teachers from her pupils.

Source: Life of Leofgyth (Leoba) by Rudolf of Fulda §9.

2.25   BONIFACE THE MORALIST   746

Boniface and seven missionary bishops to the King of Mercia. To the dearest lord King Aethelbald, preferred above all other kings in the love of Christ, who wields the glorious sceptre of imperial rule over the English, archbishop Boniface [and seven other bishops] send eternal and loving greetings in Christ.

We hear you give very many alms and it rejoices us greatly because those who give alms to the least of our brothers in need will hear this merciful sentence on the day of judgment: 'Come ye blessed of my Father, possess the kingdom prepared for you from the foundation of the world' (Matt. 25, 34). We also hear that you firmly prohibit iniquities such as theft, perjury and plunder and are known to defend widows and the poor, and that you keep a firm peace in your kingdom. And in this too we rejoice, praising God, for the Truth himself and our Peace, which is Christ (Eph. 2, 14), said: 'Blessed are the peacemakers, for they shall be called the children of God' (Matt. 5, 9):

But with these tidings comes a report of an evil sort, about your Excellency's style of life ... that you have neither taken a lawful wife nor kept chaste for God's sake, but that, swayed by lust, you have blotted the fame of your glory by lechery and adultery. We are extremely sorry for this because it is both shameful in the sight of God and the ruin of your reputation among the people.

What is worse, we are told that you commit this crime in the monasteries with holy nuns and virgins consecrated to God. That is certainly to double the sin. For example, what punishment should a servant incur from his master if he commits adultery with his master's wife? How much worse then for that man who in the filth of his lust violates a bride of Christ, the creator of heaven and earth!

Not only Christians but even heathens look on this as shameful, for they do what is right by the natural law decreed by God from the beginning, they preserve the bonds of marriage with their own wives and punish fornicators and adulterers. Thus in Old Saxony if a maiden disgraces her father's house by fornication, or if a married woman commits adultery, they sometimes force her to kill herself by hanging; and when the body has been cremated they hang her seducer over the pyre.... And the Wends, a very foul and wicked race, maintain the mutual love of the married state so zealously that a woman refuses to live after her husband is dead. She is honoured if she kills herself and burns on the same pyre as her husband.

And note that under this crime lurks another monstrous one— murder, because when either nuns or laywomen give birth in sin to children conceived in evil, they generally kill them.

2.26   BONIFACE TAKES CARE FOR THE MORROW   752

Boniface, servant of the servants of God, bishop by the grace of Christ, to his very dear fellow-churchman Fulrad the priest, sends eternal greetings in the love of Christ.

... It seems that I am coming to the end of this temporal life, the daily journey through infirmities. I therefore pray you to ask your gracious King Pippin, in the name of Christ the Son of God, that he will deign to let me know while I am still alive what kindness he will show to my disciples in the future. For almost all are foreigners. Some are priests ordained to minister to churches and people in many places, some are monks in monasteries, some children learning to read, some are those who have long laboured and lived with me and now grow old. I am anxious for all these lest after my death they be scattered like sheep with no shepherd, unless they have his Highness' support. The people living on the pagan borders must not forfeit the law of Christ.

Therefore I urgently crave his Grace's mercy in the name of God to appoint my son and suffragan bishop Lul—God willing and if it pleases his Grace—to minister to the people and churches as preacher and teacher of the priests and people. And I hope, God willing, that the priests may find him a master, the monks a teacher of their rule, and the Christian people a faithful preacher and pastor. I particularly beg this to be done because my priests live near the pagan borders in much poverty. They can get bread to eat but no clothing unless someone elsewhere supports them as I have done. *Source:* Letters of Boniface.

The Fury of the Northmen

The golden age in England ended with the coming of the heathen Vikings. They came first as raiders, later as conquerors and settlers. The first of these extracts is from a letter of sympathy which Alcuin of York, the foremost Englishman of his day and Charlemagne's principal courtier, wrote to the king of Northumbria when Lindisfarne was sacked. He puts forward one theory to account for the disaster, a theory of a kind beloved by moralists. There was perhaps something in it, but it leaves out of account the tempestuous out-thrust of adventure-and-booty-loving Vikings.

The end of the period of acute danger to Christianity in England came when Alfred defeated the Danes in 878. The Anglo-Saxon Chronicle records that 'the enemy gave him preliminary hostages and great oaths that they would leave his kingdom, and promised also that their king should receive baptism. And they kept their promise.' King Guthrum's baptism at Athelney was as important in its more restricted sphere as the baptism of Clovis had been 400 years before.

The second extract comes from Alfred's preface to his translation of Gregory the Great's *Pastoral Care*. It is a melancholy record of the ground that had been lost, written by a king who was determined that it should be regained and competent to undertake it.

2.27   THE SACK OF LINDISFARNE   793

Alcuin to Ethelred, King of Northumbria
It is nearly 350 years since we and our fathers occupied this most lovely land, and never has such terror been seen in Britain as the terror we now suffer from a heathen race; nor did any think that such an invasion could be made from the sea. Lo, the church of

St. Cuthbert spattered with the blood of the priests of God, robbed
of all its adornments! The holiest place in all Britain plundered
by pagans! The place where, after St. Paulinus left York, the
Christian faith arose in our race, there misery and disaster have
started. . . .

Brother, consider very carefully: was this new unheard of evil a
judgment upon unheard of evil deeds? I do not say that there was
no fornication among the people of old, but from the time of King
Aelfwold fornication, adultery and incest have swept the country,
so that these sins have been perpetrated without shame, even against
maids dedicated to God. And what can I say about avarice, robbery,
harsh judgments? It is clearer than daylight that these crimes have
increased everywhere, and a plundered nation is its testimony.

Look at the clothes, the hair styles, the luxurious ways of princes
and people. See how you trim your beards and hair in the style of
the pagans. Do you not live in terror of those whose fashions you
wish to follow? Your extravagant clothes are far beyond the necessities of nature and the customs of our forefathers. The superfluity
of princes is the poverty of the people.

2.28   ALFRED THE GREAT AND PASTORAL CARE   *c.* 890
King Alfred greets bishop Waeferth with loving and friendly words.
Let it be known to you what has often come into my mind; that
once there were wise men throughout England, whether men of God
or men of the world; what happy times they were through England;
how the kings who had power over folk in those days obeyed God
and his ministers, and fostered peace and virtue and order at home
while they enlarged their lands abroad; how they sped in war and
wisdom; and also the clergy, how eager they were in teaching or
learning and in all the services they rendered to God; and how
men from overseas came hither in search of wisdom and instruction,
and how we should have to get them from abroad now, if we would
have them.

So far had learning fallen in England that there were very few
on this side of Humber who could understand the liturgy in English
or translate a letter from Latin into English; and I believe that not
many beyond the Humber could. There were so few of them that
I cannot remember a single one south of the Thames when I began
to reign. Thank almighty God that we have any teachers among
us now. . . .

I remembered, before everything was plundered and burnt, how the churches throughout all England stood filled with treasures and books; and there were very many servants of God, but they had very little knowledge of the books, for they could not understand anything in them because they were not written in their language....

Then I remembered how the law was first found in the Hebrew tongue and again, when the Greeks had learnt it, they turned the whole of it into their own language and many other books also. And again the Latins similarly, when they had learnt it, turned it into their own language through wise interpreters; and also all other Christian nations have translated some part of it into their own language. Therefore I think it is better, if you agree, that we should also translate some books—those most needful for all men to know—into the language we can all understand, as we easily may with God's help if we have peace....

Among various and manifold troubles of this realm, I began to translate into English the book which is called in Latin *Pastoralis* and in English *Shepherd's Book* (lit. Herdbook), sometimes word for word, sometimes according to the sense, as I had learnt from Plegmund my archbishop, and Asser my bishop, and Grimbold my mass-priest, and John my mass-priest ... and I will send a copy to every bishopric in my realm; and on each there is a clasp worth 50 marks. And I command in God's name that no man take the clasp from the book or the book from the minster.

The Conversion of the North

2.29   THE SAXONS: 'MEN CONVINCED AGAINST THEIR WILL'
Charlemagne was determined both for political and religious motives to make sure that the pagan Saxons just across his eastern frontier were both tamed and Christianized. His long wars against them were ferocious and had something of the spirit of the Moslems' 'holy wars'. It was, according to K. S. Latourette in his *History of Christianity*, 'the most naked use of armed force for the spread of the faith which Christianity had yet seen.' Alcuin criticized Charlemagne for his compulsory and indiscriminate baptism of 'converts', declaring that no one should be baptized without adequate preparation. Augustine, whose *City of God* was Charlemagne's favourite book, would whole-heartedly have agreed. This extract comes from the *Life of Charlemagne* by his friend Einhard.

The Saxon war flared up again after a lull. No war was ever longer or crueller. No war demanded greater effort by the Franks. For the Saxons, like most of the races that live in Germany, are naturally fierce, devoted to the worship of demons, and hostile to our religion.

They do not think it dishonourable to break and defeat the laws of God and man. Besides there was always a risk of incidents that might lead to the peace being broken. Across the open plain there is no natural boundary between us and them except in a few places where there is a forest belt or a range of hills. Consequently on both sides murder, robbery, and arson were endemic. The Franks became so irritated by these incidents that they decided it was time to give up punitive raids and to make full-scale war against the Saxons.

So war was declared, and was waged for thirty years with very great ferocity on both sides. The Saxons lost more than the Franks. The end might have come sooner but for the bad faith of the Saxons. It is hard to say how often they acknowledged defeat, surrendered unconditionally to King Charles, promised to obey his orders, gave hostages as soon as they were asked, and received the ambassadors sent to them. Sometimes they were so cowed and broken that they promised to stop worshipping devils and to submit willingly to Christ. But though they were sometimes ready to profess obedience to the orders of Charles, they were always eager to break their promise. All through the war there was scarcely a year in which they did not both make a promise and break it. One cannot say which came more naturally to them.

But the high courage of the king and the steadfastness of his mind, which was undeflected either by success or failure, was proof against their vacillation. War-weariness could not force Charles to give up. He never allowed those who swore and forswore themselves to go scatheless, but he either led an expedition against them himself, or sent one under the command of his counts, to punish their perfidy and inflict a suitable penalty. At last, when all who resisted had been defeated and brought under his power, he took ten thousand men from either bank of the Elbe, with their wives and children, and settled them in many groups in various parts of Germany and Gaul. And at last the war, which had lasted so long, was finished on terms proposed by the king and accepted by the Saxons. They were to abandon the worship of devils, to give up their national ceremonies, to receive the Christian sacraments, and then to become one people with the Franks.

2.30   SWEDEN: GOD MOVES IN A MYSTERIOUS WAY

This extract comes from Rimbert's *Life of Anskar*, the Frank who served as a missionary in Sweden and became archbishop of Hamburg in 857. It describes some of the difficulties the pioneer missionaries had to meet.

God did not let this crime [the murder of a missionary] go unavenged, and nearly all who participated were punished in different ways. . . . The son of an influential man had joined in the plot and had put the spoils in his father's house. The father's property began to diminish, especially his flocks and household goods. The son himself was struck by divine vengeance and died, and soon afterwards his wife, son and daughter also died. When the father saw that he had lost everything but one little son, he began in his misery to fear the anger of the gods. Surely he was suffering because he had offended some god? . . .

He consulted a soothsayer to discover by casting lots which god he had offended. . . . The soothsayer said that all their gods regarded him favourably, but the Christian god was very angry with him.

'Christ has ruined you. Something hidden in your house is consecrated to him, and is the cause of all the evils you have suffered, and you will not be free of evils as long as this remains in your house' . . .

Then he remembered that there was a certain book among the spoils his son had brought into the house. He was filled with horror, for there was no priest nearby; what was he to do with the book, which he dared not keep any longer in his house? At last he thought of a plan. . . . He wrapped it up carefully and tied it to a fence with a notice attached stating that anyone who wished could take it. He also promised to make amends to the Lord Jesus Christ for the sin he had committed. One of the Christians took the book to his own home. We were assured of this by the man himself, who later showed such faith and devotion that while he was with us he learnt to say the Psalms by heart.

2.31   ICELAND: A HIGHLY SECULAR APPROACH   1000
When the Norsemen came to colonize Iceland in 870 Ari the Learned noted: 'The Christian men whom the Norsemen call Popes were here; but afterwards they went away because they did not wish to live there with the heathen men, and they left behind Irish books, bells, and crooks. From this it could be seen that they were Irishmen.' Iceland was settled partly direct from Norway and partly by Norsemen who had been in Scotland, the Orkneys, Shetlands and Faroes, or in Ireland. There was thus a certain strain of Celtic blood mixed with the Scandinavian and a certain contact with Christianity. Throughout the tenth century there was a slowly growing number of families who had become Christian, though the culture of the island remained thoroughly pagan. But in the year 1000 the Icelanders decided in their assembly (the Althing) to go over as a people to Christianity. The story was recorded by Ari the Learned about 130 years later.

'I came,' said Ari, 'when seven winters old to Hall, one winter after the death of Gelli Thorkelsson, my paternal grandfather and foster-father, and I remained there fourteen winters.... Hall, who both had a good memory and was truthful and remembered when he was baptized, told us that Thangbrand baptized him at the age of three winters; and that was one winter before Christianity was introduced here by law.'

King Olaf, son of Tryggvi, son of Olaf, son of Harald the Fair-haired, brought Christianity into Norway and into Iceland. He sent to this country a priest by the name of Thangbrand, who taught Christianity to people here, and baptized all those who embraced the faith. Hall Thorsteinsson of Sida let himself be baptized early and so did Hjalti Skeggjason of Thjorsardal and Gizur the White, ... and many other chieftains; yet those were numerous who opposed and refused it. And when he had been here a winter or two he went away, having at that time slain here two or three men who libelled him. And when he came east (to Norway) he told King Olaf all that had befallen him here, and said that it was beyond hope that Christianity yet would be received here. The king grew very angry at this, and because of it designed to kill or maim all our countrymen who were there in the east. But that same summer Gizur and Hjalti came out thither from here and persuaded the king to let those men off, promising him to use their good offices for a new trial that Christianity might still be received here, and they expressed a firm hope that this would meet with success....

Next year Gizur and his men went immediately to the mainland, and afterwards to the Althing, and they prevailed on Hjalti that he with eleven men stayed behind in Laugardal because the preceding summer he had been sentenced to the lesser outlawry for blasphemy. And the reason for that was that he had recited at the Law Rock the following ditty:

> Barking dogs I disesteem,
> And a bitch I Freya deem.

Gizur and his followers proceeded until they came to a place by Ölfus Lake called Vellankatla, and sent words from there to the Althing that all their supporters should come to meet them because they had heard that their adversaries were going to keep them from the moot field by force of arms. But before they broke up from there Hjalti came riding thither and those who had stayed behind with him. And then they rode to the moot, having before been joined by their kinsmen and friends as they had requested. The heathen men, however, gathered together fully armed, and whether it would come to a fight hung upon the slenderest thread. On the second day Gizur and Hjalti went to the Law Rock and made known their message; and it is reported that it was striking how well they spoke. But the consequence was that one man after the other called witnesses, the Christians and the heathen, each declaring themselves out of law with the other, and then they went away from the Law Rock.

Then the Christians asked Hall of Sida to proclaim the law of conformity with Christianity, but he disengaged himself from that by bargaining with Thorgeir the law-speaker that he should declare the law though he was still a heathen. And afterwards when men had gone to their booths Thorgeir lay down and spread his cloak over himself, and rested all that day and the next night, nor did he speak a word. But the next morning he sent word that men should go to the Law Rock.

And when men gathered there he began his speech, saying that he thought the people would be in a sorry plight if men in this land were not all to have the same law; and he remonstrated with them in various ways that they should not let this come to pass, saying that it would lead to disturbance, and certainly it was to be expected that there would occur such fights between men that the land would be laid waste thereby. He related how the kings of Denmark and Norway had carried on battles against one another for a long time until the people of those countries made peace between them although they did not wish it; and that counsel turned out so well that within a short time they were exchanging precious gifts, and that peace lasted so long as they both lived. 'And now it seems advisable to me,' he said, 'that we do not let their will prevail who are most strongly opposed to one another, but to compromise between them that each side may win part of its case, and let us all have one law and one faith. It will prove true that if we sunder the law, we will also sunder the peace.' And so he concluded his speech that both parties agreed that all would keep the law which he should declare.

Then it was made law that all people should be Christian and those be baptized who were still unbaptized in this land; but as to infanticide the old law should stand, and also as to eating of horse-flesh. People might sacrifice to the heathen gods secretly, if they wished, but under the penalty of the lesser outlawry, if this was proved by witnesses. But a few winters later this heathendom was abolished like the rest.

Infanticide was practised as a form of birth control to limit the supply of slaves. The interval between the adoption of Christianity and the abolition of these permitted pagan practices was probably 20 years.

2.32　　　　　THE FRONTIER WITH THE SLAVS

Most of the Slavs were brought to Christianity by missionaries from the Eastern wing of the Church; but in Central Europe there were approaches from the west as well. Either way the process was long delayed. This account of German missions and colonization among Slavs near Oldenburg comes from *The Chronicle of the Slavs* by Halmod, priest of Bosan. The events described took place in 1156—660 years after the baptism of Clovis which had taken place only 350 miles away.

On our journey across the great plain we came to a forest, the only one in that country. In it there were very old trees and among them we saw oaks sacred to Prove, the god of that land. These sacred oaks were within an enclosure with a wooden fence which had two gates in it. Each village and house had its own idols, but this was the central holy place for the whole land.... Nobody was allowed to enter it except the priest, worshippers making a sacrifice, and fugitives seeking sanctuary in fear of death. They were never denied asylum.

　　The Slavs have many forms of idol worship.... Some temples contain weirdly shaped idols like that of the god Pogada at Plön. Other gods, of whom no images are made, live in woods and sacred groves, like Prove, the god of Oldenburg. The Slavs also carve idols of gods with two, three, or more heads. They do not, however, deny that there is one god in the heavens ruling over all the other gods; the gods of plains and woods, sorrows and joys. But they believe that this all-powerful god is concerned only with matters that take place in the heavens....

　　When we came (on Sunday, January 8, 1156) to that wood and the unholy place, the bishop told us to lose no time in destroying the sacred grove. Leaping from his horse he used his pastoral staff to break up the decorated gates. We entered the enclosure, heaped together the material of the fence against the sacred trees and made a pyre.... We were a little afraid that the people might start a riot and overwhelm us, but we were protected by heaven. After this we went to the Lodge where Thesseman received us with great ceremony. We did not enjoy the entertainment which the Slavs gave us because we saw the shackles and various instruments of torture which they used on Christians brought here from Denmark. We saw there priests of God whom the bishop was unable to help either by force or by entreaty. They were grown thin from their long imprisonment.

The following Sunday (January 15) all the people of the land assembled in the market place of Lübeck. The lord bishop came and urged them to give up their idols and worship the one God who is in heaven, to receive the grace of baptism and to renounce their evil works—namely, robbing and killing Christians. When the bishop had finished speaking to the gathering, Pribislav, speaking for the others, said '... Your princes are so bitter and severe towards us, imposing such taxes and burdensome labour services, that we find death is kinder to us than life.... How can we, who have always to be thinking about flight, be free to build churches for this new religion and to receive baptism?... What fault is it of ours if, driven from our fatherland, we have troubled the sea and those who travel by it, Danes and merchants? Is not this really the fault of your princes who hunt us?'

To this the lord bishop replied: 'It is no wonder that up to now our princes have maltreated your people since they do not think they can be greatly wronging people who worship idols and are without God. It is rather for you to return to Christian worship and submit yourselves to your Creator before whom even those who carry the world on their shoulders bend in obedience. Do not the Saxons and other Christian peoples live in tranquility, content with what is rightly theirs? Indeed it is because you alone dissent from the religion of all men that you are liable to be plundered by all....'

[Pribislav did in fact receive baptism.]

... The bishop summoned Bruno the priest from Faldera and sent him to Oldenburg to provide for the salvation of that people. Bruno was undoubtedly sent by God for his task. At night in a vision he saw himself holding a chrismal [a vessel containing the holy oils used in baptism] from which came a young green sapling which grew into a fine large tree. And in truth his mission turned out as he expected. As soon as he came to Oldenburg he started with great zeal on God's work. On the one hand he cut down the sacred groves and abolished the sacrilegious rites; on the other he urged the Slavs to receive the grace of regeneration in baptism. Because the citadel of Oldenburg, where there had once been an episcopal church and see, was deserted, the bishop persuaded the count to settle a colony of Saxons there, partly so that the priest might have the comfort of neighbours whose language and customs he knew.... The count ordered the Slavs to bring their dead for burial in the churchyard and on feast days to assemble in the church to hear the word of God. To them Bruno, God's priest, brought a full ministry of the word of God, preaching to them at appointed times in their own Slavonic speech.

CHAPTER THREE

THE CHRISTIAN EAST:
HOLY WISDOM, HUMAN FOLLY

The Christian East in the sixth century—roughly the Balkans, Turkey, Syria, Israel, Egypt, Libya—differed greatly from the West. It was a unified, civilized state with a powerful emperor, supported by an efficient bureaucracy, working under an effective code of laws. Small wonder then that the most important man in Eastern Christendom was the Emperor himself, layman though he was. He could, and did, play an active part in church affairs, deposing one patriarch and setting up another. He did that not only or mainly because the patriarchs played politics or set a bad example, but for theological reasons. Only the western patriarch, the Pope of Rome, was effectively beyond his control. There was, however, one great practical limit to his power—the strength of the mob in the great cities, and especially in Constantinople (Byzantium) and its ardent participation in theological debate (3.1).

In 532 the Emperor Justinian nearly lost his throne, and the cathedral was destroyed, in five nights of rioting which started in the arena over a dispute between supporters of the Green and Blue chariot teams (cp Celtic and Rangers) over a theological nicety. An earlier riot is described in 3.1.

In Byzantium, where so many were so intensely concerned with religious issues, there developed a distinctive spirituality which found characteristic expression in the Orthodox Liturgy and an appropriate setting in the domed Byzantine churches and supremely in the Emperor Justinian's St. Sophia, the Holy Wisdom of God (3.2).

At the same time men sat pretty lightly to the theological enthusiasms of the day. There was much superstition and, among the educated, a greater readiness to conform than to believe. Thanks to a great historian, Procopius, it is possible to make something like a balance sheet of the state of religion in the East (3.5–3.7).

Beyond the bounds of the Eastern Empire Christianity was still making progress, but the expansion was more often Nestorian than Orthodox or Catholic (3.8–3.10).

In Constantinople

3.1   FOUR FEARFUL WORDS   512

Religious controversy and religious riots, if not religious wars, still flourished in the empire. The Alexandrians had been Monophysite—so deeply attached to the unity of Christ's nature that they believed that as God he was born and as God he died. The Syrians had on the whole been Nestorians, denying that Mary was rightly called the Mother of God. A compromise had been found at the Council of Chalcedon in 451 (See Vol. I p. 268). It now defines the orthodox Christian belief, but for a considerable time after its formation it satisfied only some. Among its most vociferous and belligerent supporters was the mob of Constantinople; but the emperor, Anastasius, an old man of 81, was a Monophysite and so were most of the upper class in the capital. As always, some symbol had to be found to serve both as a rallying cry and as a mark of division. In 512 it took the form of four Greek words (five in English: 'who was crucified for us') which the Monophysites added to the Trisagion (Holy, holy, holy: Isaiah 6, 1–3) in the Liturgy. The following extract comes from Marcellinus, a contemporary who was a courtier of the Emperor Justinian.

On Sunday the choir added to the Trisagion the four words which speak of the death of God. This was done in the presence in their official seats of Marinus [the Praetorian Prefect] and Plato [the prefect of the city] at the order of the Emperor Anastasius. Many of the orthodox who sang the old words and shouted down the singers of falsehood were killed inside the sacred church or thrown into prison where they perished. But on Monday there took place in the porch of the church of St. Theodore a still greater slaughter of Catholics who suffered for the one true faith. Because of this on the next day, Tuesday, November 6, the day on which Constantinople keeps the anniversary of the covering of all Europe with volcanic ash, crowds of the orthodox from all over the city assembled in the forum of Constantine. [In 472 there had been severe earthquakes in Asia Minor and the sky at Constantinople had been black with ash from Vesuvius.]

Some of them spent the whole day and night singing the Trisagion to Christ, rushing through the city and putting to the sword and fire those (few) monks and monasteries who sided with the Emperor Anastasius. Others brought the keys of the city gates and the standards of the legions to the forum where a religious camp was set up on military lines. They shouted for Areobinda to be made emperor in place of Anastasius, whose pictures and statues were thrown down. The houses of Marinus and Pompey were burned.[1] They drove back with a storm of stones Celer and Patricius who were sent to mediate and calm them down.

[1] Another account describes how a monk was found hiding in the house of Marinus. The mob decided that it was he who had advised the use of the heretical Trisagion so they cut off his head and paraded with it on a pole shouting, 'See the head of an enemy of the Trinity'.

Most of them made their way to the Circus Maximus and there, in front of the imperial box where Anastasius sat, they sang the Trisagion in the Catholic way, brandishing the Gospels and the cross of Christ and demanding that Marinus and Plato as the instigators of the perverted Trisagion should be thrown to the wild beasts. The Emperor Anastasius promised them everything, but falsely and hypocritically, and on the third day after they had assembled in the forum he persuaded them to go back to their homes having accomplished nothing.

3.2   THE BUILDING OF ST. SOPHIA   560

The church which Justinian built in place of the old cathedral still stands, one of the architectural glories of the world, perhaps the fairest of Christian churches (See Plate 3). But it is no longer a church. It is now a museum after serving for 900 years as a church and 550 as a mosque. The following extract, like several others in this chapter, comes from Procopius, a high official of Justinian's court. His book on Buildings is an enthusiastic survey of the Byzantium Justinian created.

Regardless of expense and eager to begin the work of construction Justinian began to collect craftsmen from the whole world. The most experienced and skilled architect, not only of his own time but in comparison with those of old, was Anthemius of Tralles. He fed the fire of the emperor's enthusiasm, specified the work of the various craftsmen and drew the plans of the buildings to be constructed. Associated with him was another master-builder, Isidorus the Milesian, an intelligent and worthy assistant....

So the church has become a vision of marvellous beauty, overwhelming the beholder, incredible to those who know it only by hearsay. It soars to a height that matches the sky. Thrusting up among the other buildings it stands on high and looks down on the rest of the metropolis. It adorns the city because it is a part of it, and it glories in its own beauty because though a part of the city it dominates it....

Sunlight floods over it and is mirrored from its marble. Even the interior is not so much illuminated by the sun as bathed in its own radiance generated within.

Procopius proceeds to give a detailed description of the building's architectural construction, the climax of which is the dome which seems to 'float in the air on no firm basis ... suspended from heaven'.

He who enters this church to pray knows at once that this work has been so finely shaped not by human power or skill alone, but by the influence of God. So his mind is raised to heaven and exalted. He feels that God cannot be far away, that God must love to dwell in this his chosen place. And this happens whenever one sees the church, not only for the first time but again and again; the experience comes anew each time.

Orthodox Worship

3.3 THE DIVINE LITURGY

The Liturgy, or form of Eucharistic worship, used in the East in Justinian's time and substantially still today, was ascribed to John Chrysostom, the 'golden-tongued', (*c.* 345–407: see Volume I, p. 213). It followed the pattern of the earlier Liturgy of Basil. Note the emphasis on Wisdom in relation to the Gospel. To understand the service it is important to remember that in all Orthodox (Eastern) churches the sanctuary, where the altar is, is divided from the rest of the church by a screen called the Iconostasis because it holds the icons or sacred pictures. This explains the important part played in the ceremonial by the two Entrances or processions through the screen—the Little Entrance before the Gospel in the Mass of Cate-chumens or Ministry of the Word, and the Great Entrance near the beginning of the Mass of the Faithful when, as Symeon of Salonika (d. 1429) put it, 'the procession of the divine gifts (the bread and wine) is with great pomp of Reader, Deacons and Priests, with the lamps and holy vessels going before and after, because this symbolises the last Advent of Christ, when he shall come with glory.' As time went on symbolic explanations were given to all the ceremonial acts. Thus the puzzling expression 'The Doors' after the Offertory, which was almost certainly a signal that the doors of the church should be shut against non-Christians, was interpreted as an injunction to the faithful to shut out all worldy cares so that they could 'attend in Wisdom'. Similarly the fans waved before the divine gifts during the canon were originally intended to keep flies away, but had come to be made of silver in the shape of wings to recall the Seraphim who beat their wings around the throne of God.

The language of the service was that of the country—Greek, Syriac or Coptic—just as it was Latin in the West. The Liturgy, which was usually preceded by Matins, took about three hours, but worshippers were free to come and go. Much of it was unaccompanied singing. Our text comes from a MS of about 790 in the Bibliotheca Barberina, Rome.

THE MASS OF THE CATECHUMENS

Priest: Blessed be the kingdom of the Father and of the Son and of the Holy Spirit, now and for ever and from all ages to all ages.

[Prayers follow, in the form of a litany, with responses sung by the choir. Then there are three antiphons or anthems with accompanying prayers. The prayer of the 3rd antiphon is the 'Prayer of St. Chrysostom' in our English prayer-book. The words of the 3rd antiphon on Sundays were the Beatitudes of Matt. 5, 3–11.]

The first antiphon is sung by the choir and the priest says the prayer of the first antiphon. The deacon, having made a reverence, leaves his place and stands before the icon of Christ, taking hold of his orarion [stole] with three fingers of his right hand.

While the third antiphon is being sung by the choir, the priest and deacon make three reverences before the altar. Then the priest, taking the Holy Gospel, gives it to the deacon, and thus, going through the north portion of the sanctuary preceded by lamps, they make the Little Entrance. The prayer of the entrance, said secretly by the priest:

Master, Lord, and our God, who hast disposed in heaven troops and armies of angels and archangels, for the ministry of thy glory:

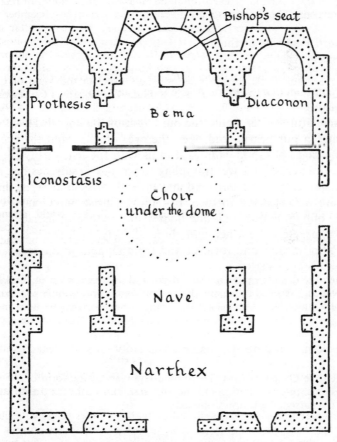

Plan of the Church of St. Theodore, Athens

grant that with our entrance there may be an entrance of holy angels, ministering together with us, and with us glorifying thy goodness.

The deacon stands before the priest and shows the Holy Gospel, saying with a loud voice:

Wisdom [sophia], stand up!

The deacon lays the Holy Gospel on the altar and the choir sing the trisagion:

Holy God, Holy and Mighty, Holy and Immortal, have mercy upon us.

[This 'thrice-holy' is sung five times while the priest says secretly the prayer of the trisagion. Then after an alleluia from the reader, a verse and sung response, the Epistle is read.]

Priest: Peace be to thee.

Reader: Alleluia.

While the Alleluia is being sung the deacon censes the altar and the whole sanctuary and the priest. The priest says the Prayer before the Gospel:

O merciful Master, cause the pure light of the knowledge of thee to shine in our hearts, and open the eyes of our mind to perceive thy messages of Good Tidings. Fill us with the fear of thy blessed commandments, that we, trampling down our fleshly desires, may seek a heavenly citizenship, and may do and consider all those things that are well-pleasing to thee. For thou, Christ our God, art the source of light to our souls and bodies, and to thee we ascribe glory, with thine eternal Father and thine all-holy, righteous, and life-giving Spirit, now and for ever and from all ages to all ages.

[Then the deacon takes up the Gospel and asks the priest to bless him, after which, preceded by tapers, the deacon stands on the ambo—a reading platform which later became a pulpit—and the priest turns to the west and says:]

Wisdom, stand up. Let us hear the Holy Gospel. Peace to all.

[Then the Gospel is read. There follow prayers in the form of a litany, for bishops, priests, monks, and the imperial family and for the departed. Then the catechumens are dismissed.]

THE MASS OF THE FAITHFUL

[This begins with a litany for peace followed from Justinian's time by the Cherubic Hymn:]

We who now mystically
Portray the Cherubim
Praise with thrice-holy hymn the life-giving Trinity.

Banish life's cares while we
Welcome the King of All,
Coming with angels attending invisibly.
Alleluia, alleluia, alleluia.

[Meanwhile the priest says a secret prayer:]

... Cleanse my soul and heart from an evil conscience, and strengthen me that have been endued with the grace of priesthood with the might of thy Holy Spirit, that I may stand by this holy altar and sacrifice thy holy and spotless Body and Blood....

[Then the deacon censes the altar and sanctuary. He and the priest say the penitential Psalm 51.]

Then they go to the prothesis [credence table] ... and the deacon, having censed the holy things and said to himself,
God be merciful to me a sinner,
saith to the priest,
Sir, lift up.
And the priest raises the veil and puts it on the left shoulder of the deacon, saying,
Lift up your hands in the sanctuary and bless the Lord.
Then, taking the holy discus [paten or dish], he puts it with all care and reverance on the deacon's head, the deacon also holding the censer with one of his fingers. And the priest, taking the holy chalice in his hands, they go through the north part, preceded by tapers, and make the GREAT ENTRANCE.

[Returning to the sanctuary, the priest places the chalice and paten on the altar, covers them with the veil and censes them three times. A litany of supplication is said by the deacon, with responses by the choir. Then the priest says the Offertory prayer, the Prayer of Oblation:]

O Lord God Almighty, who only art holy, who dost accept the sacrifice of praise from those who call upon thee with their whole heart, admit to thy holy altar and accept the prayer of us sinners, enabling us to offer unto thee gifts and spiritual sacrifices, both for our sins and the ignorances of the people. Count us worthy to find such favour with thee that this our sacrifice may be acceptable unto thee, and that the good Spirit of thy grace may dwell with us and these gifts presented unto thee, and with all thy people.

[The priest and deacon then adore the holy gifts three times, kissing the veil that covers them. Then the deacon exclaims:]

The doors! the doors! Let us attend in Wisdom!
The people join in the Creed.
The deacon then fans the Oblation reverently while the priest takes the veil from the holy gifts and lays it on one side.
Priest: The grace of our Lord Jesus Christ and the love of God the Father, and the fellowship of the Holy Spirit be with you all.
Choir: And with thy spirit.
Priest: Let us lift up our hearts.
Choir: We lift them up unto the Lord.
Priest: Let us give thanks unto the Lord.
Choir: It is meet and right to worship the Father, the Son, and the Holy Spirit, the consubstantial and undivided Trinity.
Priest: It is very meet and right to hymn thee, to bless thee, to praise thee, to worship thee in all places of thy dominion, for thou art God indescribable, incomprehensible, invisible, immeasurable, always existing as thou dost exist, thou and thy only begotten Son and thy Holy Spirit. Out of nothing thou hast brought us into being, and when we fell away thou didst raise us up again, and until thou hast done everything thou dost not cease to bring us to heaven and give us thy coming Kingdom. For all these things we give thanks to thee and thy only-begotten Son and to thy Holy Spirit, for all the things we know and do not know, for the seen and unseen blessings we enjoy. We give thanks to thee also for this service which thou dost deign to receive at our hands, although there stand by thee thousands of archangels and ten thousands of angels, and Cherubim and Seraphim that have six wings and are full of eyes and soar aloft, singing the shouting the triumphal hymn:
Choir: Holy, Holy, Holy, Lord of Sabaoth; heaven and earth are full of thy glory. Hosanna in the highest; blessed is he that cometh in the name of the Lord; hosanna in the highest.

[There follows from the priest, speaking in a low voice, a commemoration of the institution of the sacrament by Christ:]

... Who took bread in his holy, pure, and sinless hands, and gave thanks, and blessed and hallowed and broke it, and gave it to his holy disciples and apostles saying *(aloud)*, 'Take, eat: this is my body which is broken for you for the remission of sins.'

Choir: Amen.

Priest (in a low voice): Likewise after supper he took the cup saying *(aloud)*, Drink ye all of this: this is my blood of the new covenant, which is shed for you and for many for the remission of sins....

... We commemorate the command of our Saviour and all that he endured for our sake, the cross, the grave, the resurrection after three days, the ascension into heaven, the enthronement at the right hand of the Father, and the second and glorious coming again. We bring before thee thine own, from thine own, in all things and for all things.... Send down thy Holy Spirit upon us and these gifts we offer....

Deacon (pointing with his stole towards the holy bread, says in a low voice): Sir, bless the holy bread.

Priest (making the sign of the cross three times on the holy gifts): And make this bread the precious Body of thy Christ.

Deacon: Amen. Sir, bless the holy cup.

Priest: And make that which is in this cup the precious Blood of thy Christ.

Deacon: Amen. *Then, pointing with his stole to both the holy things:* Sir, bless.

Priest: And change them by thy Holy Spirit.

[Then, while the deacon fans the Oblation, the priest begins the Great Intercession.]

... Unite us all, as many as share the one bread and cup, in the fellowship of the one Holy Spirit ... that we may find mercy and grace together with all the saints which have been well-pleasing unto thee since the world began, our forefathers and fathers, patriarchs, prophets, apostles, preachers, evangelists, martyrs, confessors, teachers, and with all the spirits of the just in faith made perfect....

[The priest continues with the commemoration of the Mother of God and all saints, general and particular, for 'every orthodox bishopric' and the clergy.]

... We pray for our most faithful kings, beloved of Christ, all their court and army. Grant to them, Lord, a peaceful reign, that we, in their peace, may lead a quiet and peaceable life in all godliness and honesty....

Remember the city in which we dwell and every town and district and the faithful who live there. Remember, Lord, them that voyage and travel, that are sick, that are labouring, that are in prison, and keep them safe. Remember, Lord, those that bear good fruit, who do good deeds in thy holy churches and help the poor. And send forth on us all the riches of thy compassion ... for thou art the help of the helpless, the hope of the hopeless, the saviour of the tempest-tossed, the haven of them that sail, the physician of the sick....

Deacon: Having prayed for the oneness of the faith and the participation of the Holy Spirit, let us commend ourselves and each other and all our lives to Christ our God.

Priest: And make us worthy, O Lord, with boldness and without condemnation, to dare to call upon thee, our God and Father who art in heaven, and to say:

People: The Lord's Prayer.

Priest: ... Hear us, O Lord Jesus Christ our God, out of thy holy dwelling-place, and from the throne of the glory of thy kingdom, and come and sanctify us, thou that sittest above with the Father, and art here invisibly present with us. By thy mighty hand make us worthy to partake of thy spotless Body and precious Blood, and through us all thy people.

And when the deacon sees the priest stretching forth his hands and touching the holy Bread to make the holy elevation, he exclaims,

Let us attend!

And the priest, elevating the holy Bread, exclaims,

Holy things for holy persons!

Choir: One holy, one Lord, Jesus Christ, to the glory of God the Father.

[The priest then makes his communion, saying as he takes the elements:]

The blessed and most holy Body of our Lord and God and Saviour, Jesus Christ, is communicated to me, N., priest, for the remission of my sins and for everlasting life.

I, N., priest, partake of the pure and holy Blood of our Lord and God and Saviour, Jesus Christ, for the remission of my sins and for eternal life.

[After the deacon is given communion he opens the doors of the sanctuary and says to the people:]

Approach with the fear of God, faith, and love.

[Each communicant bowed and crossed his hands over his breast, and received the bread and wine together, put into his mouth with a silver spoon. A brief thanksgiving follows; then the priest says:]

Let us go in peace.... Give thy peace, O God, to thy world, to thy churches, to our priests and kings, to the army and all thy people....
The blessing of the Lord be upon you.
Glory to thee, our God: glory to thee.
People: Glory. Now and evermore.

[The holy vessels are removed to the prothesis. The deacon returns to gather all the holy things, 'even the smallest particle', and the priest comes forth to give the antidoron to the people. This is the remains of the five loaves which had been offered for the service of the altar and blessed in the prothesis, but not actually used, small pieces having been cut off each loaf for that purpose.]

3.4   HYMNS OF THE EASTERN CHURCH

Hymns played a great part in the worship of the church. In the Liturgy the hymns changed daily and were sung in a special mode for each day of the week. In the East as in the West a new rhythmic verse had replaced the old classical forms based on long and short quantities. The most prolific writer was Romanos, called 'the singer', a deacon who wrote first at Beirut in Lebanon and later at Constantinople where he worked in the first half of the sixth century. Altogether he wrote a thousand hymns, rivalling Charles Wesley,—not only in quantity but in quality. A modern editor considers him 'the greatest poet of the Byzantine age, and perhaps the greatest ecclesiastical poet of any age'. Below is an almost literal translation of the first four verses of his hymn for Palm Sunday. Each hymn of this type had about 25 verses of varying length, often in acrostic form.

Two hundred years later Greek hymn-writing entered a new phase, characterized, it is said, by 'an increase in artistic finish and a falling off in poetical vigour'. Perhaps the best known writer of this period is John of Damascus whom we shall meet again as a theologian (see 4.27). His Easter hymn, 'Come ye faithful, raise the strain' is familiar in J. M. Neale's version to most English congregations.

> With branches once they hymned him,
> With clubs they seized him then,
> They, Jews insensible,
> Him, Christ the God.

But we with faith unchangeable
Honour him ever as saviour;
So let us loudly hail him:
> *Blessed are thou that comest*
> *To raise up Adam's race.*

Borne on a throne in heaven,
On the foal of an ass on earth,
You, Christ the God!
You accepted the praise of angels
And the children's hymn,
As they shouted to you:
> *Blessed are thou that comest*
> *To raise up Adam's race.*

When you had fettered hell,
And made a corpse of Death,
And resurrected Earth,
With palm-leaves infants praised you
As conqueror, O Christ,
Shouting to you today:
> *Hosanna to the Son of David.*

No more, they say,
Shall babes be killed,
Thanks to the babe of Mary;
You only will be crucified
For the old man and the child.
No more shall the sword come against us,
But the spear shall pierce your side;
Wherefore we say, rejoicing,
> *Blessed are thou that comest*
> *To raise up Adam's race.*

Taking Stock with Procopius

3.5   THE DISCREET AGNOSTIC   534

The description of St. Sophia by Procopius (3.2) was almost certainly
commissioned by Justinian. The real Procopius comes out more clearly in
his other books. He was a civil servant whose career ran from 511 to 552.
For fifteen years, from 527 to 542 he was closely associated with Justinian's
famous general Belisarius whom he served as something like a Judge
Advocate General, legal adviser and counsellor. They became close friends,

though later there was a quarrel. Procopius's main claim to fame is the excellent histories he wrote of the general's campaigns in Iraq, Africa and Italy.

Procopius probably never got down to writing the book he planned about 'the things for which Christians quarrel among themselves', or, if he did, it has been lost. We, therefore, have to be content with passing references which, fortunately, are graphic and revealing. This particular story, from his *Gothic War*, makes his own religious position clear. We are dealing with an informed but uncommitted writer, a theist but not, except officially, a Christian.

Among the Goths was one Theodatus, son of Amalfida, Theodoric's sister, a man of advanced years, versed in Latin literature and the teaching of Plato. He was unpractised in war and never aspired to the seats of justice, yet he was extremely avaricious.... So he plotted to deliver Tuscany to the Emperor Justinian for a great sum of money; he was also to be made a Senator and live in Constantinople.

Meanwhile ambassadors came from Constantinople to the bishop of Rome. They were Hypatius of Ephesus and Demetrius from Philippi in Macedonia and they came about questions which Christians of different opinions dispute among themselves. The questions I know but will not repeat. To search into the nature of God I hold to be madness. Man cannot exactly understand human nature, much less the nature of God. Let me therefore be discreetly silent, only not denying that which in God is honoured. Let priests or private men speak what they believe. All I can say about God is that he is absolutely good and has all things in his power.

Theodatus met these ambassadors privately and gave them orders to inform the emperor of his aforementioned plot.

Source: Procopius, *The Gothic Wars* I, 2.

3.6 THE TRUE CROSS OF APAMEA 540

This extract comes from Procopius' *Persian War* II, 8 as translated by Sir Henry Holcraft in 1653. Chosroes (d. 579) was the greatest of the Persian Sassanid dynasty. In 540 he sacked Antioch and extended his power to the Black Sea and the Caucasus. For the True Cross see Vol. I p. 149.

Chosroes much desired to see Apamea, only for curiosity, he said, and the ambassadors unwillingly yielded on condition that, having seen the city and received 1,000 pounds weight of silver, he should retire without sacking it.... Then Chosroes and his army went to Apamea.

In Apamea there is a piece of wood a cubit long [18″], part of

Christ's cross, brought thither long ago by a Syrian. The inhabitants, believing this to be a great defence to them and their city, have put it in a casket set all with gold and precious stones, and committed it to three priests to keep. One day yearly the whole city brings it out and adores it.

The Apameans were afraid of the Persians coming, hearing too how in Chosroes was no truth, and they entreated their bishop, Thomas, to show them the wood of the cross that they might do it their last reverence. Then a miracle happened above reason and belief. While the priest was carrying and shewing the wood, a bright flame hovered above it and the roof above shone with an extraordinary light. As the priest moved round the church the light went along, keeping its place in the roof directly above him. The Apameans were ravished with delight at the miracle, at once rejoicing and weeping and now confident of their preservation. Thomas, after he had gone round the church, put the wood into the casket and covered it; and suddenly the shining ceased. . . .

Chosroes rode into the city with 200 of his best men. And no sooner in but he broke his promise to the ambassadors and commanded the bishop to give him not 1,000 lb weight of silver only, nor tenfold that, but all their treasures of gold and silver which were very great. I do not doubt that he would have sacked and enslaved the whole city if God had not manifestly hindered him. . . .

When Chosroes had taken their treasures and Thomas saw that he was drunk with abundance, he brought the wood of the cross and opening the casket showed it to him saying:

'O excellent king, this is all that is left. This casket beautified with gold and precious stones we do not grudge you. Take it with all the rest. But this piece of wood is our preservative and precious to us. I beg and beseech you to give it to us, sir.'

Chosroes granted this; and to show magnificence he willed the people to go to the circus and the charioteers to run their races and was himself a keen watcher of their sports.

3.7   RELIGIOUS PERSECUTION

Men often write books not to be published during their life-time. These are often at variance with what they publish at the time. Procopius was such a man. In old age he wrote his *Anecdota* which is full of bitter criticism and gossip about Justinian and Belisarius. What he says is suspect where it is not supported by other evidence. This caution, however, does not apply to the following passage.

It shows Justinian as persecutor, which he was—though not on the scale of some later rulers. It shows the strength of heretical churches, some of which were more like English nonconformists than heretics. For the Montanists see Vol. 1 pp. 91–94. The Samaritans are the descendants of the Biblical sect of whom a tiny minority still survive in Samaria.

The reference to 'the followers' of the old gods' and the 'Greeks' is important for two reasons. It shows the persistence of a non-Christian philosophical tradition 150 years after the failure of Julian the Apostate to restore the old religion. It refers to the efforts that Justinian made to put it down. Of these the one that is best remembered, though it is not referred to by Procopius, is the closing of the schools, or university, of Athens in 529. From this time higher education was confined to guaranteed Christian hands.

This passage in Procopius (*Anecdota* XI) points to a good deal of religious apathy, illustrated by a readiness to change faiths when required.

In the Roman empire there are many rejected Christian doctines which they call 'heresies', such as those of Montanists, Sabbatians, and all others which lead man's judgment astray. Justinian ordered all these heretics to renounce their old beliefs; if they refused he would not allow them to bequeath any property to their children or relatives. Now the churches of these so-called heretics, especially the Arians, contained fabulous treasures. Neither the Roman Senators nor any other group of citizens possessed the wealth of these sanctuaries. Their gold and silver and precious stones could not be counted. They owned quantities of houses and villages and lands in all parts of the world, in fact every kind of wealth—naturally, because no previous ruler had disturbed them. Many orthodox believers also depended on them for a living. So Justinian began by confiscating the property of these churches, stripping them suddenly of their wealth. Many lost their livelihood.

Everywhere they tried to force people to change their traditional faith. But farmers thought this would be a sin and determined to resist the demand. Many were killed by the soldiers; many, stupidly thinking that it was a righteous act, committed suicide; most went into exile. The Montanists, who live in Phrygia, shut themselves up in their churches and set them on fire, so that they and their building perished senselessly together. The whole Roman empire was filled with murdered corpses and homeless men.

There was great confusion in Palestine when a similar law was passed against Samaritans. People in my own Caesarea and the other towns thought it foolish to suffer for a silly dogma, so they gave up their own label and called themselves Christians, and by this ruse escaped the legal penalty. All the most prudent and intelligent showed no hesitation in joining the faith, but the majority resented being forced to abandon the faith of their fathers against their will and they turned to the Manichaeans and to the worshippers of the old gods.

[A peasant rising was bloodily suppressed and the land left derelict, but Christian owners still had to pay taxes on it.]

Justinian then persecuted the so-called 'Greeks', punishing their bodies and plundering their property. Even those who became nominal Christians to avoid trouble did not escape for long, for they were soon arrested while pouring libations, performing sacrifices or other pagan acts....

Beyond the Bounds

These three extracts deal with Christianity outside the Roman empire in Africa and Asia. The first tells a familiar story though in an unusual form— the scandal of competing churches in a pagan world. The unfamiliarity of the form lies in the fact that this particular competition was caused by the rivalry of Justinian and his wife Theodora. Justinian was an orthodox Christian who accepted, and enforced, the doctrine of the person of Christ as defined by the Council of Chalcedon. The Empress Theodora was a Monophysite (see Vol. 1 p. 270). The story comes from John of Ephesus, a Monophysite leader of the Syriac speaking church and an important contemporary historian. One of his achievements was to preach to the surviving pagans in Asia Minor. He claimed to have baptized 70,000.

The second extract (3.9) comes from Procopius. It shows two important things—the persistence of the old pagan religion in Arabia and the strength of the Jewish colony there. (For Christianity in Ethiopia see Vol. 1 pp. 270–272.)

3.8   RIVAL MISSIONS IN THE SUDAN   *c.* 540

Among the clergy in attendance on the patriarch Theodosius (of Constantinople) was a proselyte named Julian, a good old man, who formed an earnest spiritual wish to bring Christianity to the nomads who live on the eastern borders of the Thebais below Egypt. They were not only not part of the Roman empire but received a subsidy on condition that they kept out of it and did not pillage it. The blessed Julian, therefore, went and spoke about them to the late empress, Theodora, (who) ... received the proposal with joy and promised to do everything in her power for the conversion of these tribes from the errors of idolatry.... But when the emperor (Justinian) heard that the person she intended to send was opposed to the council of Chalcedon, he was not pleased, and made up his mind to write to the bishops of the Thebais who agreed with him and tell them to go and instruct the Nobadae.... He sent thither without a moment's delay ambassadors with gold and baptismal robes and gifts of honour for the king of that people. He wrote also to the governor of the Thebais ordering him to take every care of the embassy and escort them to the territory of the Nobadae.

When, however, the empress discovered this she quickly wrote a letter of her own to the governor and sent an officer of her household with it. The letter said: 'Both his majesty and myself propose to send an embassy to the Nobadae. I am now sending out a holy man called Julian. I am determined that my ambassador should reach the Nobadae before the emperor's. Take warning that if you allow his ambassador to get there first, and do not hold him up by one excuse or another until mine shall have passed through your province and reached his destination, your life shall answer for it. I shall send immediately and have your head cut off.'

Soon after the governor got this letter the emperor's ambassador arrived. The governor said to him, 'You must wait a little while we find suitable transport and men who know the desert. Then you will be able to go on.' Thus he held him up until the arrival of the empress's embassy. These found horses and guides ready waiting. They pretended to force the governor to let them have them, and set out the same day without delay. The governor made his excuses to the emperor's ambassador (blaming the empress)....

The blessed Julian and the ambassadors who went with him meanwhile reached the border. They sent word to the king of the Nobadae and his princes of their arrival. An armed escort was sent to greet them and bring them to the king. And he too received them with pleasure. The emperor's letter was presented to him, read and explained. The Nobadae accepted also the magnificent gifts of honour sent to them, the many baptismal robes and all the other things richly provided for their use. Immediately with joy they yielded themselves up, abjured the errors of their ancestors, and confessed the God of the Christians, saying 'He is the one true God, and there is no other beside him.'

And after Julian had given them much instruction and teaching, he told them about the council of Chalcedon. He told them the reasons why the empress had sent him to the Nobadae. It was because there had been disputes between Christians about the faith which had led to the blessed Theodosius being ordered to accept the decrees of the council. When he refused, the emperor deprived him of his patriarchal throne but the empress took him in and rejoiced that he had stood firm for the right faith and left his throne rather than conform. 'This is why the empress has sent us to you that you may walk in the ways of pope Theodosius, and stand in his faith, and imitate his constancy.'

[When the emperor's ambassadors arrived they were told the Nobadae would follow the teaching of Theodosius (Monophysitism) and not 'the wicked faith' of the emperor.]
Source: John of Ephesus III. 4, 6–7.

3.9   ETHIOPIA AND THE YEMEN   524–5
The king of Ethiopia, a very devout Christian, found that the Himyarites on the opposite continent were grievously oppressing the Christians there. Many of these Himyarites were Jews and many revered the old religion which was now called Greek. So he gathered a fleet and an army, came against them, conquered them, killing many of the Himyarites including their king [Dhu Novas, a Jew by religion]. He made Esimiphaeus king, a Himyarite by birth and a Christian, imposed a tribute and went home.

In the Ethiopian army there were many slaves and adventurers who would not go back with their king. They remained behind with the Himyarites because they coveted some of their land because it was very good. Soon these men and others imprisoned Esimiphaeus and made Abram their king. He had been a slave to a Roman merchant engaged in shipping at the port of Adulis in Ethiopia, and Abram was also a Christian. [The Ethiopians sent several expeditions against Abram, but failed to dislodge him.]
Source: Procopius, *The Persian Wars* I, 16.

3.10   CHRISTIANS IN CHINA   638
Meanwhile Christianity had been working its way slowly eastward from Syria to China (3.10). In 635 a mission arrived at Changan in the province of Shensi. It was courteously received and a Christian church grew up. The story of its foundation was recorded 150 years later on a stone monument inscribed by 'Lu Siu-yen, Secretary to the Council, formerly Military Superintendent for Taichau, while the Bishop Ning-shu had the charge of the congregations of the Illustrious in the East.' It is signed by 'the High Statesman of the sacred rites, the Imperially-conferred purple-gown Chief Presbyter and Priest, Yi-Li.' On the edges are the names of 67 priests with Syriac names and 61 with Chinese. The date was 781. The stone is known as the Nestorian Stone, for the mission to China was led by men whom orthodox Christians condemned as heretics. Our translation is by A. Wylie

in 1909. Christianity in China was known as the 'Syrian Illustrious Religion'. In 845 it suffered an eclipse as a result of an edict primarily directed against Buddhists. (For later Chinese Christians see pp. 279–284; for Nestorianism see Vol. I pp. 264–270.)

In the time of the accomplished Emperor Taitsung, the illustrious and magnificent founder of the dynasty, among the enlightened and holy men who arrived was the most virtuous Olopun, from the country of Syria. Observing the azure clouds, he bore the true sacred books; beholding the direction of the winds, he braved difficulties and dangers. In the year A.D. 635 he arrived at Changan. The Emperor sent his Prime Minister, Duke Fang Hiuen-ling, who, carrying the official staff to the west border, conducted his guest into the interior. The sacred books were translated in the imperial library. The sovereign investigated the subject in his private apartments, when, becoming deeply impressed with the rectitude and truth of the religion, he gave special orders for its dissemination. In the 7th month of the year 638 the following imperial proclamation was issued:

'Right principles have no invariable name, holy men have no invariable station; instruction is established in accordance with the locality, with the object of benefitting the people at large. The greatly-virtuous Olopun, of the kingdom of Syria, has brought his sacred books and images from that distant part, and has presented them at our capital. Having examined the principles of this religion, we find them to be purely excellent and natural. Investigating its original source, we find it has arisen from the establishment of important truths. Its ritual is free from perplexing expressions; its principles will survive when the framework is forgotten. It is beneficial to all creatures, it is to the advantage of mankind. Let it be published throughout the Empire, and let the proper authority build a Syrian church in the capital ... which shall be governed by 21 priests. When the virtue of the Chau dynasty declined, the rider on the azure ox ascended to the west, the principles of the great Tang became resplendent, illustrious breezes have come to fan the East.'

... The Emperor Kautsung respectfully succeeded his ancestor, and was still more beneficent toward the institution of truth. In every province he caused illustrious churches to be erected, and ratified the honour conferred upon Olopun, making him the great conservator of doctrine for the preservation of the State. While this doctrine pervaded every channel, the State became enriched and tranquillity

abounded. Every city was full of churches, and the royal family
enjoyed lustre and happiness....

> The Lord is without origin,
> Profound, invisible, and unchangeable;
> With power and capacity to perfect and transform,
> He raised up the earth and established the heavens.
>
> Divided in nature, he entered the world
> To save and help without bounds....
>
> The true doctrine how expansive!
> How difficult to name it,
> To elucidate the three in one!

CHAPTER FOUR

ISLAM AND CHRISTIANITY

In world history the seventh century is decisively Mohammed's, and the most important thing in Christian history then, and for several centuries afterwards, was the Prophet's impact on it. Equally, the most important external influences on Mohammed were Judaism and Christianity—in that order.

Mohammed was born in Mecca about 570, a posthumous child, soon to be an orphan. As a young man he travelled backwards and forwards with the trading caravans from Mecca, outside the Roman empire, to Syria, which lay within it. Not until he was 40 did he receive a vision of the archangel Gabriel (to Christians the angel of the Annunciation). Gabriel urged him to 'recite in the name of God, the most bountiful one, who by the pen has taught mankind things they did not know.' This was the origin of the Koran, which is Arabic for 'Recital'. The Koran is the infallible Word of God to Moslems. God is always the writer, Mohammed the pen. It is a formless succession of chapters written at many different times over the next twenty odd years. It has given rise to as many different and difficult expositions as the Bible has.

When he was fifty Mohammed was taken on a visionary Night Journey from Mecca to Jerusalem and thence to the Seventh Heaven, the event which makes Jerusalem a sacred city to Moslems as well as to Jews and Christians. Some two years later in 622, came the Hegira, the migration of Mohammed and his followers from Mecca to Medina which is used as the chronological base line of the Moslem calendar. In 630 Mohammed returned and conquered Mecca whose whole population accepted Islam. Islam is the name given to the religion taught by Mohammed. It is an Arabic word meaning 'surrender' and like the Christian's self-surrender implies submission to the will of God.

The political and religious situation in Arabia in Mohammed's youth was confused. It was a land of competing tribes, some Jewish, some Christian, most pagan. Mecca was predominantly pagan with its cult directed to the Ka'ba ('Cube' probably a meteorite) which was already an object of pilgrimage before it became the most sacred spot in the Moslem world. The Christian tribes were closely linked with Ethiopia, the Christian state 'beyond the bounds' of the Roman empire. The New Testament and Christian elements in the Koran derive chiefly from Ethiopian sources.

The Pillars of Islam

The essential features of Islam are its stress on the unity of God (and hence the power of God) and its basic simplicity. The Koran is told in the eastern story-teller's elaborate style, and Islam is capable of the most refined theological elaboration; but what is required of every Moslem is simple, easy to understand, and, in general, not too difficult to achieve. Islam welcomes all who accept it.

There are five traditional Pillars of Islam, to which a sixth, the Holy War, has sometimes been added.

4.1   THE PILLAR OF THE RECITAL OF THE CREED

La ilaha illa-llaha. There is no God but Allah.

Compare the first of the Old Testament commandments: 'I am Yahweh your God who brought you out of the land of Egypt, out of the house of slavery. You shall have no other gods except me.' (Deut. 5, 6–7: Jerusalem Bible.) Allah was the name of the male god worshipped by the people of Mecca, just as Yahweh was the sacred name of the god of the Hebrews. Both have been universalized and are correctly interpreted as 'There is no god but God'.

Muhammad rastel allahi. Mohammed is the Prophet of God.

This is the second section of the Moslem creed with no counterpart in the Ten Commandments, but the role of Moses as an intermediary provides an analogy: 'On the mountain from the heart of the fire Yahweh spoke to you face to face, and I stood all the time between Yahweh and yourselves to tell you of Yahweh's words' (Deut. 5, 4–5). Until a short time ago Christians spoke of Mahommedanism or the Mahommedan religion. This Moslems never do. They feel it detracts from the uniqueness of God.

4.2   THE PILLAR OF PRAYER

Recite your prayers at noon, at nightfall, and at dawn: the dawn prayer has its witnesses. Pray during the night as well, an additional duty for which your Lord may exalt you to an honourable station. Say: 'Lord, grant me a good entrance and a good exit and give me your sustaining power.' ... Pray neither with too loud a voice nor too softly. Say: 'Praise be to Allah who has never begotten a son, who has no partner in his kingdom nor any to defend him from humiliation.' Proclaim his greatness. (Koran 17: The Night Journey.)

4.3   THE PILLAR OF FASTING

Believers, a fast is ordained for you as it was ordained for those before you [Jews and Christians]; perhaps you will guard yourselves against evil. Fast a certain number of days, but if any is sick or on a journey let him fast a similar number of other days. Or it may be redeemed by feeding a poor man, but to fast is better if you but knew it.

In the month of Ramadan the Koran was revealed, a book of guidance with proofs of guidance, distinguishing right from wrong. Therefore whoever is at home in that month let him fast. But he who is sick or on a journey shall fast a similar number of other days.

Allah desires to make things easy and not difficult for you. Fulfil the days of the fast and glorify him for guiding you and give thanks. (Koran 2: The Cow.)

4.4 THE PILLAR OF ALMSGIVING

Have faith in Allah and his prophet and give in alms from that which he has made your inheritance; for unto those who believe and bestow alms shall be given a great reward. (Koran 57: Iron.)

4.5 THE PILLAR OF PILGRIMAGE

The first temple ever to be built for men was that at Mecca, a blessed place, a focus for the nations. There Abraham stood. Whoever enters it is safe. Pilgrimage to this house is a duty to Allah for all who can make the journey. (Koran 3: The Imrans.)

Perform the pilgrimage to Mecca and visit God. But if you are besieged send such offerings as are easiest and do not shave your heads until the offerings have reached their place of sacrifice.... Make the pilgrimage in the appointed (three) months. He who intends to perform it in these months must abstain from sexual intercourse, not transgress or quarrel on the way. (Koran 2: The Cow.)

4.6 JEHAD, THE HOLY WAR

When you meet the unbelievers strike off their heads, make a great slaughter among them and put them in bonds. Then grant them their freedom or take ransom from them, until war shall cease. Thus shall you do. Had Allah willed, he could have punished them himself but this way he tests you, the one by the other. As for those who die in defence of Allah's true religion ... he will admit them to Paradise.... Where flow rivers of unpolluted water, rivers of milk that never sour, rivers of delicious wine and rivers of clearest honey. There they shall eat of every fruit and receive forgiveness from their Lord. (Koran 47: Mohammed.)

4.7 ISLAM AND THE SECOND COMMANDMENT

The second commandment, 'Thou shalt not make to thyself any graven image' ... was accepted as a fundamental law by Mohammed. In mosques abstract design replaces pictorial representation. There was no conflict here between Jew and Moslem, but there was a deep difference between Christian practice and theirs in the seventh century. A little earlier there would have been no such conflict since the introduction of sacred pictures (icons) and statues into Christian churches was of a relatively late date (see Vol. 1, 131). Mohammed's protest was followed, as we shall see, by an accompanying protest against images inside the Christian world. The passages in the Koran which refer to idolatry, however, are directed in the first place against the still pagan tribes in Arabia rather than Christian excesses, though they could be and were applied to them. These are characteristic passages.

Idolatry is worse than bloodshed. . . . Fight until idolatry ceases and the religion of Allah reigns supreme (2: The Cow). Allah will not forgive idolatry. He will forgive all other sins to whom he wills (4: Women). On the day Allah gathers all together he will say to idolaters: 'Get to your place, you and your idols!' And he shall separate them. And the idols shall say to the idolaters: 'It was not us you worshipped. Allah is witness enough between us that we knew nothing about it' (10: Jonah).

The Koran and the Bible

The Koran assumes and incorporates a whole world of Biblical story-telling. There is much embroidery, much misunderstanding—perhaps hardly more, though, than recent investigations into the knowledge of British school-children have shown to exist today. The Bible stories in the Koran throw light not only on what Moslems believe, but on what ordinary seventh century folk in Arabia, Ethiopia and Syria—many of them Christians—believed. Allah is always the speaker in the Koran.

4.8   THE CREATION AND SATAN

We created man from dry clay, from black moulded mud, after creating the devil from smokeless flame. Your Lord said to the angels: 'I am creating man from dry clay, from black moulded mud. When I have completed him and breathed my spirit into him, fall down and worship him.' All the angels worshipped except Satan who refused to join them.

'O Satan,' said Allah, 'why do you not worship?'

He answered: 'It is not fitting that I should worship a man made from dry clay and black moulded mud.'

'Be gone!' said Allah. 'You shall be driven away with stones. My curse shall be on you until the day of judgment.'

'Lord,' said Satan, 'reprieve me till the day of resurrection.'

'You are reprieved until the appointed day.'

'O Lord,' said Satan, 'since you have seduced me, I will seduce men on the earth. I will seduce them all except those who serve you faithfully' (15: Al Hijr). [Cp. Gen. 2, 4–7; 3, 1–6, 13–15; Job 1, 6–12; 2, 1–7.]

4.9   MOSES AND PHARAOH

After them we sent Moses with our signs to Pharaoh and his princes, who took them to be false. See the fate of the evil-doers.

Moses said: 'I am a prophet from the Lord of Creation and justly say nothing of Allah but the truth. I bring you a sign from your Lord: let the children of Israel depart with me.'

Pharaoh answered: 'Show us your sign, if what you say be true.'

Moses threw down his rod, whereupon it changed into a veritable serpent. Then he drew out his hand and it appeared white to all beholders.

Pharaoh's elders said: 'This is a skilled enchanter who seeks to take away your kingdom. What would you have us do?'

Others said: 'Put them off a while, him and his brother, and send heralds to your cities to summon every skilled magician.'

So the magicians came to Pharaoh and said: 'Shall we be rewarded if we win?'

'Yes, you shall be close friends to me.'

They said: 'Moses, will you have first throw of your rod, or we?'

'You throw yours,' he replied.

And when the magicians had done so, they put a spell on people's eyes and terrified them by a display of great enchantment.

Revealing ourselves to Moses we said: 'Throw down your rod!' and lo, it swallowed up what they had transformed. They were defeated and put to shame. And the magicians prostrated themselves in adoration, saying:

'We believe in the Lord of Creation, the Lord of Moses and Aaron.'

Pharaoh said: 'You believe in him without my permission? This is a plot of your devising to turn my people out of their city. But you shall see. I will cut off your hands and feet on alternate sides and then crucify you all' . . .

We smote Pharaoh's people with dearth and famine to warn them, but when good things happened they said: 'It's our due,' but when evil befell them they ascribed it to the ill-luck of Moses and his people. Yet was not their ill-luck from Allah though most knew it not?

They said to Moses: 'Whatever sign you show us to bewitch us, we will not believe in you.'

So we plagued them with a flood, with locusts, lice, frogs and blood—all clear miracles, yet they remained a scornful and wicked people. When each plague smote them they said:

'Moses, entreat your Lord for us, according to the covenant he has made with you. If you lift the plague from us, we will believe in you and let the children of Israel go with you.'

But when we lifted the plague from them they broke their promise. So we took vengeance on them and drowned them in the sea (Koran 7: The Heights). [Cp. Exodus 5–11, and 14.]

4.10   THE BIRTH OF JOHN THE BAPTIST

Remember your Lord's goodness to his servant Zacharias when he besought him secretly saying:

'O Lord, my bones grow weak, my hair whitens with age, yet never have I prayed to you in vain. I now fear my nephews who will succeed me, for my wife is barren. Give me a son who will be my heir and an heir to the house of Jacob, who will be acceptable to thee.'

'O Zacharias, you shall be given a son and he shall be called John, a name no man has borne before him.'

'How shall I have a son, Lord, seeing my wife is barren and I well stricken in years?'

The Lord said: 'This is easy for me since I created you when you were nothing before.'

'O Lord, give me a sign.'

'For three days and three nights you shall be dumb, though otherwise in perfect health.'

Then Zacharias came out from the shrine and made signs to the people to praise Allah morning and evening (Koran 19: Mary). [Cp. Luke 1.]

4.11   THE NATIVITY

Remember Mary, how we sent her our spirit in the likeness of a full-grown man.

'I fly for refuge,' she said, 'to the Merciful one to defend me. If you fear him—'

'I am the messenger of your Lord,' he replied, 'and have come to give you a holy son.'

'How shall I bear a child, seeing that no man hath touched me. I am no harlot.'

'Yet it shall be so. Your Lord says: "This is easy for me. He shall be a sign unto men and a blessing from us. It is decreed."'

Then she conceived and retired to a place far off; and the pains of child-birth came upon her by the trunk of a palm tree.

'Would to God I had died before this and been forgotten,' she cried.

'Grieve not,' said a voice from below. 'Allah has provided a brook that runs at your feet, and if you shake this palm tree's trunk it will drop ripe dates upon you. Eat, drink, and be at peace. Should you meet a man say to him: "I have vowed a fast to the Merciful and will not speak with any man today."'

So she carried the child to her people.

'O Mary,' they said, 'you have acted strangely. Sister of Aaron, your father was never a whore-monger, nor your mother a whore.'

She made a sign towards the child, but they replied:

'How can we speak with a baby in a cradle?'

Whereupon he spoke to them: 'I am the servant of Allah. He has given me the book [of the gospel] and ordained me a prophet. His blessing is upon me wherever I go, and he has commanded me to pray and give alms as long as I live, to honour my mother; he has purged me of vanity and wickedness. His peace is with me on the day I was born and on the day I shall die and on the day when I shall be raised to life.'

Such was Jesus the son of Mary: the Word of truth which they are loth to believe. It is not for Allah to have any son. Allah forbid! When he decrees a thing he need only say: 'Be!' and it is (Koran 19: Mary).

4.12   THE TRUE BREAD

'Jesus, son of Mary,' the disciples said, 'can your Lord send down to us from heaven a table of food?'

'Fear Allah and be true believers,' he answered.

'We wish to eat of it so that we may reassure our hearts and know that what you have told us is true, and that we may be witnesses of it.'

'Lord,' said Jesus, son of Mary, 'send to us from heaven a table of food, that it may become a feast day for us and those who come after us, and be a sign from thee. Give us our food for thou art the best provider.'

'I am sending one down to you,' answered Allah. 'But if any of you disbelieves after this, he shall be punished as no one has ever been punished before.'

Then Allah will say: 'Jesus, son of Mary, did you ever say to man "Take me and my mother as two gods beside Allah?"'

'Glory to thee,' he will answer, 'how could I say what I have no right to say?' (Koran 5: The Table.) [Cp. John 6, 30–59.]

4.14   JESUS, PROPHET OF MOHAMMED

Jesus son of Mary said: 'O children of Israel, I am sent to you by Allah to confirm the Torah [Law] already revealed and to bring good news of a prophet who will come after me whose name is Ahmed,'

Yet when he did miracles for them they said: 'This is plain magic' (61: Battle Array). [Cp. John 14, 26; 16, 7.]

Behind this lies a confusion between the 'parakletos' ('Comforter' in the A.V.) of the Greek New Testament and 'periklutos' which is the Greek for the 'renowned' or 'praised' one, roughly the same as Ahmed or Mohammed which are derived from the Arabic verb 'to praise'.

4.15   THE TRINITY

Unbelievers are those who say: 'Allah is the Messiah, the son of Mary.' For the Messiah himself said: 'Children of Israel, serve Allah, my Lord and yours.' Whoever proposes that Allah has a companion shall be excluded from Paradise and cast into hell-fire, and none shall help him.

They are certainly unbelievers who say: 'Allah is one of three.' There is no god but Allah. If they do not refrain from saying so a painful torment shall surely be inflicted on them. Will they not therefore turn to Allah and seek forgiveness? For Allah is gracious and merciful.

The Messiah, the son of Mary, was no more than a prophet, and other prophets went before him. His mother was a truthful woman. They both ate earthly food (5: The Table).

4.16   HOPE FOR CHRISTIANS

While it is easy to quote passages unfriendly and threatening to Christians, there is, as so often in the Koran, something said also on the other side. This extract makes it possible to see why Christians were able to live un-molested in freedom in Moslem lands.

You will surely find that the most violent in their opposition to the faithful are the Jews and the idolaters, and that the nearest in friendship with true believers are those who say: 'We are Christians.' That is because there are priests and monks among them, and because they are free from pride.

When they listen to that which was revealed to the Prophet, you will see their eyes fill with tears as they recognise its truth. They say: 'Lord, we believe. Count us among your witnesses' (5: The Table).

The Upper Reaches of Islam

The lands conquered and ruled by the Moslems had in the middle ages a high civilization. The words 'algebra' and 'alchemy', parent of chemistry, come from the Arabic, and real mathematics had to wait for the introduction of Arabic numerals. It is, therefore, not surprising that Moslem theology and Moslem devotion reached up into a sphere where inter-faith conflict is replaced by dialogue. There was in fact a good deal of contact between deeply religious Moslems and deeply religious Christians in the conquered lands. Thus Sufi, the name given to Moslem mystics, probably comes from the Arabic for wool because a Sufi wore a simple white woollen dress like an English monk's. Any Christian might indeed be glad to have written the following passages.

The first three come from a woman called Rabia (717–801) who was born in Basra and spent most of her life there. Her parents died while she was still young. She was kidnapped and sold as a slave. But her master freed her when he heard one night how she prayed in these words: 'O my Lord, you know that the desire of my heart is to obey you, and that the light of my eye is in the service of your court.' Many disciples came to learn from her; Sufis for many centuries looked back with devotion to her. The first passage explains why she rejected the many offers of marriage she received.

The fourth passage is from Jalal-ud-Din Rumi (1207–1273), the greatest of Persian mystics, who spent most of his life in Konia, the ancient Iconium, in Asia Minor. The fifth and sixth come from the poet Jani (1414–1492).

The last of these extracts is by Avicenna (980–1037), best known of Moslem medical men whose books were translated into Latin and widely studied in the West. He was also a philosopher, theologian and politician— his philosophy was basically Aristotelian with an infusion of Neoplatonic ideas. He was born in Bokhara in Central Asia, lived mainly in Persia, but travelled widely.

4.17   FROM RABIA

A. Why she chose celibacy

> My peace, O my brothers, is in solitude,
> And my Beloved is with me always,
> For his love I can find no substitute,
> And his love is the test for me among mortal beings,

O Healer of souls, the heart feeds upon its desire,
The striving after union with thee has healed my soul.

B. 'Not for the hope of gaining aught . . .'
O my Lord, if I worship thee from fear of hell, burn me in hell,
and if I worship thee from hope of Paradise exclude me thence. But
if I worship thee for thine own sake, then withhold not from me
thine eternal beauty.

C. At night in old age on the roof-top
O my Lord, the stars are shining and the eyes of men are closed,
and kings have shut their doors and every lover is alone with his
beloved, and here I am alone with thee.

4.18   FROM JALAL-UD-DIN RUMI
The Prophet said that God had declared, I am not contained in
aught above or below. I am not contained in earth or sky or even
in highest heaven. Know this for a certainty, O beloved!
             I am contained in the believer's heart!
             If you seek me, search in your hearts.

4.19   FROM JANI
A.
        O Lord, none but thyself can fathom thee,
        Yet every mosque and church doth harbour thee.

B. To a ruler

        Thou art a shepherd, and thy flock the people
        To help and save, not ravage and destroy.
        For which is for the other, flock or shepherd?

4.20   FROM AVICENNA: ON PRAYER
Prayer is divided into two parts, one being outward (the part of discipline, that appertains to the body) and one inward (the real prayer,
that concerns the soul). The outward part of prayer is that prescribed
by the religious law and recognized as a fundamental duty of religion.
Our Lawgiver (Mohammed) imposed it as an obligation for every
man, calling it salat and making it the foundation of faith. . . .
    The postures of prayer, composed of recitation, genuflection, and
prostration, and recurring in regular and definite numbers, are visible

evidence of that real prayer which is part of the rational soul. They act as controlling the body, to bring it into tune with the general harmony of the universe.... The Lawgiver realised that all men are not capable of mounting the steps of reason; they therefore required some regular bodily training and discipline to oppose their natural inclinations ... and prevent them from imitating the beasts....

As for the second or inward part or truth of prayer: this is to contemplate God with a pure heart, and a spirit abstracted and cleansed of all desires.... This is the kind of prayer that is exclusively the concern of the intellect; reason confirms this statement, bearing in mind the Prophet's words, 'The man at prayer is in secret converse with the Lord'. It is obvious to the intelligent man that such converse is not effected through the physical parts and the audible and visible tongue, because conversation can only take place with somebody contained in space and determined by time.... The True and Absolute Being is absent from the sensible world and is neither seen nor contained in space.... Pure souls that are abstracted and free from events in time and directions in space contemplate God intellectually, to behold him with spiritual, not corporeal vision. It is thus evident that true prayer is spiritual contemplation, and that pure worship is spiritual divine love.

Source: Avicenna, *Kitab al-Najat.*

Christians under Moslems

For more than three hundred years the very great majority of Christians, and all those in the old Christian heart-lands, had been living in states that were, in a political sense, actively Christian. This was now to change. Moslem armies spread Islam with bewildering speed. Mohammed died in 632. Antioch, where men were first called Christians (Acts 11, 26), fell in 635; Jerusalem in 637; and Alexandria in 640. Carthage was taken and utterly destroyed in 698; Moslem armies were across the Straits of Gibraltar and Cordova was captured in 711. Constantinople itself endured a long siege from 668–675 and again from 717–718. (See Map 2.)

Christian Africa (except Ethiopia), the greater part of Christian Asia, and the larger part of Christian Spain was in Moslem hands. But normally the Christians were neither deported, massacred nor forcibly converted. They were free to practise their religion; they were employed in important public work—the architect of the Dome of the Rock in Jerusalem, the first major Moslem place of worship, was a Christian; but they were without political influence. Gradually many conformed and accepted Islam, but the process was slow, and important Christian communities still survive with a continuous history from before Moslem times. But Christianity began to contract instead of expanding; it fossilized instead of developing in its old centres; and the outlying churches of Ethiopia and Persia and beyond were cut off from contact with their fellow believers. The intellectually stimulating controversies between Monophysites, Nestorians, and Chalcedonians (the Orthodox, as we should say) ended as the 'heretics' passed under Moslem rule. Theology in the East, inside and outside the Empire, soon ceased to be a thought-provoking debate. The two following extracts illustrate the terms under which Christians existed after the Moslem conquest.

4.21   THE CALIPH OMAR TAKES JERUSALEM:

                THE TERMS OF CAPITULATION   637

The following are the terms which I, Omar, the servant of God, the Commander of the Faithful, grant to the people of Jerusalem. I grant them security for their lives, their possessions, and their children, their Churches, their crosses and all that appertains to them in their integrity, and their lands, and to all of their religion. Their Churches therein shall not be impoverished, nor destroyed, nor injured from among them; neither their endowments, nor their dignity and not a thing of their property; neither shall the inhabitants of Jerusalem be exposed to violence in following their religion, nor shall one of them be injured.

4.22   ABDULLAH'S TERMS OF PEACE WITH CHRISTIAN NUBIA   653

In the name of God, the Merciful, the Compassionate. This is a treaty granted by the Emir Abdullah Ibn Saoud to the chief of the Nubians and to all the peoples of his dominions, a treaty binding on all, great and small, among them from the frontier of Assouan to the frontier of Alwa. Abdullah ordains security and peace between them and the Moslems. You Nubians, you shall dwell in safety under the safeguard of God and his apostle Mohammed, the Prophet, whom God bless and save. You shall protect Moslems or their allies who come into your lands. . . . You shall put no obstacle in the way of a Moslem, but render him aid until he quit your territory. You shall take care of the mosque which the Moslems have built in the outskirts of your city and hinder none from praying there. You shall clean it, light it and honour it. Every year you shall pay 360 head of slaves to the leader of the Moslems, of the middle class of slaves of your country, without bodily defects, males and females, but no old men, nor old women, nor children.

Christian Imagebreakers

They are usually called 'Iconoclasts', but in common usage the word has lost its precision. The Greek word icon covers any image whether two or three-dimensional. In practice in the Eastern Church the images were normally two-dimensional paintings or mosaics—'icons' in the restricted sense.

Islam's tenacious attachment to the Second Commandment found its counterpart inside Christendom among the Imagebreakers. Like the earlier Arians, they came near to complete and permanent triumph through a succession of strong emperors who shared their faith. Like the Arians they were in the end destroyed when they lost control of the state machine. Their movement was a protest, as its name implies, at the state of Christian practice, especially in the east of the empire, in the seventh century. Certainly things had moved far since 326 when the great Christian historian Eusebius answered a request from the emperor's sister for a likeness of Christ with these words: 'What, and what kind of likeness of Christ is there? Such images are forbidden by the second commandment.' Already images were dressed up to act as godparents, and communion was sometimes administered at the hands of a statue.

The main support of the Imagebreakers came from a rather curious alliance of civil servants and soldiers. The first, and greatest of the Imagebreaking emperors, Leo the Isaurian, was a rough soldier who came from a mountainous district in the centre of Asia Minor where primitive puritan habits still survived. Warfare, too, had brought him into contact with Moslems, and Christian defeats—though he himself was a notably successful soldier—may have seemed a punishment for Christian idolatry. The main support of the Imageworshippers came from monks and women. The first seventy years of Imagebreaking supremacy were ended by the Empress Irene; after an Imagebreaking revival the final restoration of the icons was brought about by the regent, Theodora in 843.

4.23   WESTERN CAUTION   *c.* 600

Wise western leaders such as Pope Gregory the Great were aware that images and pictures had their dangers as well as their uses. In this letter, written of course before the coming of Islam and a century before the first Imagebreaking emperor, he sets out a balanced view:

Gregory to Serenus, bishop of Marseilles. We have been informed that, inflamed by inconsiderate zeal, you have broken the images of the saints, on the pretext that they ought not to be adored. And indeed we altogether praise you for forbidding them to be adored, but we blame you for breaking them. Say, brother, what priest has ever been heard to have done what you have done? Ought not this consideration to have checked you, and kept you from despising your brethren and setting yourself up as the only one that is holy and wise? For it is one thing to adore a picture, another to learn what is to be adored through the history told by the picture.

What Scripture presents to readers, a picture presents to the gaze of the unlearned. For in it even the ignorant see what they ought to follow, in it the illiterate read.

4.24   LEO'S PURGE   727

Leo the Isaurian started his reign in 717 with the glorious defence of Constantinople against a very strong Moslem army. By 725 he was already thinking of stopping the superstitious use of images. In the following autumn there was a volcanic eruption near the island of Thera which he took as a warning to him to remove the images. This he at once put in hand. What he did met with opposition. Over the great gate of the Imperial Palace, there stood a very famous and cherished figure of Christ either in mosaic or in wood. A soldier brought a ladder and climbed up to take it down. Angry women shook the ladder until he fell; then they stabbed him to death. Later a tablet recorded the substitution of the cross for the figure of our Lord (the translation is by E. J. Martin):

> The emperor Leo and his son Constantine
> Thought it dishonour to the Christ divine
> That on the very palace gate he stood,
> A lifeless, speechless effigy of wood.
> Thus what the Book forbids they did replace
> With the believer's blessed sign of grace.

4.25   CONTRARY COUNCILS   787

Leo's son, Constantine V, in 753 assembled at Constantinople a general council attended by 338 bishops who endorsed the full policy and doctrine of the Imagebreaking party. In 786 the Empress Irene called a new general council to reverse the doctrine. It met in a church at Constantinople, but broke up in disorder when a party of Imagebreaking soldiers broke into the building and turned the bishops out. Next year Irene tried again in the quieter air of Nicaea. There the new patriarch Tarasius, Irene's private secretary and a layman, presided over 350 bishops who obediently and unanimously made the following definition:

Following the divinely inspired teaching of our holy fathers, and the tradition of the Catholic Church (for we know that this tradition comes from the Holy Spirit which dwells in the Church), we define with all care and exactitude that: venerable and holy icons, especially those of our Lord and God and Saviour Jesus Christ, and of our immaculate Lady, the mother of God, of the honourable angels and of saintly and holy men, whether made of mosaic or painted or made of other fit material, are to be set up in churches and portrayed on sacred vessels, on vestments, on walls, in houses or by the roadside in the same way as the precious and life-giving cross is represented.

As often as a man looks at these pictures he is stimulated to think about and to imitate the originals. Therefore it is right to give them honour and veneration but not that peculiar worship which belongs solely to the Godhead. We therefore follow the pious custom of antiquity and pay these icons the honour of incense and lights just as we do to the holy gospels and the venerable and life-giving cross. For the honour paid to the icon passes to its original; he who adores an icon, adores the person it depicts.

Source: Theophanes, *Chronographia.*

4.26   THE THEOLOGICAL OBJECTION TO ICONS   *c.* 820

Because the Imagebreakers lost, their writings have disappeared. We have to reconstruct their views from quotations in their opponents' work. They go deeper than the danger of superstitious abuse and question the possibility of representing Divinity. Thus Mammon (i.e. Constantine V) is reported in a later hostile work as saying:

How is it possible that there can be a drawing, that is an image, made of our Lord Jesus Christ, when he is one person of two natures in a union of the material and the immaterial which admits of no confusion? Since he has an immaterial nature conjoined to the flesh, and with these two natures he is one, and his person or substance is inseparable from the two natures, we hold that he cannot be depicted.... For what is pictured is one person, and he who draws that person has plainly outlined the divine nature which cannot be thus confined.

Source: Antirrhetici I. 232a, 236c.

4.27   JOHN OF DAMASCUS AND THE CASE FOR ICONS   *c.* 730

John of Damascus, the last of the Fathers of the Church, spent his whole life in a land where Islam prevailed. He was born about the year 700 and succeeded his father as a financial officer under the Caliph of Damascus. His work as a hymn writer has already been noticed (3.4); he also wrote the classic exposition of dogmatic theology of the Eastern church, which translated into Latin was known to and influenced Thomas Aquinas. But his most decisive work was his leadership in the intellectual case against the Imagebreakers. He formulated this in *Three Orations*, written about the year 730. He died soon after 750—probably in 752. He acquired the title of Chrysorrhoas (gold-pouring) because of his eloquence (cf. John Chrysostom—golden-tongued); his Arabic name, Mansur, means Victor. The first passage is designed to show that it is legitimate to make icons of our Lord; the second argues that they may rightly be worshipped as, in a sense, an extension or analogy of the incarnation.

These injunctions (against idols) were given to the Jews on account of their proneness to idolatry. We, on the contrary, are no longer in leading strings. Speaking theologically, it is given to us to avoid superstitious error, to be with God in the knowledge of the truth, to offer service to God alone, to enjoy the fulness of his knowledge.... The Scripture says, 'Ye have not seen his likeness.'... How depict the inconceivable? How give expression to the limitless, the immeasureable, the invisible?... It is clear that when you contemplate God who is pure in spirit becoming man for your sake you will be able to clothe him in human form. When the Invisible One becomes visible in flesh you may then draw a likeness of his visible form. When he who is without form or limitation, immeasurable in the boundlessness of his own nature, existing as God, takes upon himself the form of a servant in substance and stature and a body of flesh, then you may draw his likeness and show it to anyone willing to contemplate it.

Devils have feared the saints and have fled from their shadow. The shadow is an image and I make an image that I may scare demons. Material things are endured with a divine grace because they bear the names of those they represent.... Material things in themselves demand no veneration, but if the person who is represented is full of grace, the material becomes partaker of grace metaphorically, by faith.

Source: John of Damascus, *Three Orations* I, 1237, 1264.

4.28   THE ICONS RESTORED

Most people think of the Greek Anthology as a collection of short poems commemorating the life, death and loves of Greeks who lived before the coming of Christianity or were untouched by it. Most of it fits happily into this description, but there are also a number of Christian poems. Here is a translation of one celebrating the return of the icons to the churches (1, 106).

> The beam of truth shines out again,
> Blinding the eyes of the teachers of lies;
> Reverence grows tall and error falls,
> Faith comes into flower and grace opens wide.
> For see! the pictured Christ again
> Shines at the summit of the seat of power
> And overthrows the gloomy heresies.

Over the entry, like a holy door,
The guardian Virgin is portrayed;
Emperor, Patriarch, with their fellow-workers
Are figured nearby as refuters of error,
And all around, as sentries of the house,
Are spirits, disciples, martyrs, priests.

CHAPTER FIVE

PILGRIMS AND CRUSADERS

The Peace of God

The ninth and tenth centuries were filled with local fighting between lawless lords. They caused widespread physical and spiritual distress. Something had to be done about it. The abbots of Cluny took the lead. The 'peace of God' was an idea first brought forward in the South of France in 990. The following extract comes from a meeting called by four diocesan bishops at the Cluniac daughter house of Sauxillange to settle a devastating petty war. The four bishops and many barons and lesser laymen swore to ban certain types of military action.

5.1   THE PACT OF SAUXILLANGE   *c.* 995

Since we know that without peace no man may see God, we adjure you, in the name of the Lord, to be men of peace, that henceforward in these bishoprics and in these counties no man may break into a church, nor bear off the horses, foals, oxen, cows, asses, sheep, goats, or pigs of the labourer and the serf, or the burden he bears upon his shoulders; that no man may kill any of these beasts; that he may exact nothing except from his own servants and his immediate dependants; that to build or to assault a fortress he may only take the men of his own land, his allod, *bénéfice* or *commende*; that clerks may not bear arms borne by laymen; that no man may ever insult a monk, or those who walk with him, if they are unarmed; that no man may dare to invade the lands of churches, cathedrals, chapters, or monasteries, or to waylay their agents and despoil them. May every thief and evil-doer who infringes this or refuses to observe it, be excommunicate, anathema, and driven from the threshold of the church, until he make amends; and if he refuse, let the priest refuse to sing mass for him, or to celebrate any sacrament; and at his death let him be deprived of Christian burial.

The deed was confirmed by the Archbishops of Bourges and Vienne. It set a precedent which was widely followed. Often there was provision for physical sanctions, if need be, by a diocesan militia which all above the age of fifteen were expected to join.

5.2   THE TRUCE OF GOD   1042

The Peace of God was soon broadened into the Truce of God which imposed a regular weekly close season for fighting, enforceable by the same sanctions. There were also seasonal prohibitions during Advent, Lent, and at the major festivals. Neither Peace nor Truce, however, achieved more than mediocre success, though they show the tone and direction of Christian thinking. The following extract, from a letter written in 1042 to Italy by the Abbot of Cluny and the French bishops points forward in the last clause quoted to what was to prove a more successful antidote:

From the hour of vespers on Wednesday until sunrise on Monday let there reign a settled peace and an enduring truce between all Christians, friends and enemies, neighbours and strangers, so that for these four days and five nights at all hours there may be safety for all men, so that they can devote themselves to business without fear of attack. Let those who, having pledged themselves to the truce, break it, be excommunicated, accursed, and abominated, now and forever, unless they repent and make amends. Whosoever shall kill a man on a day of truce shall be banished and driven out of the country, and shall make his way into exile at Jerusalem....

Pilgrimages

Cluny used its influence to encourage men to go on pilgrimages, especially to the major Christian shrines—to Rome, to St. James at Compostella in the north-west of Spain, and above all to Jerusalem. It built hostels at key points on the route to give pilgrims shelter. There were many reasons for going on pilgrimage—to fulfil a vow of gratitude to God or his saints, to satisfy a spiritual longing, or to carry out a penance, a spiritual discipline which removed the sinner from the scene of his sin which was often a crime of vengeance. A desire for adventure and a traveller's curiosity played their part. Some pilgrims went singly or in small groups; more joined great pilgrimages thousands strong.

5.3   GUIDE TO ST. JAMES OF COMPOSTELLA   *c.* 1125

You enter Compostella by the north gate and the Inn of the Poor Pilgrims is close by. At the end of the street where that famous inn stands, there is an enclosed court, which you enter by descending nine steps. At the bottom is the most beautiful fountain in the world, given for the benefit of the pilgrims to St. James. It is a great bowl of stone, so large that 15 men can bathe in it together in comfort; and it is raised on a high platform. In the middle is a seven-sided column of bronze, supporting four lions, from whose mouths clear sweet water gushes into the basin below. Beyond the fountain extends the stone-paved court, where they sell scallop-shells, wine skins, shoes, deerskin wallets, purses, straps, belts, medicinal herbs, drugs and many other articles....

In the basilica the great altar of St. James covers the saint's marble tomb, which contains the whole body, though some other churches have claimed to possess some of his relics. The body is divinely adorned by paradisal garnets, blessed by sweet heavenly perfumes, illuminated by brilliant celestial tapers, and surrounded by angels. A simple altar is immediately over the tomb and above that is the great altar, the front of which is all of carved gold and silver. Its canopy is square and rests on four beautifully proportioned pillars, and is covered inside and out with paintings and designs.

The basilica of St. James was begun in 1078 and from that day to this miracles have been wrought here. The sick have been healed, the blind have seen, the dumb have spoken, the deaf have heard, the lame have walked in ease, the possessed have been freed from evil spirits. Furthermore, the prayers of the faithful have been answered, their vows have been fulfilled, their chains have fallen; heaven has opened to those who knocked, and the suffering have been consoled. Pilgrims come from every quarter to St. James, and all are made welcome and given help.

5.4   PALMERS, PILGRIMS AND ROMEOS

The failure of the crusades did not mean the end of pilgrimages. After the death of Beatrice in 1290 Dante wrote a sequence of sonnets, connective narrative and analysis called *La Vita Nuova*. In this extract he meets a group of pilgrims passing through Florence.

And so, when they had passed from my sight, I decided to write a sonnet in which I would set forth what I said to myself; and to make it more moving I decided to write as if I had spoken to them. So I wrote the sonnet which begins, *O pilgrims*....

I called them pilgrims in the general sense of the word. For 'pilgrim' may be understood in two ways, one general and one particular. Anyone journeying from his own country is a pilgrim, but in the particular sense pilgrim means someone who journeys to the sanctuary of St. James and back. It should be understood that those who travel in the service of the Almighty are of three kinds. Those who travel overseas [i.e. to Jerusalem] are called palmers, as they often bring back palms. Those who go to St. James' shrine in Galicia are called pilgrims, because the burial place of St. James was further away from his country than that of any other apostle, and romeos are those who go to Rome, which is where those whom I call pilgrims were going.

Pilgrim, with scallop shell of Compostella on his scrip, and staff for support & protection. 14 Cent. MS, B.M.Harleian 4826

5.5   CHAUCER'S MUCH-TRAVELLED WIFE OF BATH

Chaucer, in his Prologue to the *Canterbury Tales*, describes how every springtime there was a great popular urge to go on pilgrimages. Among his very mixed crowd of Canterbury pilgrims was a group of craftsmen: a haberdasher, carpenter, weaver, dyer, and carpet-maker, 'clothed in one livery, of a solemn and a great fraternity'. They were members of a guild, whose economic and religious purposes were inextricably mixed (see 11.4; 11.6). Here is one provision from the rules of the guild of Tailors of Lincoln, founded in 1328:

'If anyone wishes to make a pilgrimage to the holy land of Jerusalem, each brother and sister shall give him a penny, and if to St. James or Rome a halfpenny. And they go with him outside the gates of the city of Lincoln, and on his return they shall meet him and go with him to his mother church.'

Chaucer's Wife of Bath might be described as a free-lance pilgrim.

> And she had thrice been at Jerusalem;
> She had passed over many a strange stream.

She'd been to Rome and also to Boulogne,
St. James of Compostella and Cologne.
Well knew she how to wander on the way.

The church of Notre Dame at Boulogne is still a place of pilgrimage; Frederick Barbarossa brought the relics of the Three Kings (Magi) to Cologne from Milan in 1162.

The First Crusade

In the second half of the eleventh century the Seljuk Turks from Central Asia, who played a role in Islam not unlike that of the Normans in Christendom, inflicted overwhelming defeats on the Christian Eastern Empire and drove out the Egyptian Moslem dynasty which was ruling in Palestine—the two great Powers on whose peaceful administration the pilgrims depended. The Eastern Emperor appealed to the West for help; the abbot of Cluny and each returning pilgrim underlined the need for something to be done.

The man who did it was Pope Urban II. Odo de Lagery, the son of a noble family in Champagne, had become a monk of Cluny in 1070 when he was about twenty-eight. In 1088 he was elected pope. He spent the autumn of 1095 in France. In November he held a council at Clermont which defined and enforced the Truce of God (see 5.2). Then on Tuesday November 27 the pope addressed not only the Fathers of the Council but all who could come. There were far too many for the cathedral, so an open air meeting was held. The pope was tall, bearded, courteous, a practised orator. Three reports survive from men who heard him speak. None was a skilled reporter, but each conveys admirably the effect of the pope's words on him. The first of the two used here is by Fulcher of Chartres who was thirty-seven at the time. He was a chaplain to Stephen of Blois, William the Conqueror's son-in-law, and went on the Crusade with him. The second is by Robert the Monk, of Reims, who about 1120 wrote what became the most widely read history of the First Crusade. Most of it is a working over of other men's work, but occasionally he could, as here, provide first-hand information.

5.6 THE SERMON AT CLERMONT: FULCHER OF CHARTRES REPORTS

I implore and urge you both poor and rich—and it is God, not I, who implores and urges you as Christ's heralds—to be quick to drive that vile breed from the country inhabited by our brothers, and bring aid to those worshippers of Christ before it is too late. I say it to those present, I will proclaim it to the absent, but it is Christ who commands....

If those who go lose their lives on the journey either on land or sea, their sins will be forgiven them immediately. I grant this by the power God has given me....

Let those who have fought wrongfully against brothers and relatives now rightfully fight the infidel, let those who have been robbers
become soldiers of Christ, let those who were hirelings for a few
pieces of silver now win eternal rewards.... Pledge yourselves now;
soldiers, put your affairs in order and collect what you will need
to spend; then when winter is over and spring has come, set out
with happy hearts to take the road under the guidance of the Lord.

THE SERMON AT CLERMONT: ROBERT THE MONK REPORTS

Stop hating one another, stop quarrelling, stop fighting.... Undertake the journey to the Holy Sepulchre. Capture the land the heathen
have seized, the land God gave to the children of Israel, the land
the Bible describes as all milk and honey.

Jerusalem is the navel of the world, no land more fruitful, a
second paradise of delights. This is the land lightened by the coming
of man's Redeemer, made lovely by his life, made holy by his passion,
saved by his death and sealed by his burial. This royal city, centre
of the world, is now held captive by enemies ignorant of God and
is made to serve their heathen ceremonies. It looks and longs for
freedom, unceasingly it implores you for help, and it expects it
especially from you because God has given you more military glory
than any other nation. So undertake the journey for the forgiveness of your sins, sure of a glory that never fades in the kingdom
of heaven.

The effect of this speech was immediate. It was punctuated by shouts of
'Deus le volt' (God wills it). When the pope ended the bishop of Le Puy
at once knelt before the pope's throne and asked leave to join the Crusade.

5.7   PETER THE HERMIT AND THE PEOPLE'S CRUSADE

The Crusade was a complex military operation in which many great lords
and their followers took part. It was also a spontaneous popular movement.
Peter the Hermit, or 'Little Peter' as his contemporaries called him, was
an oldish man, born at Amiens. He started preaching the Crusade on his
own in Central and Northern France, working eastwards into the Rhineland.
By the time he reached Cologne at Easter in 1096 he may have had 15,000
followers. Guibert, abbot of Nogent (1053–1124), who knew Peter personally, has left us an account of the man and his recruits:

As far as I know, Peter came from the city of Amiens. He lived
as a hermit in a monk's habit somewhere in the north of France

and when he left there—for what purpose I do not know—we saw him going through towns and cities under the pretext of preaching. He was surrounded by greater crowds, received richer gifts, and was more famed and praised for holiness than anyone I can remember.

From the riches he received he gave generously to the poor, and reclaimed prostitutes by providing them—not without dowries— with husbands. With amazing authority he everywhere restored peace and concord in place of strife. All he did or said was accepted as little short of divine. Folk went so far as to pull hairs from his mule as relics—not because they loved truth but because it was something new. He wore a plain woollen shirt with a hood and over this an ankle-length sleeveless cloak, and his feet were bare. He lived on wine and fish and seldom or never ate bread.

Such a burning zeal inflamed the poor that no one paused to consider his lack of means, nor if it was wise to leave his house, vineyards or fields, but each sold his best goods for a price less than if he had been a prisoner in cruel captivity and forced to get himself a quick ransom ... you could hear of 7 sheep sold for 5 deniers [instead of 1 for 8], an astonishing example of the sudden and unexpected drop in all values....

You could see astounding things which could only make you laugh: poor people shoeing their oxen as though they were horses, harnessing them to two-wheeled carts, on which they piled their few provisions and small children and led them away. And when these little children saw a castle or a town, they were eager to know whether that was the Jerusalem they were going to.

Though the Apostolic See appealed especially to the Frankish nation, there was almost no Christian people who did not pour out in force and try to join the Franks and share their dangers, thinking that they owed God a like allegiance. You could see crowds of Scots [i.e. Gaels from Ireland or Scotland], who were savages at home, unskilled in the arts of war, bare-legged, wearing cloaks of shaggy skins, with their provisions slung in sacks over their shoulders, hurrying from their mist-shrouded homeland. Many, whose arms are absurd compared with ours, came to offer us the aid of their faith and vows. God is my witness that I heard of men who had landed at one of our ports from some barbarous nation unknown to me, who spoke a language so unknown that no one could understand them. They laid their fingers over one another in the form of a cross, to show by signs instead of words that they wished to further the cause of faith.

5.8 'LITTLE PETER'

They reached Constantinople on August 1, 1096. The Emperor's daughter, Anna Comnena described the scene:

These people burnt with a divine fire, surging around Little Peter with their horses, arms, and provisions. Men with happy faces, full of zeal for the holy cause, swarmed in every street. Behind the Celtic warriors you could see a countless mob of ordinary people with their wives and children, all with the Red Cross on their shoulders....

But in truth Peter's followers had become an awkward thievish lot; the local people suffered bitterly from their behaviour. Within eleven weeks the Turks had almost completely wiped them out. Next year Fulcher of Chartres saw a mass of skulls and bones as he passed the scene of their defeat. Peter himself was absent in Constantinople and so escaped. He joined the main Crusading army next year.

5.9 A CRUSADER'S LETTER TO HIS WIFE 1098

The main Crusading armies gathered in Constantinople in 1097 and slowly fought their way eastward. They arrived before the almost impregnable city of Antioch in October. At Easter, 1098 the Crusaders were still outside the city when Count Stephen wrote this cheerful letter home. But two months later the Crusaders' position seemed hopeless and Stephen and his men deserted only 24 hours before an Armenian officer of the garrison, a Christian, let the Crusaders in. Stephen's wife Ada, a daughter of William the Conqueror, was furious when he got home and sent him back. He went, and was killed in battle in 1102.

Count Stephen to Ada, his most sweet and loving wife, to his dear children and all the vassals of his lineage, greeting and blessing.

Be sure my dearest, that the messenger I send to give you comfort has left me safe and sound before Antioch and, by the grace of God, in the greatest prosperity. Until now we, with the whole army chosen by Christ and richly endowed by him, for the past 23 weeks, have continually been drawing nearer to the home of our Lord Jesus. And know for certain, my well-beloved that I have doubled the gold, silver, and all the other valuables that you lovingly handed me when I left you; for all our princes, with the complete consent of the army, yet against my own wish, have so far made me the principal head and leader of the expedition....

[He was neither the commander-in-chief nor the politico-religious head, but probably what we should call Quartermaster-General. Stephen describes how the army had fought its way through Asia Minor.]

But the bravest of the Turkish soldiers entered Syria and by forced marches day and night made haste to enter the royal city of Antioch before us. When they heard this, the whole army of God gave thanks and praise to the Almighty and hurrying towards Antioch laid siege to it. Many a battle have we had there with the Turks and seven times, with fierce courage and under Christ's leadership, we fought the people of Antioch and the countless hosts who came to their aid. We won all those seven battles with the help of the Lord God and killed a great number of enemies, but in those same battles, to tell the truth, and in the many attacks launched against the city, many of our fellows were killed and their souls borne to Paradise.

In front of that city, all through the winter, we endured extreme cold and tremendous torrents of rain for the sake of Christ our Lord. People said that it would be impossible to bear the heat of the sun in Syria, but that is not true, because the winter here is just like ours in the West. . . .

While Alexander, my chaplain, was hurriedly writing this letter on Easter Day, some of our men reconnoitering the Turks fought a victorious battle against them, capturing 60 horsemen, whose heads they brought back to camp.

These are only a few of the many things we have done, dearest, I cannot tell you all I am thinking, so just advise you to do good, to take care of my lands, and do your duty to your children and vassals. You will see me as soon as I can return to you. Farewell.

5.10 THE CAPTURE OF JERUSALEM

It was not until the summer of 1099 that Jerusalem itself was taken. This account of the final struggle is by an unknown soldier in the army of the Norman Bohemond of Taranto. His work must have been published either in 1100 or 1101 for the German abbot Ekkehard read it in Jerusalem in the latter year.

We attacked the city on Monday (June 13th) so fast and furiously that it would have been taken, if only the ladders had been ready. As it is, we destroyed the lesser wall and set a ladder against the main wall, and some knights climbed up and attacked the Saracen defenders with swords and spears. Many of our men, but more of theirs, found death there.

During this siege we could get no bread for ten days, when a carrier from our ships arrived; and we suffered from such a burning thirst that we had to trudge up to six miles in fearful danger to water our horses and other animals. The Pool of Siloam, at the foot of

Mount Sion relieved us, but the water was sold to us at too high a price. . . . The Saracens were laying traps for our people and poisoning the cisterns and springs. They killed and cut in pieces all of us they could find; they hid their animals in caves and ravines.

Our lords were planning to attack the city with the aid of machines, so that we could enter it and worship the sepulchre of our Saviour. They built two wooden castles and many other machines. Duke Godfrey and Count Raymond each constructed a castle equipped with contrivances [wheels and catapults], built with wood fetched from afar [the forests of Samaria].

When the Saracens saw our people building these machines, they fortified the city amazingly, strengthening the defences of the towers over-night. Then our lords, finding that the weakest side of the city was on the east, got our wooden castle and machines moved there during Saturday night (July 9–10). They set them up at dawn and through Sunday, Monday and Tuesday fitted out the castle and manned it. In the southern sector Count Raymond of Saint-Giles prepared his appliance. By this time we were suffering so much from thirst that a man could not buy enough water to quench it even for a denier.

On Wednesday and Thursday we fiercely attacked the city from all sides. But before the assault the bishops and priests exhorted us in their sermons to make a procession around the walls of Jerusalem to the glory of God, coupled with prayers, alms and fasts. (This took place on Friday, July 8th.)

Early in the morning of Friday (July 15th), we launched a concerted attack on the city but were not able to damage it and this surprised us and filled us with fear. Then, as the hour approached when our Lord Jesus Christ consented to suffer the agony of the cross for us, those of our knights who were posted in the wooden castle—Duke Godfrey, his brother Count Eustace and others—fought furiously, and one of our knights named Litold got to the top of the wall. As soon as he reached it, the defenders all fled from the walls through the city, and our men pursued and smote them, cutting them down and killing them as far as the Temple of Solomon, where there was such a slaughter that our men waded ankle-deep in blood.

Count Raymond on his side had led his army and wooden castle near the wall to the south, but between wall and castle ran a ditch. It was announced that any who carried three stones into the ditch should have a denier, and this took three days and nights to fill, when the castle was brought close to the wall. The defenders fought hard against our men, using fire and stones.

['Greek' fire was tow steeped in nitre, sulphur, and naphtha, to set fire to the wooden castle. The crusaders had covered the wood with skins as a protection.]

The Count, hearing that the Franks were inside the city, shouted to his men, 'What are you waiting for? All the Franks are already inside!'

The governor (Iftikhar) commanded the Tower of David, but surrendered to the Count and opened the gate where the pilgrims used to pay tribute (the Jaffa Gate). Once inside the city our pilgrims pursued the Saracens right up to the Temple of Solomon, slaughtering all the way. There the Saracens joined up their forces and fought our people most furiously all through that day, so that the whole Temple flowed with their blood. After crushing the pagans our men captured the Temple and a great number of men and women, whom they killed or spared as they thought fit. A large group of the pagans of both sexes had taken refuge on the roof, and Tancred and Gaston of Béarn gave them their banners (as a sign that their surrender had been accepted). Soon the crusaders were running all over the city, seizing gold, silver, horses and mules, and plundering the houses, which were crammed with treasures.

Then, full of gladness, weeping for joy, our people went to worship the Sepulchre of our Saviour Jesus and pay their thanks to him. Next morning they climbed to the roof of the Temple, attacked both the men and women of the Saracens and, drawing swords, cut off their heads. Some threw themselves down from the roof. When he saw this, Tancred was filled with indignation....

Orders were given that all the dead Saracens should be thrown out of the City because of the horrible stench, for almost the whole city was filled with their corpses. The living Saracens dragged out the dead, and heaped them almost as high as the houses in front of the gates. No one had ever seen, no one had ever heard of such a butchery of pagans; funeral pyres were set up like milestones—God alone knows how many.

Steven Runciman, the historian of the Crusades, comments: 'Many even of the Christians were horrified by what had been done; ... It was this blood-thirsty proof of Christian fanaticism that recreated the fanaticism of Islam.

When, later, wiser Latins in the East sought to find some basis on which Christian and Moslem could work together, the memory of the massacre stood always in the way.' (I. 287).

5.11 The King of Jerusalem: 'Where Christ had worn a Crown of Thorns'   1099

No scene more exactly catches the spirit of the Crusaders, their genuine and simple piety and their adroit political jockeying, than the story of the election of a ruler in Jerusalem. This account is by William of Tyre (*c.* 1130–*c.* 1190) who was what present-day Israelis would call a Sabra—not a Crusading settler, but a man born in the Latin Kingdom of Jerusalem. He rose to be its Chancellor and Archbishop of Tyre. Here he is describing something which happened before he was born, but of which he possessed both first-hand written accounts and still living oral tradition. The translation is by Caxton.

To the end that they might the better know the conduct of all the barons, they ordained that wise men should search the life of each of them and their manners. They made such men as were most privy of (intimate with) the barons to come before them, and took each of them apart by leave of their lords. And they took oaths of them to say the truth of what they should be examined, which was the life and manner of their lords, without lying and failing of the truth.... The wise men that made this inquest were true men and held all things secret that ought not to be known....

They that were most privy of the Duke Godfrey, when demanded of his manners and tetches (characteristics), answered that he had one manner right grievous and annoyous; for when he heard Mass and the service of our Lord, he could not depart out of the church, but sent unto painters and glaziers, unto the clerks and governors of the churches. He heard gladly the ringing of the bells and attended so long that it much displeased his fellowship and servants. And oft times his meat was spoiled because of his long tarrying in the monasteries and holy places.

When the wise men heard this and that this was the greatest vice that could be found in the Duke, they had much great joy, for they thought well that he did this for love of our faith and for the honour of our Saviour....

When he was chosen to be king, all the barons required him to be crowned and receive the honour of the kingdom as highly as the other kings in Christendom do. He answered that in this holy city, where our Saviour Jesus Christ suffered death and had borne a crown of thorns upon his head for him and for sinners, he would never bear, if it pleased God, crown of gold nor of precious stones. To him it seemed enough for that coronation that he had the day of His Passion to honour all Christian kings that should be after him in Jerusalem. For this cause he refused the crown.

Unfortunately Godfrey died within the year. Baldwin of Boulogne did not share his brother Godfrey's inhibitions. He took the title of King of Jerusalem as soon as he reached the city and was crowned in the Church of the Nativity in Bethlehem on Christmas Day, 1100.

Christians and Moslems in Palestine

The next four extracts deal with the settlers from the West and their relations with the people of the land, both Christian and Moslem. The first, from Caxton's translation of William of Tyre, discusses the motives which had sent them on Crusades. The second, by Fulcher of Chartres, shows the process of assimilation. The third and fourth are from Moslem sources, the first of which is from a circular letter from Saladin at the time of the Third Crusade (Richard Lionheart's). Admittedly it is designed to stimulate Moslem recruiting, but the picture it gives of Christian fervour cannot be altogether discounted. The last shows the process of assimilation at work from a Moslem angle. The writer is Usama Ibn Mundqidh, an Arab aristocrat who lived in Damascus for many years. In his old age—he lived to be ninety-three—he wrote a volume of memoirs.

5.12   WHY MEN CAME

You should have seen the husband depart from his wife, and the fathers from the children, and the children from the fathers. And it seemed that every man would depart from what he loved best in this world, for to win the joy of that other. There was so great affray and so great a moving through all the land that you should scarcely have found a house but that someone had enterprised this voyage.

I say not that all that went were wise and of pure intention toward our Lord, for some monks went out of their cloisters without leave of their abbots or priors, and the recluses went out of the places where they had been closed in and went forth with the others. Some went forth for love of their friends, to bear them fellowship. Others went forth for bombast, lest they should be reputed for evil and not good. And some there were that would withdraw from their creditors and have respite of their debts. . . .

And it was of great need that this pilgrimage was chosen at that time, for there were in the world so many sins that they withdrew the people from our Lord. And it was well behoveful that God should send to them some direction by which they might come to heaven, and give them some travail, as it were a purgatory before their death.

| 5.13 | ASSIMILATION | c. 1120 |

We who had been Occidentals have become Orientals. The man who was once a Roman or a Frank has here become a Galilean or a Palestinian, he who used to live in Rheims or Chartres now discovers himself a citizen of Tyre or Antioch. We have already forgotten the places where we were born; many of us do not know them or at least no longer hear them mentioned. Some of us already own houses and servants in this country by hereditary right. Another has married a wife of another country, a Syrian or Armenian woman, or even a Saracen who has received the grace of baptism. One houses either son-in-law, daughter-in-law, father-in-law, or stepson; another is surrounded by nephews or even grand-nephews. One cultivates his vines, another his fields; they speak different languages, but have already learnt to understand one another. Very different idioms are now common to many nations, and races utterly unlike each other learn to live in mutual trust.

| 5.14 | SALADIN ON HIS ENEMIES | c. 1190 |

We are amazed to see the war-like spirit of the infidels and the indifference of the true believers. Does a single Moslem answer our entreaty and come when called? Yet look at the Christians! See how they come in crowds, how they vie with each other in their haste, how they support each other, how they sacrifice their riches, subscribe together, submit to the most extreme privations. Every one of their kings or lords, every island and city, every man of any importance sends his peasants and subjects, and makes them act in this brave theatre. There is not a mighty man among them who does not join this campaign.... They think they are serving their religion, and that is why they consecrate their lives and wealth to this war. Their one aim is to serve the cause of the God they adore, the glory of him they believe in.

Source: Abu Shama, *Book of the Two Gardens.*

| 5.15 | A MOSLEM IN THE TEMPLE | c. 1140 |

Everyone who is a fresh emigrant from the Frankish lands is ruder in character than those who have become acclimatized and have held long association with the Moslems. Here is an illustration of their rude character.

Whenever I visited Jerusalem I always entered the Aqsa Mosque, beside which stood a small mosque which the Franks had converted into a church. When I used to enter the Aqsa Mosque, which was occupied by the Templars, who were my friends, the Templars would evacuate the little adjoining mosque so that I might pray in it. One day I entered this mosque, repeated the first formula, *Allah is great*, and stood up in the act of praying. Upon this one of the Franks rushed on me, got hold of me and turned my face eastward.

'This is the way thou shouldst pray!' he said.

A group of Templars hastened to him, seized him, and repelled him from me. I resumed my prayer. The same man, while the others were otherwise busy, rushed once more on me and turned my face eastward.

'This is the way thou shouldst pray!' he said.

The Templars again came in to him and expelled him. They apologized to me:

'This is a stranger who has only recently arrived from the land of the Franks and he has never before seen anyone praying except eastward.'

Thereupon I said to myself, 'I have had enough prayer.' So I went out and have ever been surprised at the conduct of this devil of a man, at the change in the colour of his face, his trembling and his sentiment at the sight of one praying towards the Qiblah [to Mecca].

5.16 The Templars

The roads in Palestine were infested by pockets of Moslem resistance operating from inaccessible strongholds and by incursions of Bedouin raiders from across Jordan. Nine knights, who had taken part in the siege of Jerusalem, vowed to devote themselves to seeing pilgrims safely to Jerusalem. They lived together and, after a time, took vows which made them soldier-monks —they remained laymen, of course, calling themselves 'Poor Fellow-soldiers of Jesus Christ'. The Patriarch of Jerusalem received their three-fold monastic vow of obedience, chastity, and poverty (individual, but not corporate). In 1118 they were granted as their headquarters the 'Temple of Solomon', recently the Mosque el-Aqsa, which had started life as Justinian's church of the Virgin. From this they were called the Knights Templar.

Soon it became necessary to draw up a new rule of life which would fit the needs of these strange hybrids, soldier-monks. There was one obvious man to do it—Bernard, abbot of Clairvaux, 'the oracle of Europe' as Gibbon called him. Hugh de Payens, the first Grand Master, came home with five of his knights, visited the Pope, and went on to consult Bernard. The result was the rule from which the following extracts are taken.

In the Holy Land the two military orders, Templars and Hospitallers (Knights of St. John), became the small standing army of professionals on which the defence of the Kingdom of Jerusalem depended. Throughout Europe men flocked to join the orders and to endow them with property. Their priories and preceptories served as regimental depots for those on active service in Palestine. One of their castles in Syria is shewn in Plate 4.

15. Although the reward of the poor is doubtless the kingdom of heaven (Matt. 5, 3) we order you to give a tenth of your daily bread to the almoner for distribution to them as the Christian religion surely urges us to do.

18. Knights who are tired because they have been on duty need not rise for matins as others must, but with the approval of the master or his deputy they may rest.

30. Each knight should have three horses, poverty allowing no more at present....

31. For the same reason we give to each knight only one squire and if he serves without pay out of charity he must not be abused or beaten for any fault.

37. Gold or silver, signs of private wealth, should never be seen on bridles, breastplates or spurs, and no one may buy such accoutrements. If one is given them in charity he must paint over the gold and silver parts so as not to appear more proudly distinguished than his fellows.

41. No brother may receive letters from his parents or anyone without the permission of the master or the preceptor....

42. Idle words lead to sin and how will those who like to brag of past misdeeds answer their Judge? We therefore forbid brothers to tell tales of their silly doings and sinful fears while they were in the world or on military campaigns. No one must retail stories of other's failings or of sexual adventures with unhappy women.

46. No one should follow the sport of catching one bird with another. Such worldly pleasures are not in tune with the religious life....

47. All religious men should be well-behaved and humble, avoiding laughter, speaking only a little, sensibly and quietly. A brother must not go shooting in the forest with long bow or crossbow, nor accompany hunters except to protect them from infidels. He must not shout the 'view hallo!' nor use a hound nor spur his horse to be in at the kill.

51. We believe that this new kind of religious life was begun by divine guidance in the holy land, uniting war and religion, so that religion advances by the sword and smites the enemy without committing sin. Therefore we believe it right for the Knights Templar to have estates and tenants and serfs working on the land, and all services should be rendered particularly well for you.

5.17   BERNARD ON THE NEW CHRISTIAN CHIVALRY

Not once or twice but three times, my dearest Hugh [Grand Master of the Templars], unless I am mistaken, you have asked me to write something to encourage you and your fellow-knights, and use my pen since I may not use a lance against the tyrant foe.

The soldiery of the world

In secular war there is great danger either that, although you may kill your opponent, he will destroy you spiritually, or that you will be killed yourself both body and soul. The peril or the victory of a Christian has indeed to be reckoned not by whether he wins but by the state of his conscience.…

You worldly soldiers cover your horses with silver trappings. I know not how much fine cloth covers your coats of mail. You paint your spears, shields and saddles; your bridles and spurs are ornamented with gold and silver and gems. In all this pomp, with shameful fury and reckless insensibility, you rush on to death. Is this military equipment or woman's trinkets? Will an enemy's sharp sword respect gold, spare gems, fail to cut through silk? As you yourselves know by experience, a soldier must be bold, active, and wary; fast on his feet, quick on the draw. But you make yourselves an eye-sore by wearing your hair like a woman's, enveloping your feet with long, flowing garments, and burying your delicate and tender hands in large, wide sleeves. You go to war or pick a quarrel only because of a fit of sudden, thoughtless anger; or through a mad lust for glory; or because you covet another man's land or goods. For such purposes it is neither safe to kill nor be killed.…

The soldiery of God

But the soldiers of Christ are secure when they fight the battles of their Lord. They fall into no sin when they kill the enemy, nor are they in danger should they die. Death given or received for Christ bears no touch of crime but much of glory.…

And now, to set an example, or to confound other soldiers who clearly make war for the devil, not for God, here is a brief description of the life of the Knights of Christ in the field and in the convent which makes plain the difference between the soldiery of God and the soldiery of the World.... The soldiers of Christ live a pleasant, frugal common life, unmarried, uncumbered by children. So that they may live as the Gospel bids them, they live together without any individual property of their own, in one house, under one rule, careful to preserve the unity of the Spirit in the bond of peace. You may say that the whole army has only one heart and one soul since no man follows his own way but each whole-heartedly carries out the Master's wishes. They are never idle or at a loose end. When they are not in the field, they are busy looking after their armour or their clothes, or doing some job which the Master assigns them or which springs from the needs of their life together. In this way they do not eat their bread in idleness. Among them there is no distinction of persons: the best and most virtuous rank highest, not the most nobly born. They share each other's honour, they bear one another's burdens, that they may fulfil the law of Christ.... They detest cards and dice, they avoid field sports, take no pleasure in the ludicrous pastime of hawking which men are fond of indulging in. Jesters, fortune-tellers, and bards; scurrilous songs, pageants, and games, they treat with contempt as vanity and mad folly. They cut their hair short, knowing that, according to the Apostle, it is not ooomly for a man to have long hair. Their hair is never combed; they seldom wash; but they go about with rough, neglected hair, foul with dust; their skin is brown from the sun and coarsened by their coats of mail.

Before battle they arm themselves with faith within and steel without, not with gold. Thus armed and not adorned, they strike terror into the enemy instead of arousing his lust for plunder. They take great trouble to secure strong, swift horses; but they do not trick them out with ornaments, for they are concerned with battle-worthiness not with pomp and show. They want to inspire fear rather than admiration....

These are the men God has chosen for his own, and brought together to be his servants from the ends of the earth, from among the bravest of Israel. They vigilantly and faithfully guard the Holy Sepulchre, armed with the sword and most learned in the art of war....

5.18 Jerusalem Lost

In 1187 Jerusalem was surrendered to Saladin (1138–1193), Sultan of Egypt and Syria. It had really been lost at a disastrous battle near the Sea of Galilee three months before. Balian of Nablus escaped and defended Jerusalem with a scratch force. There were only two knights in the city so he knighted all boys of noble families who had reached the age of sixteen. This account of the last days of Christian Jerusalem is by Ibn al-Athir (1160–1233) of Mosul. Several thousands for whom no ransom could be found were made slaves, but Saladin and his brother freed many out of compassion—a sentiment insufficiently developed in the Christian Patriarch to overcome his desire to protect the treasures of his church.

The Franks showed great courage at first. For both sides this was a religious war. The soldiers needed no orders from their leaders to encourage them; they defended their positions fearlessly; those who attacked never looked behind them. The besieged made daily sorties into the plain. After one of these attacks, when a noble emir had been killed, the Moslems advanced as one man to avenge his death, and put the Christians to flight. Then they reached the ditch and made a breach, while archers from their posts nearby drove the Christians from the ramparts with their arrows, thus protecting the workers. At the same time they dug a tunnel and filled it with wood ready for burning. At this crisis the Christian leaders thought it best to surrender and some of the chief citizens came in a deputation to Saladin.

'I shall treat you as the Christians treated the Moslems when they took the Holy City,' he said. 'I shall slay the men with the sword and reduce the rest to slavery. In short, I shall return evil for evil.'

When he got this answer Balian son of Basran, the commander of Jerusalem, asked for a safe conduct to treat with the Sultan personally. It was granted; he came and argued with Saladin but he was not to be shaken. Balian sank to prayers and entreaties. As Saladin remained relentless, Balian cast caution to the winds.

'O Sultan,' he said, 'God alone knows how vast are the numbers of our people. They do not want to fight, because they hope for such terms of surrender as you have granted to so many others. They fear death and cling to life, but if death becomes inevitable, I swear by the God who hears us we shall kill our women and children and burn all our possessions. We shall not leave you a sou. You shall find no women for slaves, or men to put in irons. We shall destroy the Church of the Sakka (Dome of the Rock) and the Mosque al-Aqsa, and all the holy places. We shall slaughter all the 5,000 Moslems imprisoned in our walls. We shall not leave one beast of burden alive. Then we shall come out against you and fight to the death. For every one of us who dies, many of yours will perish. We shall die free or triumph gloriously.'

At these words Saladin consulted with his emirs, who advised him to agree to a surrender.

'Let the Christians come out on foot bringing nothing without showing it to us. We shall treat them as prisoners at our mercy and they will have to ransom themselves at a price to be agreed.'

Saladin accepted this completely. It was agreed that every man in the city, whether rich or poor, should pay ten pieces of gold for his ransom, each woman, five, each child, two. This had to be paid within 40 days, when all who had not found the money would count as slaves, but those who had paid were free to go where they liked. As for the poor—about 18,000 in number—Balian himself promised to pay 30,000 pieces of gold for them.

This agreed, the Holy City opened its gates and the standard of Islam was hoisted on the walls. It was then Friday, the 27th of Rajab. [The anniversary of Mohammed's Night Journey to Jerusalem and the Seventh Heaven.]

5.19   A Soldier Pilgrim of the Third Crusade   1192

The loss of Jerusalem provoked the Third Crusade in which King Richard Lionheart took part. He failed to recapture Jerusalem, but secured another hundred years of life for what remained of the Latin Kingdom. When he and Saladin made peace in 1192 parties of Christian soldiers were allowed to go unarmed as pilgrims to the Holy Places before they returned home. This account is translated by M. J. Hubert from the Old French of Ambroise, a jongleur who versified a prose account, now lost, by a foot-soldier in Richard's army. One result of this parting pilgrimage was that the Bishop of Salisbury saw Saladin, got on well with him, and was given as a leaving gift the right to send Catholic priests to the Holy Places in Jerusalem, Bethlehem, and Nazareth which had been returned in 1187 to the Orthodox Church, to which most Palestinian Christians belonged. Henceforth the Moslem authorities rationed the use of the Holy Places among the Christian sects, retaining control themselves. Pilgrims from the West continued to visit them. Line 21 refers to a lost relic. The bishop of Acre had been killed in the battle near the Sea of Galilee in 1187 with the relic of the True Cross in his hands. After the Third Crusade the Christians tried to buy it back from Saladin, but were refused.

> The Sultan sent his men to stay
> And guard the road in loyalty
> The while the pilgrim folk marched by,
> So that we passed secure from ills.
> And then we climbed into the hills
> And soon we reached the Montjoie's height.
> Then in our hearts was great delight

To see Jerusalem. We felt
Such joy that on the ground we knelt,
As all who come there ought to do.
We saw the Mount of Olives, too,
The place whence started the procession
When the Lord God went to his passion.

We went next on our pilgrimage
To where God won his heritage,
The city. Those who rode first were
Allowed to kiss the Sepulchre;
The knights and those men who were mounted,
When they were with our troop, recounted
How Saladin showed and disclosed
That holy cross, the which was lost
During the battle, and saw fit
To have them kiss and worship it.
We others were on foot, and we
Saw all the things that we could see.

We saw in truth the monument
Wherein God's body evident
Was laid away when death he suffered.
There a few offerings were offered.
But since the Saracens would take
What offerings we chose to make
We offered little. But large share
We gave to the poor captives there,
The Franks and Syrians detained
In wretched bondage and enchained.

5.20   The Fate of the Templars   1307

After the loss of Palestine the Military Orders continued to defend Christendom from a succession of island bases—Cyprus, Rhodes, and Malta. But the wealth of the Templars whetted the King of France's appetite, and their rule of secrecy gave him a pretext for action against them. A deal was done with the pope, and on October 13, 1307 the Grand Master, Jacques de Molay and all the other Templars within reach were arrested. This sober account is by Giovanni Villani (*c.* 1280–1328), the Florentine historian. Dante endorsed Villani's judgment when he described Philip the Fair as 'the cruel new Pilate who brings into the Temple his greedy sails'. So did Döllinger, the great nineteenth-century German Catholic writer, when he wrote, 'If I were to name one day in the whole history of the world which appears to me in the truest sense as a *dies nefastus* (an unhallowed day, day of wickedness), I should be able to name no other than the 13th of October, 1307.'

The king was moved by avarice and made secret arrangements with the Pope (Clement V), getting his promise to destroy the Order of the Templars. He brought many counts of heresy against them, but his real reasons were said to be more the hope of getting great sums of money from them, and the fact that he had taken offence against the Master of the Temple and the Order.... The Pope fixed a day on which all Templars throughout the world were to be arrested, and on which all their churches, houses, and possessions, which were almost innumerable in power and wealth, were to be sequestered. [In fact the first arrests were in France; other countries followed later.] All those in France the king's courts took over. In Paris the Master of the Order, Jacques, of the family of the lords of Molay in Burgundy, was arrested together with sixty knights, friars, and gentlemen. They were charged on several counts with heresy; with vile sins against nature which they were said to practise among themselves; with taking an oath at their profession to support the Order right or wrong; with idolatrous worship and with spitting on the Cross....

The king had them tortured in various ways to extract a confession, but they would neither confess nor admit anything. He kept them in prison a long time (three years) in great misery, not knowing how to bring their trial to a conclusion. At last fifty-six of the Templars were executed outside Paris at St. Antoine (and there were similar executions at Senlis). In a great open space enclosed by a wood the Templars were bound to separate stakes. The executioners began to set fire to their feet and their legs, little by little. They reminded the Templars one after the other that anyone who would acknowledge the error and sins with which he was charged might escape death. During this martyrdom their kinsmen and friends urged them to confess and not to allow themselves to be thus vilely slain and destroyed. Not one of them, however, would confess, but with weeping and cries they defended themselves as innocent and faithful Christians, calling upon Christ and St. Mary and the other saints. Burning to ashes, by this martyrdom they ended their lives.

The case of the Master and of some others was held over and they were brought to Poitiers before the Pope in the presence of the King of France and promised forgiveness if they would admit their error and sin. It is said that they made some kind of confession. When they had returned to Paris two cardinal legates came there to pass judgment, condemning the Order on this confession and punishing the Master and his companions. When the legates had mounted a great platform opposite the church of Notre Dame and had read the indictment, the Master of the Temple rose to his feet, demanding to be heard. When silence was proclaimed, he denied that ever such heresies and sins as they had been charged with had been true, and maintained that the rule of their Order had been holy and just and Catholic. But he said that he himself certainly deserved death, and would endure it in peace, because through fear of torture

A Crusader receives Communion
13th century figures on the central porch of Reims

and yielding to the persuasion of the Pope and the king, he had by deceit been led to make a partial confession. His speech was interrupted, and the court's judgment was left unfinished. The cardinals and the other prelates went away and consulted the king. Then the Master and his companions were put to martyrdom in the Isle of Paris in front of the king's hall in the same way as the rest of their brethren. As the Master burnt slowly to death, he continually repeated that the Order and their religion was Catholic and righteous, and he commended himself to God and St. Mary. And so did the brother of the Dauphin. Brother Hugh of Peraud and the other man, through fear of martyrdom, confessed and confirmed what they had said before the Pope and the king, and they saved their lives, but afterwards they died miserably. . . .

The night after the Master and his companion had been martyred, their ashes and bones were collected as sacred relics by friars and other religious and carried away to holy places. In this manner was destroyed and brought to nought the rich and powerful Order of the Temple at Jerusalem in the year of Christ 1310 [in fact 1314].

Contemporaries were not slow to notice that Philip the Fair, King of France, and Pope Clement V, the first of the popes to leave Rome and settle at Avignon, both died in the same year as the Grand Master. Many saw significance in this.

5.21 Chivalry—the Ideal of the Christian Aristocrat

The Crusades left behind them the doctrine and, to a markedly less degree, the practice of chivalry. The imagination of the West was long touched by the ideal best known to us through Chaucer's knight, who had ridden into battle 'no man further':

> '(Yet) of his bearing meek as is a maid.
> He never yet no villainy had said
> In all his life unto no manner wight.
> He was a very perfect gentle knight...
> He was but lately come from his voyage
> And now he went to do his pilgrimage.'

In the last years of the Middle Ages William Caxton printed a book about knights, at the end of which he wrote:
'This little book I present to my most redoubted natural and most dread sovereign lord, King Richard, King of England and of France (Richard III), to the end that he command this book to be had and read unto other young lords, knights, and gentlemen within this realm, that the noble order

of chivalry be hereafter better used and honoured than it hath been in late days past.'

Caxton's 'little book' was already 200 years old, the work, though he did not know it, of Ramon Lull (*c*. 1235–1315), one of the most remarkable Christians of the Middle Ages (see 7.7). The following extracts from the *Book of the Order of Chivalry* show the Christian context of knighthood.

Of the Office that Appertaineth to a Knight

The office of a knight is the end and beginning (purpose) for which the order of chivalry began. Then if a knight does not carry out his office he is contrary to his order and to the beginning of chivalry. By which contrariety he is not a very knight howbeit that he bear the name. For such a knight is more vile than the smith or the carpenter who do not their office as they ought after they have learned to do it. The office of a knight is to maintain and defend the holy catholic faith by the which God the Father sent his son into the world to take human flesh in the glorious virgin, our Lady, saint Mary. And to multiply the faith he suffered in this world many travails, despites, and the anguish of death. Then in like manner as our Lord God has chosen the clergy for to maintain the holy catholic faith with scripture and reasons against the miscreants and unbelieving, in like wise the God of Glory has chosen knights so that by force of arms they may vanquish the miscreants which daily labour for to destroy holy church. And God holds such knights for his friends, honoured in this world and in that other when they keep and maintain the faith by which we intend to be saved.

In What Manner a Squire ought to be Received into the Order of Chivalry

At the beginning before a squire enters the order of chivalry he ought to confess him of his faults that he has done against God, and ought to receive chivalry with the intention that in it he will serve our Lord God which is glorious. And if he be clean from sin he ought to receive his Saviour (i.e. in communion). The day of some great feast such as Christmas, Easter, Whitsuntide or some other solemn day is proper for to make and dub a knight because, by reason of the honour of the feast, many people assemble in that place where the squire ought to be dubbed knight. And God ought to be adored and prayed that he give to him grace for to live well after the order of chivalry.

The squire ought to keep the vigil of that feast in honour of the saint whose feast it is; and he ought to go to the church for to pray God, and ought to wake the night and be in his prayers. And he ought to hear the word of God and of the deeds of chivalry. For if he should otherwise hear jongleurs [minstrels] and ribalds that speak of corruption and of sin he should begin then to dishonour chivalry. On the morning after the feast at which he is to be dubbed he should cause a solemn mass to be sung. And the squire ought to come to the altar and offer to the priest, who holds the place of our Lord to whom he must undertake to submit himself to keep the honour of chivalry with all his power, saying 'In thy name, and with the intention to serve thee, and honour thee, my sovereign Lord God, and thy dear mother Mary, and all thy holy saints of paradise, I take this day this worthy order.' [The words of the oath are from an earlier translation into Scots.]

Then the prince or baron that will make the squire and dub him knight must have in himself the virtue and order of chivalry. For if the knight that maketh knights is not virtuous, how may he give that which he hath not?... The squire ought to kneel before the altar and lift up to God his eyes, corporal and spiritual, and his hands to heaven. And the knight ought to gird the squire with his sword in sign of chastity, justice and charity. [This rather than the accolade seems to have been the essential act in knight-making.] The knight ought to kiss the squire and to give him a palm to remind him of that which he receives and promises.... And after, when the knight spiritual, that is the priest, and the earthly knight have done what belongs to their office as touching the making of a new knight, the new knight ought to ride through the town and to show himself to the people to the end that all men know and see that he is newly made knight.

5.22   EPITAPH ON A KNIGHT

A great number of medieval French romances in rhymed verse were sung by the 'jongleurs' (minstrels) in cloisters and courts in the twelfth to four-teenth centuries. The Lancelot stories of the Arthurian cycle have been attributed to Walter Map, archdeacon of Oxford, *c.* 1200. These were turned into English prose by Sir Thomas Malory in 1469 in the *Morte d'Arthur*, a book which has kept the Middle Ages alive for us ever since. Here is Sir Ector's lament for Sir Lancelot in the last chapter.

Ah Lancelot, he said, thou were head of all Christian knights, and now I dare say, said Sir Ector, thou Sir Lancelot, there thou liest, that thou were never matched of earthly knight's hand. And thou were the courteoust knight that ever bare shield. And thou were the truest friend to thy lover that ever bestrad horse, and thou were the truest lover of a sinful man that ever loved woman. And thou were the kindest man that ever struck with sword. And thou were the goodliest person that ever came among press of knights. And thou was the meekest man and the gentlest that ever ate in hall among ladies. And thou were the sternest knight to thy mortal foe that ever put spear in the rest.

CHAPTER SIX

CLUNY AND CITEAUX

Two place names, insignificant in themselves—indeed sought out because they were insignificant—dominate the spiritual, the cultural, and to an astonishing extent the political history of Western Europe from the beginning of the tenth to past the middle of the twelfth century. It is the spiritual domination from which the rest flows. It was for the spiritual life, the 'work of God', that the monasteries of Cluny, Citeaux, and Clairvaux were founded. The modern palate will perhaps most easily place Cluny geographically by its nearness to Mâcon, and Citeaux as forming the eastern apex of an equilateral triangle with Chambertin and Nuits St. Georges.

6.1 The Founding of Cluny

Why did a noble found a monastery? This is not quite the same question as why did a man become a monk, though it is allied to it. William of Aquitaine sets out his reasons in the charter by which he founded Cluny in 910. He combined realism ('no pockets in shrouds'), a fitting concern for himself (no harm in that), a vivid sense of the inter-dependence of all Christian people 'past, present and to come' with confidence in the practical value of what the monks of Cluny would do in return (a belief, that is, in intercessory prayer). These might have been by themselves enough to prompt his gift. But there was something more not mentioned in his charter. Joan Evans recalls in her 'Monastic Life at Cluny' a little difference of opinion about the site of the monastery. Berno, abbot of Baume and abbot-designate of Cluny, had made his choice. 'William of Aquitaine held other views; he objected that Cluny was the best hunting-ground in all his domains. "Drive your hounds hence," said Berno, "and put monks in their place; for you know which will serve you better before God, the baying of hounds or the prayers of monks": and William, with murder on his conscience, could only agree.' In an age of violence and ungovernable tempers, when men believed unhesitatingly in the Last Judgment, fear and remorse were potent spurs to works of charity. In later times men were to laugh at such 'fire insurance'. In the middle ages it was no laughing matter.

I, William, by the grace of God count and duke, having pondered these things and wishing while there is yet time to make provision for my salvation, have found it right, yea necessary, to dispose for the good of my soul of some of the temporal possessions which have been bestowed upon me. For since I appear to have increased them much, I would not wish to deserve the reproach in the hour of death that I had used them only for the needs of my body, but would rather, when my last moment shall take them all from me, give myself the joy of having used a part for my soul: the which may not be better done than by following the precept of our Lord: 'I will make myself friends among the poor'. That this benefaction may endure not only for a time, but may last for ever, I will provide at my expense for men living together under monastic vows, with this faith and hope that if I cannot myself despise all the things of this world, at least by sustaining those who despise the world, those whom I believe to be righteous in the eyes of God, I may myself receive the reward of the righteous.

To all those who live in the unity of faith and who implore the mercy of Christ, to all who shall succeed them and shall be living so long as the world endures, I make known that for the love of God and of our Saviour Christ Jesus I give and deliver to the Apostles Peter and Paul the village of Cluny, on the river Grosne, with its curtilage and its house, with the Chapel that is dedicated in honour of St. Mary Mother of God and of St. Peter, Prince of the Apostles, with all the property that depends thereon, cottages, chapels, serfs both men and women, vines, fields, meadows, forests, water and watercourses, mills, crops and revenues, land tilled and untilled, with no reservations. All these things are situate in the county of Mâcon or near it, each enclosed within its bounds. I, William, with my wife Ingelberge, give these things to the aforesaid Apostles, first for the love of God, then for the soul of my lord the King Eudes, for the souls of my father and mother, for me and my wife, that is for the salvation of our souls and bodies, for the soul of Ava, my sister who left me these properties by will, for the souls of our brothers and sisters, our nephews and of all our kindred, men and women, for our faithful servants, and for the maintenance and integrity of the Catholic faith. Finally, since as Christians we are all bound together by the bonds of our faith and charity, may this gift be made also for the faithful of times past, present and to come.

I give on condition that a Regular Monastery be established at Cluny in honour of the apostles Peter and Paul; that monks shall form a congregation there living under the rule of St. Benedict; that they shall for ever possess, hold and order the property given

in such wise that this honourable house shall be unceasingly full
of vows and prayers, that men shall seek there with a lively desire
and an inner fervour the sweetness of converse with Heaven, and
that prayers and supplications shall be addressed thence without
ceasing to God, both for me and for those persons commemorated
above....

6.2 The Monk's Vocation   *c.* 1223

The Latin word *conversio* has to do double duty. It stands for conversion
in the sense in which we use it of a religious experience today. It also has
the technical sense of the taking of monastic vows, akin to the specialized
sense in which we speak of a man's vocation to the ministry. Ideally, the
second meaning should always be concealed within the first. The first book
of a Cistercian novice-master's dialogue of instruction in the religious life
deals with conversion. The writer, Caesarius of Heisterbach in the Rhineland, has both meanings in mind:

Monk: Conversion is a turning of the heart, either from bad to good,
or from good to better, or from better to best.

The first turning is *at* the heart and that is contrition, the second
is *in* the heart, which is devotion, and the third *from* the heart, which
is contemplation. Conversion at the heart is the return from wilfulness to grace, from sin to uprightness, from vice to virtue. Conversion
in the heart is advancing in charity, and going *from strength to
strength* (Psa. 84, 7) until the God of gods appears in Sion, that is,
in contemplation. Conversion from the heart is the soaring of the
spirit in contemplation. Contemplation has its plane above the heart,
wherefore it is called in the Scripture *ascensiones in corde*.

Further the word is *con*version because it is a total and complete
turning; as it is said, 'He who forsakes one vice but still clings to
another, does indeed turn, but is not converted.'... Nor is it of any
value in the sight of God that a sinner should leave his abode (to
enter a monastery) and not his sin, should change his garment (to
a cowl) and not his heart. It is an unnatural thing to carry the
heart of a wolf beneath the clothing of a sheep.

Novice: Does this often happen?

Monk: Yes, I will give you an example... [and he gives many].
....

Monk: ... Some men seem to be 'converted' by the direct call
and inspiration of God, others on the contrary by nothing else than
an instigation from the spirit of evil, some by a certain levity of
mind; but the greatest number are 'converted' by the ministry of

others, as by the word of exhortation, or the power of prayer, or the example of a Religious life. Then again a vast number are drawn to the Order by different compulsions, such as sickness or poverty or captivity or shame for some fault, or some danger to life, or by the terror and foretaste of the pains of hell, or by a longing for the heavenly country. All these are illustrations of those words of the Gospel: *Compel them to come in* (Luke 14, 23).

Novice: Though all these causes seem likely enough, yet I shall be much better satisfied if you will give me examples of each.

Monk: I will begin then with an example from which you may understand how men are 'converted' by the direct call of God. When St. Bernard was preaching the Crusade in Liège ... a certain canon of the Cathedral lying prostrate in prayer before one of the altars, heard a voice from heaven saying to him: 'Go out and listen, for the gospel has come to life again.' ... He found the saint preaching the Crusade against the Saracens; he was giving the cross to some, and others he was receiving into his Order. The canon, pricked to the heart, and led by the inward unction of the Holy Spirit, took up the cross, not indeed of that overseas expedition, but of the Order. He judged it better for his soul's health to imprint the enduring cross for ever upon his heart than to sew the short-lived sign upon his garment for a season....

Novice: You think then that the Order is a higher vocation than a pilgrimage?

Monk: It is judged higher, not by my authority, but by that of the Church....

6.3   WHY MEN BECAME MONKS   898

Odo, abbot of Cluny, told this story to his pupil and biographer, John of Salerno. Odo had been a weak baby. His father dedicated him to St. Martin. The boy throve. His father changed his mind and sent Odo to court, but he still took trouble about his son's religious education. Then, Odo said:

A.

God began to frighten me in dreams and to show me my life turning swiftly to evil. He changed all the pleasures of the chase into weariness for me; the more I took part in such diversions the more I returned overwhelmed with sadness and fatigue. About this time my father advised me to keep the eves of the great festivals as he did himself. A few years later, after I had spent in this fashion a part of the night of Christmas Eve in prayer, it suddenly came into my mind to ask help from the Mother of our Lord Jesus concerning my way of life. 'O Lady and Mother of Mercy,' I cried, 'Thou who hast during this night given birth to the Saviour, deign to make intercession for me by thy prayers; I hide myself in the mystery of this glorious birth. I tremble lest my life be displeasing to thy Son; and since it is through thee that he is made manifest to the world, may it be through thee that he may have mercy upon me.' The rest of the night passed in prayer, in Lauds, and in the solemn celebration of the Mass, and day dawned. The albs of the canons shone white in the choir. While the psalms proper for this solemn festival sounded in the chanting of the different voices, I—young and hot with impatience—sprang into the middle of the choir and began to chant with the clerks the praises of the King of this world. I should not have done it, I confess; but yet, when I recall the saying of King David, 'Let all the nations praise the Lord, let all the peoples sing his praise' (Psa. 67.5), it seems it was not without reason that I dared to act thus. At that moment I was seized by a violent head-ache, that overwhelmed me for a time and then departed. After the Gospel it returned worse than before, and if I had not propped myself with both arms against the wall I should certainly have fallen helpless and senseless on the pavement. The pain was so acute that with each spasm I felt that I should die. This was in my sixteenth year, and for the next three years my head was torn by this pain like earth beneath the blade of a plough. They had to take me home again, where for two years they tried to cure me by all manner of remedies. But the more they tried, the less hope there seemed to be of a cure. One day my father, weighed down with sorrow and sighing deeply, told me the story of my infancy. 'So,' said he, 'O blessed Martin, the gift which I offered thee willingly thou exactest from me to-day, as a pitiless creditor demands payment of a debt. Assuredly thou art most accessible to prayer, but hard to pay in business.' Having lost all hope of regaining health, I saw no other course open to me than to take refuge with him, to take the tonsure, and voluntarily to devote myself to the service of him to whom I had once been vowed without my knowledge. [So Odo de Dole became a canon regular (i.e. living under a monastic rule) at St. Martin of Tours.]

'Conversion' might come as a political punishment as it did to Charlemagne's handsome but deformed illegitimate son, Pippin; or it might start by taking sanctuary from justice, as did the man who murdered the brother of abbot

Hugh of Cluny according to the account of Hugh's life by Hildebert of Le Mans:

B.

Finding no place where he might find a refuge from the vengeance of his victim's kindred, he found a noble protection in his (Hugh's) bosom. Admitted to Cluny, he gained the life both of this world and the next. Hearkening to the exhortation of the holy abbot and touched with compunction, he put on the habit of a penitent, and so happily ended the perilous pilgrimage of this world and only left this life for a better.

'Conversion' might also happen simultaneously to a whole group of men and women as in the case of Guy II, Count of Mâcon and thirty of his knights. Together they entered Cluny; together their wives and daughters entered the Cluniac nunnery of Marcigny. Guy himself was later made prior of Souvigny, but after a time he resigned out of humility and came back to Cluny as a simple monk.

The Oblate: 'Lent to the Lord' (1 Sam. 2, 28)

Some monks started life in a monastery in their boyhood as 'oblates', offered to God by their parents as Hannah once offered Samuel. Once entered, they were expected to remain, although some of the deeds for the admission of oblates at Cluny reserve a boy's right to withdraw if he lacks a vocation. Their chief function at Cluny, where Abbot Hugh limited their number to six, was to act as choirboys. At fifteen or sixteen they became novices, and a relatively short time afterwards they made their final profession. At Cluny the precentor, the monastic official responsible for the services, had usually been an oblate.

　The two following extracts deal with the reception and training of oblates. The first is from the Custumal of the Norman abbey of Bec when Lanfranc, Archbishop of Canterbury, was there. Bec followed Cluniac practice. The second comes from the monastery at Cerne Abbas in Dorset and was written, not in Latin but in Old English, by its abbot Ælfric (see 6.8). The state of affairs they describe is recognizably the same, but there is a world of difference between the severe tone of the regulations and the affectionate nature of Ælfric's dialogue. All the same one would have liked an oblate's view of his position also. To understand the nature of the discipline to which the oblates were exposed it is necessary to remember that the penances given to monks often took the form of beating, and that no contemporary would have reacted as we tend to do.

6.4　　　　　CLUNIAC RULES FOR OBLATES　　　　　*c.* 1060

When a boy is offered to the Order, his parents bring him to the altar after the gospel at Mass and, when the Cantor has made the

Night stairs from the Dormitory.
South Transept of Hexham Abbey, 13th century.

usual offering, the boy makes his. Then the Sacristan takes his offering [bread and wine] and the parents draw near and wrap the boy's right hand in the altar cloth. Then they kiss it so enveloped and give it into the hands of the priest, who shall receive the boy and make the sign of the cross over his head. [Antiphons and prayers are sung and said while the boy's hair is cropped and his clothes exchanged for the cowl.]

At the night services, and indeed at all the Hours, if the boys make any mistake in psalmody or chant, or fall asleep, or transgress in other ways like that, let them be stripped immediately of frock and cowl and beaten in their shirt, either by the prior or their own master, with smooth and supple osier rods kept for that special purpose....

When they sit in cloister or chapter-house, let each have a tree-trunk seat, placed so far apart that not even the shirts of their clothing can touch each other.... When necessary the boys are beaten during the talking-hour in the cloister, never after Vespers....

A master sleeps between each pair of boys in the dormitory and sits between them in the rere-dorter [lavatory], and at night all the candles of the lanterns are fixed on the spikes on the top of the lanterns, so that the boys can clearly be seen in all that they do.

When they are in bed, let a master always stand among them with his rod and, if it be night, with his candle in one hand and his rod in the other. If one happens to linger after the others he is promptly given a smart touch of the rod; for children should ever have punishment with care, and care with punishment. And note that this is the only corporal punishment they receive, to be beaten with rods or pulled smartly by the hair; they are never disciplined with kicks or fists or palm of the hand or any other way....

One boy must report another if he knows anything against him, or, if he is found to have concealed anything on purpose, he is beaten as well as the offender.

6.5   ÆLFRIC AND HIS OBLATE   *c.* 990

If the hours at Cerne were the same as at Cluny, Matins would have been at first light, and Prime an hour later. Terce, Sext and Nones would have followed at three hourly intervals counting from Matins, not Prime. Vespers would have been at sunset, and Compline at nightfall. Nocturns were at 2.0 a.m. At Cluny the Oblates attended only part of Nocturns; it looks as if they were excused them altogether at Cerne.

You, boy, what have you done today?

I did many things. This night, when I heard the bell, I got out of bed and sang Matins with the brethren. After that we sang the Lauds of All Saints and of the day, then Prime and the seven Psalms with the Litany and the first Mass; then Terce and we did the Mass of the day; after that we sang Sext, and we ate and drank and slept. Again we got up and sang Nones, and now we are here before you, ready to hear what you will say to us.

When will you sing Vespers and Compline?

When the time comes.

Have you been whipped today?

Not I. I have been careful.

And how about your fellows?

Why ask me about them? I dare not betray our secrets to you. Everyone knows whether he has been whipped or not.

What do you eat each day?

I still eat meat, because I am a child, living under the rod.

What more do you eat?

Vegetables and eggs, fish and cheese, butter and beans, and all clean things I eat with many thanks.

You are greatly greedy, then, to eat all things put before you.

I am not such a glutton as to eat all kinds of food at one meal.

How then?

I eat sometimes of this, sometimes of that, in moderation, as becomes a monk, not ravenously, because I am not a glutton.

And what do you drink?

Ale, if I can get it. If not, water.

Don't you drink wine?

I am not rich enough to buy myself wine, and wine is not a drink for children or fools, but for the old and wise.

Where do you sleep?

In the dormitory with the children.

What rouses you for Matins?

Sometimes I hear the bell and get up; sometimes my master stirs me sternly with the stick.

6.6 'The Work of God'

The 'opus Dei', the work of God, was the monk's *raison d'etre*. Strictly defined it meant the regular worship of the church; but it may legitimately be extended to include all that accompanied it—the building in which it took place, the books used in the services, the music and so on. Benedict had ordered his monks to work with their hands as their own farm labourers. Cluny relaxed this obligation, though there was still some seasonal farm work on certain days. It did this because the *opus dei* in its extended sense made ever-increasing demands on time and skill. Abbot Peter, 'the Venerable', (1122–1157) put it thus:

It is more noble to set one's hand to the pen than to the plough, to trace divine letters upon the page than furrows upon the fields. Sow on the page the seed of the word of God, and when the harvest is ripe, when your books are finished, the hungry readers shall be satisfied with an abundant harvest.

Some monks argued that the same ascetic discipline that rules a monk's personal life ought to be reflected in the setting in which he performed the *opus dei*. Cluny disagreed. Nothing could be too poor or humble for the monk, but nothing could be too rich or beautiful for God. No man could or can judge the quality of their 'work of God' itself—that only God knows—but we can still see how it was expressed. As the monks sang in the choir at Cluny—'the angels' walk', as abbot Hugh's biographer called it—they looked up at the rich and intricate carving reproduced here. It illustrates—like most medieval art it is tailored to a spiritual and moral purpose—the four rivers that sprang from Eden (Gen. 2, 1–14) and the four trees that grow beside them: the apple of knowledge, the vine of life, the fig of the Fall, and the almond of resurrection. Compare this capital, as Joan Evans does, with the passage in which a monk of Cluny, Ralph the Bald, had written rather earlier about the four rivers, linking them with the four cardinal virtues:

We must also consider with no less attention ... the river which rises in the Eden of the East and divides into four famous streams. The first of them, the Pishon, which is interpreted as the opening of the mouth, signifies Prudence that ever pours out its salutary counsels in abundance.... The second, the Gihon, or the chasm of earth, signifies Temperance, that virtue which nourishes Chastity, and which prunes with a kindly hand the evil growths of vice. The third is the Tigris, which flows through the country of the Assyrians, a word which we translate as 'the Conduits'; it certainly signifies Fortitude, since it keeps off all the vices of betrayal of trust to conduct man with God's help to eternal bliss. The fourth, the Euphrates, whose name implies abundance, evidently signifies Justice, which nourishes every soul truly devoted to it. These rivers then depict in their mystic sense the image of the four virtues of which we have spoken, as well as the image of the four Gospels....

Two other capitals represent the eight modes (see 2.19) used in the music of the church, and which form part of the music of the spheres.

But above all the monk's mind was turned towards the heavenly country which he sought. It was Bernard of Morlas in the Pyrenees, a monk of Cluny in Peter the Venerable's time, who expressed it most memorably. His work is still remembered through J. M. Neale's translations—*Jerusalem the Golden* is in almost every English hymn book. The rhythm and the complicated rhymes of the original come out better, however, in a version which that singularly un-Christian poet, Swinburne, made in his boyhood, which begins:

O land without guilt, strong city safe built in a marvellous place,
I cling to thee, ache for thee, sing to thee, wake for thee, watch
for thy face:
Full of cursing and strife are the days of my life, with their sins they
are fed,
Out of sin is the root, unto sin is the fruit, in their sins they are dead . . .

Cluniac Order: Benedictine Rule

6.7   ABBOT ODO

Not long after Odo had become a canon regular of Tours, the Normans destroyed the church in 903. Odo was active in its rebuilding, but he failed to persuade his brother canons to live a stricter life. At the age of thirty he set out with a friend to seek a monastery nearer their ideal. They ended up at Daume. When the abbot died he provided by his will that Odo should become the second abbot of the daughter house of Cluny which he ruled—mainly by the power of affection, understanding and compassion—from 926 till his death in 944.

The following story is told by John of Salerno. Odo was on his way to Rome. At Siena John, who was in charge of the purse, went round outside the walls lest his master should give all their money away in charity, for it was a time of famine. Odo went through the town, saw some tradesmen so impoverished that they had nothing but laurel berries to sell. Odo offered them a fancy price and bought the berries. He emerged from the city gate, so John of Salerno said,

at the head of a crowd of poor folk, like a man leading his troops to war. His joy was such that when I bowed to him as the custom is, he could scarce give me his blessing in return. Pretending not to know who these men were, I asked him what they wanted.

'They are,' he said, 'the serving-men of God and our labourers; therefore hasten to pay them their wages.'

I distributed alms; and then, when I saw this quantity of laurel-berries, I asked him whence he had taken them and what he wanted done with them; and then he answered us in a rush of such gay words that I have never heard the like. He made us laugh till we cried and were past speech. Then when we were a little calmer, I besought him to free us from the burden of these berries and to give them back to those who had sold them. 'No,' said he, 'for I should be afraid that they would then wish to repay us their price.'

6.8   THE MOVEMENT SPREADS: ETHELWOLD SENDS TO FLEURY

There was something about the quality of life at Cluny that made men eager to become its monks, and made others follow William of Aquitaine's example and found monasteries on the Cluniac model. Odo was also asked to reform many famous monasteries. The pope brought him in to reform the monastery of St. Paul-without-the-Walls at Rome. Duke Hugh insisted against the will of the community that he should do the same for the famous abbey of Fleury-sur-Loire where St. Benedict's bones had been since the Moslems conquered Monte Cassino. The reform of English monasteries after the wars with the Northmen was Cluniac at one remove, for it was to Fleury, just set in order by Odo, that they turned. The great protector and patron of English monastic reform was Dunstan who had been brought up by the Irish monks of Glastonbury, and became first its abbot and then from 961 to 988 archbishop of Canterbury.

Ethelwold (*c.* 910–984) had been one of Dunstan's officers in the government of the monastery at Glastonbury. In 954 he refounded the old monastery at Abingdon. Osgar, whom he sent to Fleury to see how the Cluniacs ran their houses, succeeded him as abbot of Abingdon in 963 when Ethelwold became bishop of Winchester. This account is by Ethelwold's pupil Ælfric, called 'Grammaticus' from his writings, a monk at Winchester who became abbot first of Cerne in Dorset and then of Eynsham in Oxfordshire; it was written *c.* 1005, the only surviving manuscript being in the National Library at Paris (Lat. 5362).

King Eadred was persuaded by his mother to give the venerable Ethelwold a certain place called Abingdon, where in ancient days there had been a little monastery, poorly built and possessing only 40 hides, now ruined and deserted. There were another 100 hides of land there, held by the king. It was the king's wish that, with Dunstan's permission, Ethelwold should take charge of this place and ordain monks to serve God according to rule. That servant of God came thither, followed immediately by some clerks from Glastonbury, who put themselves under his instruction; and he speedily collected a flock of monks and was consecrated as their abbot by the king's orders.

The king also gave them his royal property in Abingdon of 100 hides, with fine buildings, to increase the daily provisions and gave them much money, but his mother was even more generous. One day the king himself came to the monastery to plan the new buildings, measuring out all the foundations with his own hand....

Then Ethelwold sent the monk Osgar over the sea to the monastery of St. Benedict at Fleury, to learn the rule and its customs and then teach and explain them to the brethren at home. By this means he, Ethelwold, and those subject to him would follow the way of life of the rule, avoiding all false paths, and so he would guide his flock to the promised land.

Ethelwold, both as abbot and afterwards as bishop, was a great builder; therefore our common enemy tried to ensnare him. One day, while working on the building, a great beam fell on him, hurled him into a pit and broke nearly all his ribs on one side. He would have been completely crushed if the pit had not received him. He recovered, however, and the blessed Edgar, king of the English, chose him for the bishopric of Winchester before the church at Abingdon was dedicated and Dunstan archbishop of Canterbury consecrated him by order of the king.

Now there were certain clerics at the Old Minster, where the bishop's seat is situated, who were living in evil ways, proud, insolent and lecherous. They scorned to take their turn to celebrate Mass, they turned away wives—whom they had married unlawfully—and took others; they were continually addicted to gluttony and drunkenness. The holy Ethelwold would not endure this but, with the king's permission, he quickly expelled the evil blasphemers of God from the minster and installed monks there from Abingdon and was himself both their abbot and bishop.

This first outreach of Cluny had been through a series of *ad hoc* operations in re-modelling old monasteries and founding new ones. They were set on their feet and expected to go on without lasting control from Cluny. But before long this changed. All the Cluniac houses became embedded in a Cluniac Order. There was to be only one abbot. The heads of the daughter houses, apart from eleven honorific exceptions, were priors, not abbots, and were nominated by the abbot of Cluny. Wherever a novice made his profession, it was made to the abbot of Cluny, no matter whether he was at St. Victor in Geneva, St. Pancras in Lewes, St. Maiolo in Pavia, St. Colomba in Burgos, or St. Saviour in Galilee. Diocesan bishops could not inspect Cluniac houses, which were directly dependent on the pope, but the abbot of Cluny could. By 1100 there were over 300 Cluniac houses bound together in this way; if cells and smaller units are included the number is more than 1,400. The Cluniac Order was something new and important in Christian organization. Thanks to it, for more than two hundred years, a longer period than separates us from the French Revolution or the American Declaration of Independence, Cluny was the most consistent and influential force for good in the Christian West.

6.9   PETER THE VENERABLE

The first six abbots of Cluny were all saintly men, and at least three were also great men (Odo 926–944; Odilo 990–1049; and Hugh 1049–1109). Then the monks made a desperately bad choice. Pons de Melgueil was proud, ambitious, extravagant. Things rapidly went wrong. In 1122 he was persuaded by the pope to resign and sent off on a pilgrimage to Jerusalem. It effected no improvement. He came back, found that his successor, Peter 'the Venerable', was away visiting daughter houses, and stormed the abbey at the head of a mob of townspeople and dissident monks. The loyal party under Bernard of Auxelles, an old soldier, had barred the doors, but were driven out. Pons had the Abbey's treasures melted down to pay his troops and carried on a brisk feudal war from Lent to October, 1125. Then the pope intervened. Pons was imprisoned and died within the year; Peter was restored, the last of the great succession of first-class abbots of Cluny (1122–1157). If for nothing else Peter should be remembered for the shelter and friendship he gave the broken Abelard (see 8.11). For Pons, Peter made a tomb on which his effigy showed his feet bound, his right hand cut off, his crozier broken. For Bernard, Peter wrote this epitaph:

> Bernard the prior rests buried in this earth,
>   A rare old man, all youthful folly gone.
> His was the soldier's trade; his second birth
>   Brought him to serve in Sion's garrison.
> He fought the fight of faith, with us grew old.
> Cluny, for you his labours were untold.

6.10   SIGN LANGUAGE

Under Peter, Cluny was restored to its old humane, pious good order. When they were not in choir—and this filled the major part of the day—the monks went about their duties in silence apart from the brief periods allowed for conversation. As they worked they communicated with each other in an elaborate sign language which allowed, for instance, the work of the kitchen to be carried on. The following extract comes from William, abbot of Hirschau from 1069 to 1091, through whom and his affiliated monasteries Cluniac reforms became widespread in Germany.

For the sign of fish in general, imitate with your hand the commotion of a fish's tail in water. For a salmon, make the general sign and then put two fingers round your eye. For a cuttlefish, part all your fingers and wave them around. For the fish called carp in the vulgar tongue, make the sign for fish and add the sign for pig. For trout, draw your finger from one eyebrow to another. For an eel, clench both hands as if you were holding an eel tightly. For a barbel, move two fingers as a man who strokes his moustaches. For a crab, add the sign for scissors.

For cheese, clasp one hand slanting over the other, as he who presses a cheese. For eggs, imitate one who opens an egg-shell. For milk, clasp the little finger of your left hand with all the fingers of the right, and thus draw it out as one who draws milk from the cow. For the sign of eating, join your two top fingers and put them once to your mouth, the rest being clenched into a fist. For flesh-food, with two fingers of your right hand touch the skin of the back of your left hand and add the sign for eating. For honey, let your tongue just appear and put your fingers to it as though you would lick them.

6.11   THE LIBRARIAN

Some monks were completely happy like Peter's friend, Brother Gregory:

Wherever the business of the Order calls me, in all our houses and even in their darkest corners, I find Gregory with his Sermons, Gregory with his Epistles, Gregory with treatises, with a pile of books and notes. I see you everywhere, and everywhere in the same surroundings; the lap of your robe is full of books, your knees give way beneath their weight

But inevitably the size of the community—there were over 450 monks at Cluny itself in Peter's time, the richness of the church and the elaboration of its worship exercised pressures which were heavy on the simplicity a monk sought. There was a tendency for those who had been longest there to withdraw to the simpler life of primitive hermit-communities on neighbouring hills, but still as part of the wider community of Cluny. Thus Gerard, once an oblate at Cluny, later Prior of St. Sauveur-de-Nevers, retired to a spot above Cluny from which, 'when the rounded clouds, heavy with rain, sank down into the valleys, he could see above them the Italian Alps, and a great part of France lying below.' Peter allowed a few other monks to join him there and spent more and more time in one or other of these simple, Spartan retreats. Their existence was a sign that some compensation was needed for the changes which Cluny's world role had made in its style of life. It was also a sign that Cluny still possessed the power of adaptation and renewal.

6.12   ELECTING AN ABBOT   1182

Cluny's misfortunes under Pons underlines the importance of choosing the right man to be abbot. This passage from the Chronicle of Jocelyn of

Brakelond, a monk of St. Edmondsbury, takes us behind the scenes during
a vacancy in this great Benedictine house.

Now that there was no abbot, we often, as was right, prayed to
the Lord and to the blessed martyr, Edmund, that they would give
us and our church a fit pastor. Three times each week after the
chapter meeting we prostrated ourselves in the choir and sang the
seven penitential psalms (6, 32, 38, 51, 102, 130, 143). There were
some who would not have prayed so earnestly if they had known
who would be the next abbot. There was much difference of opinion
as to who it should be, if the king granted us free election (i.e. without
royal intervention). Every monk had his own ideas: some expressed
them openly, others in private.

Thus, one monk said of another, 'He is a good monk, a likely
candidate. He knows a good deal about the Rule and the customs
of the church. True, he has not the profound wisdom of some of
the others, but he would make quite an efficient abbot. Abbot
Ording was illiterate, and yet he was a good abbot and ruled this
monastic house wisely. After all, in the fable, the frogs did better
to make a log their king and not a snake who hissed poisonously
and then ate his subjects.'

Another monk answered, 'Come, come. How could a monk who
is illiterate preach in the chapter, or to the people on feast days?
How could a man who does not know the Bible, know how to bind
and loose? [Cp. Matt. 16, 19]. Remember the direction of souls is
the art of arts, the highest form of knowledge. God forbid that
a dumb idol should be set up in the church of St. Edmund, where
there are many learned, hard-working men.'

Another monk recommended his candidate in this way, 'He is a
well-read man, eloquent and prudent, strict in the way he keeps
the Rule. He greatly loves the monastery and has suffered much
for the good of the church. He deserves to be made abbot.' He got
his reply, 'From good clerks deliver us, oh Lord! That it may please
thee to deliver us from the cheats of Norfolk; we beseech thee to
hear us!' [The reference is to Samson, the sub-sacristan, who was
a Norfolk man.]

Similarly, it was said of another monk, 'That brother is a good
manager. You can tell that by the state of his department, by his
record in the various posts he has held, and by the building and
repairs he has carried out. He is well able to run and defend the
monastery. And he is something of a scholar, but too much learning

has not made him mad. (Cp. Acts 26, 24.) He deserves the abbot's stall.' Another monk answered him, 'God forbid that a man should be made abbot who can neither read nor sing, nor celebrate the holy office, a man who is dishonest and unjust and who maltreats the poor.'...

Yet another monk said of his friend, 'That man is very nearly as wise as all the rest of us put together, and that is true both in worldly and religious matters. He is wise in counsel, strict about the Rule, learned and eloquent. And he has a good presence. Such a prelate would do credit to our church.'

Another monk answered, 'That would be true if he was known to be of good reputation. But his character has been questioned, perhaps falsely, perhaps rightly. And though he is wise and humble. in chapter, devoted in his singing of the psalter, and strict in his behaviour inside the monastery, this is only from force of habit. For if he holds an important departmental office he looks down on ordinary monks and hob-nobs with laymen. If he is angry, he will scarcely agree to speak to a brother monk, even to answer a question.'

I actually heard another brother abused by some of the community because he had an impediment in his speech. They said that when he spoke his mouth seemed to be full of pastry or scraps. And I too, because I was young, understood as a child, spoke as a child (Cp. 1 Cor. 13, 11). I said that I would not agree to anyone becoming abbot unless he knew something of Dialectic, and how to distinguish true from false.

One monk, moreover, who thought himself clever, said, 'May Almighty God give us a stupid and foolish pastor so that he may have to fall back on us to help him out.'...

Then I saw Samson, the sub-sacristan, sitting by himself, for this little confabulation took place during blood-letting [this was done five times a year] when cloistered monks are in the habit of un-bosoming themselves and talking freely to one another. Samson was sitting quietly by, laughing to himself, noting what each monk said. Twenty years later he could still recall some of the comments I have put down above. [It was Samson who was elected abbot.]

The First Cistercians

The reforming force in twelfth century religious life (both in the narrow monastic sense and the general one) was, however, to come from a new Order, the Cistercians. Its monks, who wore white instead of the traditional black, returned to the earlier Benedictine rule of manual labour on the farm. They worked their own land by a combination of lay brothers (simple peasant monks) and choir monks instead of relying on manorial tenants as the Cluniac houses did. This was part of a general return to ascetic practices. Cistercian churches, for instance, had none of the joyful exuberance of carving that the great Cluniac churches enjoyed. Their mouldings were plain, their lines severe, they did without towers and bells. Their beauty, and it was great, depended on architectural composition alone. Cistercian monasteries were built all to the same plan with minor modifications resulting from difficulties of the site. See the ground plan of Rievaulx at the end of this extract and Plate 5 for a view of Fountains Abbey from the air. The Cistercians reduced the length of corporate worship, giving more time to private prayer and meditation. They followed, but improved upon the Cluniac pattern of a unified Order. Each Cistercian house was regularly visited (inspected) by Citeaux or one of its first four offshoots— Clairvaux, Pontigny, La Ferté and Morimond. Citeaux itself was not exempt. Each year there was a general meeting of all Cistercian abbots. William of Malmesbury (*c.* 1095–1143), the librarian of the Benedictine abbey of Malmesbury, gave this account of the founding of Citeaux in his *Gesta Regum Anglorum.*

6.13   THE FOUNDING OF CITEAUX   1098–1109

The Cistercian Order, which is now believed and asserted to be 'the surest road to heaven' (Juvenal, *Satires* 1.38) began in the time of William Rufus. To speak of this does not seem irrelevant to my history of the Kings of England since it adds to the glory of our country that it produced the distinguished founder and organiser of that rule. To us he belonged, and in our schools he passed the earlier years of his life.

His name was Harding and he was born in England of fairly humble stock. From his early years he was a monk at Sherborne; but in his youth he felt the pull of the world, grew disgusted with the monastic habit, and went first to Scotland and afterwards to France. There after some years' study in the liberal arts he woke to the love of God. And so, when he became a man and put away childish things (1 Cor. 13, 11), he went to Rome with another cleric who was a fellow student. Neither the length and difficulty of the journey, nor the short commons on which they existed, prevented them, as they went and returned, from singing the whole psalter every day. Indeed Harding was already turning over in his mind the plan which soon after by the grace of God he attempted to carry out. For in Burgundy on his way back he became a monk at Molesme, a new and magnificent monastery. Here he readily accepted the first principles of the Rule as he had formerly seen them; but when he was asked to observe other additional customs which he had neither read about in the Rule nor seen elsewhere, he began, modestly and as became a monk, to ask the reason for them, saying:

'By reason the supreme Creator has made all things; by reason he governs all things; by reason the fabric of the world revolves; by reason even the planets move; by reason the elements are directed; and by reason mankind should live. But since by sloth we too often depart from reason, many laws were made of old to guide us; and latterly a divine Rule has been promulgated by St. Benedict to bring deviant men back to the path of reason.' . . .

Sentiments of this kind, spreading as usual from one to another, justly moved the hearts of such as feared God, 'lest somehow they should run, or had run in vain.' (Gal. 2.2). After the matter had often been discussed in chapter the abbot himself agreed that all additional matter should be left on one side and that they should confine themselves to an examination of the Rule [of St. Benedict] itself. Two of the brethren, therefore, . . . were chosen . . . to inquire into the intention of the founder's Rule and then, when they had discovered it, to lay it before the rest. The abbot tried hard to persuade the whole company to agree [to what was discovered], . . . but almost all of them refused to accept the new [simplified] rule of life because they were attached to their old ways. Eighteen only, among them was Harding, otherwise called Stephen, stubbornly persevered in their holy determination and, together with their abbot, left the monastery, declaring that the purity of the Rule could not be preserved in a place where riches and gluttony warred against even the well-inclined. They came, therefore, to Citeaux; a place formerly densely covered with woods but now so translucent from the abundant piety of its monks that it is rightly reckoned to know God himself. . . .

Certainly many of the Cistercian regulations seem severe, and more particularly these: they wear nothing made with fur or linen, not even that finely spun linen garment which we call *staminium* [a kind of shirt]; nor do they wear breeches unless they are sent on a journey. If they are, they wash them when they return and hand them back. They have two tunics with cowls, but no additional garment in winter, though in summer they may wear less if they wish. They sleep in their clothes, and girt. They never go back to bed after Matins because they fix the time of that service so that it is light before Lauds begin. . . . Directly after Lauds they sing Prime after which they go out to work for a fixed period. . . .

From the 13th of September until Easter they do not take more than one meal a day except on Sunday, making no allowance for any other festival. They never go outside the cloister except to work, and they do not speak, inside or outside the cloister, except to the abbot or prior. They continue unwearied in the recitation of the canonical hours, making no addition to them except the vigils for the dead [the only Cluniac innovation they retained]. They use in the divine office the Ambrosian chants and hymns, so far as they were able to learn them at Milan. While they carefully look after

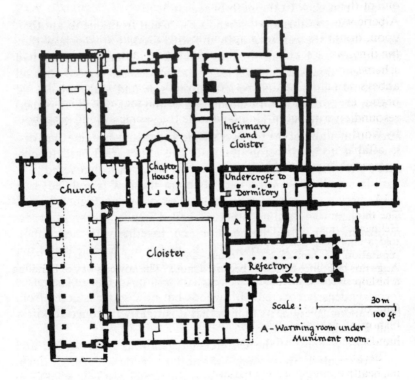

Plan of the Cistercian Monastery of Rievaulx, Yorkshire.

strangers and the sick, they inflict intolerable hardships on their own bodies for the salvation of their souls.

At first the abbot eagerly undertook these privations himself and saw that the rest of the brethren did the same. In time, however, the abbot changed his mind. He had been delicately brought up and could not well endure such rigorous daily abstinence. The monks whom he had left behind at Molesme heard of this either by messages or in letters. They recalled him to their monastery, using the obedience he owed to the pope as an excuse. Thus they compelled him to do what he had a half a mind to. As if worn out by their persistent requests, he left the narrow confines of poverty and sought again his former magnificence. All except eight of those who had gone with him returned with him from Citeaux.

The eight, few in number but great in virtue, appointed Alberic, one of themselves to be abbot, and Stephen prior. After eight years Alberic was happily called away by the will of heaven [1109]. Thereupon, doubtless by God's appointment, Stephen, though absent at the time, was elected abbot. He was the original author of the whole scheme, and is the special and famous ornament of our times. Sixteen abbeys which he has already completed, and seven which he has begun, are sufficient testimony to his abundant merit. Thus by the resounding trumpet of God he directs the people around him, both by word and deed, to heaven. He acts fully up to his own teaching, is affable in speech, pleasant in manner, and with a mind that rejoices always in the Lord.

6.14   WHOLESOME FARE

The third generation of Cistercians still preserved the founder's austerity. Hélinand, prior of Froidmont (d. *c.* 1230)—he refused to become its abbot—told a charming story about one of his novices. Hérimond had made a reputation for himself by his music and poetry at the court of Philip Augustus of France before he became a monk. The novice's way of handling a bishop shows something of the courtier's skill. Like master like pupil.

One of our young men gave an excellent and wise answer to the bishop of Beauvais, who asked him why he was more healthy and handsome in the cloister than he usually appeared while in the world.

'Because,' said he, 'I lead a regular and decent life. The first makes me healthy and the second handsome. In the world I lived an irregular and constantly changing life which brought foulness of body and sickness.'

Then the bishop asked him, 'What hast thou eaten today?'

'Enough, my lord.'

'And yesterday?'

'Enough again.'

'No, I'm not asking about the quantity, but the quality. What have you eaten yesterday and today?'

'Yesterday I ate peas and pot-herbs; today, pot-herbs and peas. Tomorrow I shall eat peas with my pot-herbs, and next day, pot-herbs with my peas.'

6.15   CISTERCIAN GENEROSITY

A good monastery might practise austerity for its members; it remembered the duty of hospitality and charity to others. There is warmth in this story of unselfishness from Caesarius of Heisterbach's *Dialogue of Miracles*.

When that most terrible famine of 1197 was raging and destroying wholesale, our monastery, poor and new though it was, gave help to many. It has been told me by those who saw the poor crowding round the gate that 1500 doles were sometimes given on a single day. Our then abbot, the lord Gerard, on every flesh-eating day before harvest, had a whole ox stewed in three cauldrons, together with herbs gathered from all sides, and dealt out a ration with bread to every one of the poor. He did the same with sheep and other foods, so that all the poor who came to us were kept alive until harvest by God's grace. And Gerard himself told me that he feared that this store would fail before the time of harvest and rebuked our baker for making his loaves so big.

'Truly, my lord, they are very small as dough and grow great in the oven; we put them in small and draw out great loaves.'

This same baker, brother Conrad Redhead, who is still alive, has told me that not only did these loaves swell in the oven, but even the meal in the bags and bins, to the wonder of all the bakers and the poor who ate them.

'Lord God! Where does all this store come from?' they exclaimed.

6.16   BERNARD OF CLAIRVAUX

Citeaux made a slow start, and at times it looked as if it might fail altogether. It was not until Bernard entered the monastery in 1112 that its success became clear. Devotion and saintliness, such as Alberic and Stephen Harding had, were not enough; charm was needed as well. Bernard's charm was irresistible. He had been born in 1090 near Dijon. He wanted to be a monk; his family were against it. But Bernard insisted and in the end did what he wanted. He brought with him about thirty friends and relatives, including five of his six brothers. The sixth joined later. Three years later Stephen Harding made Bernard the first abbot of Clairvaux. The following picture of Clairvaux is by William, abbot of St. Thierry, Bernard's friend and first biographer.

At the first glance as you enter Clairvaux by descending the hill, you can see it is a temple of God. The modest simplicity of the buildings in the still and silent valley attest the true humility of Christ's poor. In this valley full of men, where no one is allowed to be idle and all are occupied with their allotted tasks, a deep silence reigns like that of night. The only sounds are those of labour or the chanting of the brethren in the choral service. This rule of silence, and the fame of it, filled even unreligious folk with such awe that they were afraid to break it....

Glorious things are spoken of Clairvaux, because the glorious and wonderful God works great wonders there. There the insane regain their reason, and though outwardly they are wasted away, inwardly they are born again. There the proud are humbled, the rich are made poor, the poor have the Gospel preached to them (Matt. 11, 5), and the darkness of sinners is changed into light. A great crowd of blessed poor have gathered there from all parts of the world, but they have one heart and one mind....

As for me, the more closely I watch them day by day, the more I believe them to be perfect followers of Christ in all things. They pray and speak to God in spirit and in truth (John 4, 24); by their friendly and quiet words with him and their humble manner, they are clearly seen to be God's companions and friends. And when they sing God's praises in the psalms, the reverent posture of their bodies shows how pure and ardent are their minds, while their careful pronunciation and pointing of the psalms show how sweet to their lips are the words of God, sweeter than honey (Psa. 19, 10). So, as I watch them singing tirelessly from before midnight to the dawn of day, with only a short interval, they seem a little less than angels but much more than men....

At their manual labour they work patiently, calmly, with peaceful faces, in a sweet and holy order, so that though they exert themselves at many tasks, they never seem disturbed or burdened by anything they have to do....

Many of them, I hear, are bishops and earls, and many are distinguished for their birth or learning. Now, by God's grace, all distinctions are dead among them; the greater any one thought himself in the world, the more he looks upon himself as less than the least in this flock. I see them with hoes in the garden, with forks or rakes in the meadows, with scythes in the fields, and with axes in the forest. Judging by appearances, their tools, their poor and shabby clothes, they seem a race of idiots, without speech or sense. But the true thought of my mind tells me that their life is hid with Christ in heaven (Col. 3, 3).

Among them I see Godfrey of Peronne, Raynald of Picardy, William of St. Omer, and Walter of Lisle, all of whom I once knew in 'the old man' (Col. 3, 9), which I can see no trace of now, by the grace of God. I knew them proud and puffed up; I see them walking humbly under the merciful hand of God.

6.17 BERNARD AND THE UNHAPPY NOVICE

This anecdote comes from John the Hermit's Life of Bernard written a generation after Bernard's death in 1153. Accidie (torpor, despair), one of the Seven Deadly Sins, was a constant danger to good monks.

Once, having stayed away longer than usual on affairs of the Church (for much against his will he was often compelled by the pope's mandate to travel abroad to make peace, heal schism, or confute heresies) ... he seized the first opportunity to enter the cell of the novices, and called one novice aside.

'Dearly beloved son, what causes this sadness which is so fatally gnawing at the innermost recesses of your heart?'

The novice scarcely dared to speak a word for very shame. Then that truly meek and humble man, well-knowing how to show himself a true shepherd to all and no hireling, said:

'I know, beloved son, I know well, all that troubles you; and so I pity you as a father pities his own children. In my long absence, because I lacked that bodily presence of my brethren which I always desire above all earthly things, God graciously allowed me to supply in spirit all that my body was unable to do. So I returned here in the spirit, entered every corner of this house, carefully enquiring how my brethren fared. So I came then to this cell of the novices, where I found all the others rejoicing in the fear of God and their loins girded to the labours of penitence; but I groaned to see you alone drooping under a burden of sadness. When I tried to coax you to come to me, you turned your spirit and your face away, and wept so bitterly that my cowl was drenched with tears.'

With these words the holy father ... recalled the novice from his almost overwhelming melancholy into the liberty of spiritual joy.

6.18 AILRED OF RIEVAULX

The same reciprocity of affection and piety between an abbot and his monks is apparent in Walter Daniel's Life of Ailred, abbot of Rievaulx, Yorkshire, from 1146–1166. Rievaulx had been founded direct from Clairvaux in 1131. Ailred came of a long line of married Northumbrian priests. As a young man he was in the service of the Scottish king and, later, a missionary to the Picts of Galloway.

Throughout the last ten years of his life this holy man frequently underwent intense suffering, as the agonies of arthritis were added to his old distresses. So dreadfully afflicted was he that I have seen him suspended in mid air in a linen sheet, held by a man at each end of its four corners, being carried to relieve himself or from one bed to another. A mere touch affected him like a piercing wound, and his cries revealed the measure of his pain. Because of his suffering the general chapter of Citeaux allowed him to eat and sleep in the infirmary, and carefully made their necessary concessions to his bodily weakness....

He felt diffident about this generous provision for his freedom, and found it so hard to bear that he ordered a 'mausoleum' to be built for him close by the common infirmary, and, taking up his quarters there, he entrusted the care of his illness entirely to the ministrations of two of the brethren, refusing with disdain all dainties and useless blandishments.

The construction of this cot was, indeed, a great source of consolation to the brethren, for every day they came to it and sat in it, twenty or thirty at a time, to talk together of the spiritual delights of the scriptures and of the observance of the monastic order. There was nobody to say to them, 'Get out, go away, do not touch the abbot's bed.' They walked over and lay upon his bed and talked with him as a little child prattles to his mother. He would say,

'My sons, say what you will; only let no vile word, no detraction of a brother, no blasphemy against God proceed out of your mouth.'

He did not treat them with the pedantic imbecility habitual in some silly abbots who, if a monk takes a brother's hand in his own, or says anything they do not like, demand his cowl, strip him and expel him. Not so Ailred, not so.

I lived under his rule for 17 years and in all that time he, merciful as he was above all those who dwell in the world, did not expel a single monk. Four, it is true, left him without his knowledge, but the Lord led them all back save one follower of Satan.

In a corner of the cell of which I have spoken he established an inner closet and ordered that it should be closed off by a wooden partition. Here he kept a cross and relics of certain saints, and dedicated it as a place of prayer. And reflecting how 'He that keepeth

Israel neither slumbers nor sleeps' (Psa. 121, 4), he, as God's vicar, slept but little in his bed, but prayed much in that place. There when his illness allowed him the slightest relief, on bended knees, with contrite mind and in the spirit of truth, he would beset his Father with his prayers. And in that mansion he wrote many memorable works.

6.19   AILRED ON MUSIC

Broadminded and humane though Ailred was, his *Mirror of Charity* matches the later Puritan distrust of all but the simplest church music:

Why so many organs and cymbals in the church? Pray what is the profit of that terrible blast of the bellows, expressing the crash of thunder instead of the sweetness of a voice? What is the point of that contraction and infraction of the voices, one singing low, another singing something else, and a third cutting the notes short in the middle? The voice is now strangled, then swoops aloft, then held on a note long drawn out. Sometimes—I blush to say it—it is made to neigh like a horse, then gelded of all manly vigour it is sharpened to the shrillness of a woman's....

Meanwhile the common people stand in trembling awe, marvelling at the rushing wind of the bellows, the clashing of cymbals, and the harmony of the pipes, yet grinning with laughter as they watch the wanton gestures of the singers.... You would think they had come to a playhouse, not a house of prayer, to gape, not to pray.

6.20   BERNARD ON CLUNY

Bernard was, if possible, even more violent than Ailred. His attacks on Cluny began when abbot Pons was doing his worst; they continued when Peter 'the Venerable' was doing his best. Bernard objected not only to Cluny falling short of its ideals, but to what Cluny especially stood for. Like many men who have found a way to God, he did not easily recognize that there are other ways. This is from a letter to his friend William of St. Thierry.

I am amazed that monks could grow accustomed to such indulgence in eating and drinking, clothing and bedding, riding abroad and building, so that where these are pursued most actively, with most pleasure and expense, religion is thought to be best served....

I lie if I have not seen an abbot with a train of sixty horses and more. Seeing such pass by, you would say that they are not fathers of monasteries but lords of castles, not keepers of souls but princes of provinces....

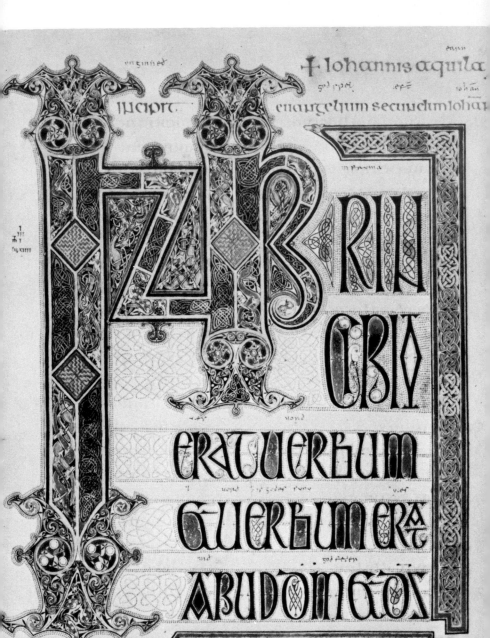

INCIPIT enangelium secundum Iohan

IN PRINCIPIO ERATUERBUM ETUERBUM ERAT ABUDOMGDS

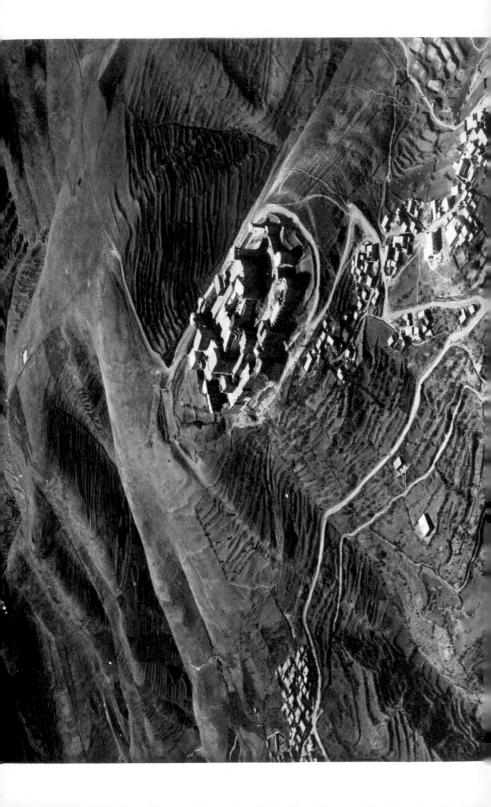

These are small things; I turn to greater matters, though they are so common that they seem smaller. I say nothing of the vast height of your churches, their unnecessary length and breadth, the expensive polished work, the curious carvings and paintings to catch the worshipper's eye and hinder his devotion. Let it pass; say it is done in God's honour. But I, a monk, ask my brother monks, 'What is gold doing in the sanctuary?'... And the jewelled crowns of light that adorn the church, the lustres like cartwheels girt around with lamps, but no less brilliant from the precious stones that stud them? Then we see candelabra like great trees of bronze fashioned with wonderful intricacy and glistening as brightly with gems as with lights. What do you think is the purpose of it all? The contrition of penitents or the admiration of sightseers? O vanity of vanities, yet no more vain than insane!

The Church is gorgeous in her buildings and beggarly in her poor; she clothes her stones in gold and leaves her sons naked; the rich man's eye is fed at the expense of the starving poor; the curious are relished here, but no needy find relief....

You may answer in the words of the psalmist (Psa. 26, 8):

> Lord, I have loved the habitation of thy house,
> And the place where thine honour dwelleth.

I grant it then; let us endure these things in the church. For though they are harmful to the vain and covetous, they are not so to the simple and pious. But what benefit can they be in the cloister to the brethren that read there ... those unclean apes, those fierce lions, those grotesque centaurs, those half-men, those striped tigers, those fighting knights, those hunters winding their horns? You may see several bodies under one head or many heads to a single body. Here is a four-footed beast with a serpent's tail; there is a fish with an animal's head. Here the front of a horse draws half a goat behind it, or a horned beast has the hind quarters of a horse. In short there are so many wonderful varieties of different forms on every side, that we are tempted to read the marble instead of our books, and spend all day wondering at these things instead of meditating on the law of God. For God's sake, if the monks are not ashamed of these follies, they might at least shrink from the expense.

6.21 The Carthusians

Contemporary with Citeaux but independent of it, this order was founded by Bruno of Cologne in 1084 at the Grande Chartreuse near Grenoble, whence the name. It was a mixture of Benedictine monasticism and hermit's austerity. The monks were vowed to silence except when they joined in the

Offices and the Mass in church. They ate together—in silence—on feast days in their humble refectory. The first English Charterhouse was founded in 1175 by Hugh, a monk of the Grande Chartreuse, later bishop of Lincoln. The best surviving remains are at Mount Grace Priory near Northallerton in Yorkshire, shown in this plan.

Each 'cell' was a two-storied little house in its own garden. A square L-shaped tunnel in the cloister wall beside each door enabled meals to be delivered without disturbance to the lives of contemplation within.

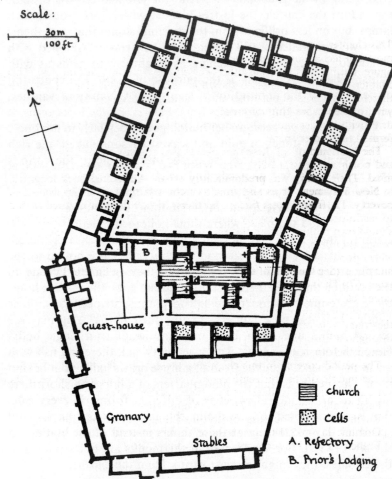

scale:

30m
100ft

N

Guest-house

Granary

Stables

🔲 church

🔲 cells

A. Refectory

B. Prior's Lodging

Plan of the Charterhouse at Mount Grace

Finally, to give an idea of the proliferation of monastic houses throughout Christendom, see Map 3, which shows those of a single county in England: Yorkshire.

CHAPTER SEVEN

FRANCIS AND OTHER REVOLUTIONARIES

This chapter is mainly about Francis of Assisi. All will have heard of him; most will feel at some sense at home with him. He is, of course, a strange figure, but his strangeness is other-worldly, not that of a distant past. This chapter tries just the same to show him as a man of his time. It contains therefore, material about other movements which have obvious affinities with, as well as striking differences from, Francis and the Franciscans. It deals with Waldensians, Albigensians, and with the Dominicans who were formed to counter them.

The heartland of all these movements was roughly the south of France and north and central Italy, areas which had been Christian time without mind. Their setting was predominantly urban. All looked back longingly to New Testament times and tried to recover the primitive simplicity and poverty. The friars (Latin *fratres*, brothers), unlike the monks, tried at first to institutionalize poverty by insisting that their Order, like its members, should own nothing. From this they became known as the Mendicant (i.e. begging) Orders. They naturally had to live and work in towns and areas where population was dense instead of seeking a wilderness as the monks had done. (See the plan of the Grey Friars by Stinking Lane in London on page 167.) Their characteristic churches were preaching halls, and they maintained close contact with the laity through their Third Orders of people who continued their secular occupations but followed a modified form of the friars' rule of life. Both Franciscans and Dominicans spread rapidly throughout Europe, and both became closely associated with the universities then in their exciting youth.

The period covered in this chapter is roughly the middle of the twelfth to the middle of the thirteenth century. The overlap in time between the various movements is illustrated by the following dates:

Peter Waldo converted 1173; excommunicated 1184

Raymond VI of Toulouse, protector of the Albigensians 1156–1222

Dominic 1170–1221 (begins mission to Albigensians 1206)

Francis 1182–1226 (conversion to poverty 1206)

Francis of Assisi

The passages that follow are intended to serve as reminders of different aspects of the work and personality of Francis.

7.1   THE BASIC RULE OF THE FRIARS   *c.* 1210

In 1210 Francis and eleven followers went to Rome to seek Innocent III's approval for the rule of life he had drawn up. As Francis wrote in his Testament, 'And after the Lord had given me some brothers, no one showed me what I ought to do, but the Most High himself revealed to me that I must live according to the form of the Holy Gospel: and I made it to be written in few words and simply; and the Lord Pope confirmed it for me.' Cardinal Ugolino, Francis's patron at Rome, tried to persuade him to adopt or adapt one of the old, established rules. But, said Francis, 'Brothers, brothers, the Lord has called me by the way of humility and he has shown me the way of simplicity; and I do not want you to mention any other rule to me, neither that of St. Augustine, nor of St. Benedict, nor of St. Bernard. And the Lord told me that he wished me to be a new fool in the world, that he did not wish to lead us by any other road than by that wisdom; for by your own wisdom and learning God will confound you.' Although the 1210 rule is lost, Dr. J. R. H. Moorman has been able to reconstruct it from the rule of 1221 in which it is embedded. What follows is his reconstruction.

The Basic Rule of St. Francis

The Rule and life of the brothers is this: to live in obedience, in chastity, and without property, and to follow the teaching and the footsteps of Christ, who says, 'If thou wilt be perfect, go and sell what thou hast and give to the poor and thou shalt have treasure in heaven, and come, follow me,' and 'If any man will come after me, let him deny himself and take up his cross and follow me', and again, 'If any man come to me and hate not his father and mother and wife and children and brothers and sisters, yea, and his own life also, he cannot be my disciple', and 'Everyone that hath forsaken father or mother or brothers or sisters or wife or children or houses or lands for my sake shall receive a hundredfold, and shall inherit eternal life'. (Matt. 19, 21; 16, 24; Luke 14, 26; Matt. 19, 29.)

If any man, by divine inspiration and willing to accept this life, shall come to the brothers, let him be kindly received by them; and he must sell all his goods and be careful to give everything to the poor. And let all the brothers be dressed in shabby clothes and let them patch them with sackcloth or other rags with the blessing of God; for our Lord says, 'They which are gorgeously apparelled and live delicately are in kings' houses'. And they may eat anything set before them according to the Gospel: 'Eat what is set before you'. (Luke 7, 25; 10, 8.)

None of the brethren shall have any power or domination, especially among themselves. As our Lord says in the Gospel, 'The princes of the Gentiles exercise dominion over them, and they that are great exercise authority over them, but it shall not be so among you'—the friars, but 'whosoever would be greatest among them let him be their minister and servant' and 'he that is greatest among them let him be as the younger'. And no one is to be called prior, but all alike shall be called Friars Minor. And let each wash one another's feet. (Matt. 20, 25–27; Luke 22, 26; John 13, 14.)

Those brothers who know how to work shall work and pursue whatever trade they have learnt, so long as it is not contrary to the good of the soul and can be honestly carried on. And for their labour they may receive all things necessary but no money. And when needful let them go and beg like the other brothers.

All the brothers must seek to follow the humility and poverty of our Lord Jesus Christ, and must remember that we ought not to possess anything in this world except what the Apostle says, 'Having food and raiment let us be therewith content' (1 Tim. 6, 8). And they ought to rejoice when they are living among common and despised people, among the poor and the weak, the sick and the lepers, and those who beg by the wayside.

When the brothers are going about the world they must carry nothing with them, 'neither scrip, nor purse, nor bread, nor money, nor staff. And into whatsoever house they shall enter, they shall first say, "Peace be to this house." And in the same house they shall remain, eating and drinking such things as they give.' They shall not resist evil, but unto him that smiteth them upon the one cheek let them offer also the other; and let them not forbid him that taketh away their cloak to take away their coat also. (Luke 9, 3; 10, 4–7; Matt. 5, 39–40.)

7.2   FRANCIS THE CRUSADER   1219

In his youth Francis, son of a rich merchant of Assisi, had enjoyed his part in his city's war against neighbouring Perugia. He was not then a stranger to military life when, on a mission to Moslems, he joined the Crusaders before Damietta in Egypt. Jacques de Vitry (1180–1240), bishop of Acre and prominently involved in this Fifth Crusade, tells the simple story of his visit behind the enemy's lines, given below. A century later, when the 'Little Flowers of St. Francis' was written, the story had become 'How St. Francis converted the Soldan of Babylon'. Francis, it was then imagined, had promised the sultan before he left his camp to send him two friars. Francis died, but the sultan lived on, still patiently hoping that Francis would keep his word. When at length the sultan himself lay dying Francis appeared to two friars and told them to go at once to the sultan, which they did. 'He received holy baptism from these brothers; and thus regenerated in Christ he died of the illness from which he was then suffering, and his soul was saved by the merits and prayers of St. Francis.'

We saw the founder of this Order whom all the others obey as their prior, a simple unlearned man named Brother Francis, beloved of God and men. Fervour of spirit so intoxicated him that when he reached the Christian camp outside Damietta he moved on towards the camp of the sultan of Egypt, made bold and given strength by the shield of faith. When the Saracens captured him on the road he said,

'I am a Christian. Lead me to your lord.'

They dragged him into the presence of their sultan [Saladin] and that cruel beast became gentle when he saw the look on the face of the man of God, so that he listened most attentively for some days while Francis preached to them the faith of Christ. At last he became afraid that some of his people would be converted to the Lord by the power of his words and go over to the Christian army. So he gave orders that Francis, with all reverence, should be escorted safely back to our camp, and said to him at parting:

'Pray for me that God may reveal to me that law and that faith which is most pleasing to him.'

Source: Jacques de Vitry, *Historia Orientalis.*

7.3   FRANCIS THE PREACHER   August 15, 1222

This description of the impression that Francis made upon an overseas student from Split in Dalmatia has, like the previous extract, the advantage of coming from one who stood outside the Franciscan order. Thomas of Spalato (*c.* 1200–1250) was the author of a history of his own people.

That year, on the feast of the Assumption of the Mother of God, when I was a student at Bologna, I heard St. Francis preach in the piazza in front of the Palazzo Publico, where nearly the whole town was assembled. 'Angels, Men, and Devils' was the theme of his address. He spoke so wisely and well of these three rational spirits, that many learned men present much admired the discourse of this unlearned man. Although the whole style of it was that of a revolutionary rather than an expositor, yet its whole effect was to dispel quarrels and make peace.

His tunic was filthy, his figure contemptible and his face far from handsome. Yet God gave such force to his words that many factions of the nobility, the fury of whose ancient feuds had shed so much blood among them, made peace together. The reverence and devotion of the people towards him was so great that men and women rushed upon him, trying to touch the hem of his garment and carry off pieces of his clothing.

7.4   FRANCIS AND LADY POVERTY

This and the following extract come from Thomas of Celano's *First Life* of St. Francis. Thomas (*c.* 1200–1255) was born at Celano in the Abruzzi in south Italy, and joined Francis about the year 1214. He wrote the book from which these extracts are taken in 1228, only two years after the death of Francis, at the request of Pope Gregory IX, the former Cardinal Ugolino, who canonised Francis.

Placed in the vale of tears, that blessed father set at naught the common paltry wealth of the sons of men, and in his ambition to attain a more exalted height longed after Poverty with all his heart. . . .

He would tell his sons that she was the way of perfection, that she was the pledge and earnest of eternal riches. No one was so greedy of gold as he of Poverty, no one more careful in guarding a treasure than he in guarding this pearl of the Gospel.

He taught his brethren to make poor habitations, of wood, not of stone, and to build them as small houses on a humble plan. And often when talking of poverty he would urge on the brethren that Gospel saying: 'The foxes have holes and the birds of the sky have nests; but the Son of God had not where to lay his head' (Matt. 8, 20). . .

One Easter day the brethren at the hermitage of Greccio laid the table more carefully than usual, with white table-linen and glass vessels. The father came down from the cell, went to the table, and noticed that it was placed on high, and decked in vain fashion. But on the smiling table he by no means smiled. Stealthily and gradually he withdrew, put on his head the hat of a poor man who was there, and went out of doors, carrying a staff in his hand. He waited outside at the door for the brethren to begin; for they used not to wait for him when he did not come at the signal. When they began to eat, that true poor man cried at the door:

'For the love of the Lord God give alms to this poor sick pilgrim.'

'Come in, good man, for the love of him whom thou hast invoked,' the brethren answered.

He came in at once, and appeared before them as they were eating. What, think you, was the amazement the pilgrim caused to the inhabitants? They gave him a dish, at his request, and sitting alone on the ground [by the fire], he made the ashes his table.

'Now I am sitting like a Lesser Brother'; he said. 'The example of the poverty of the Son of God should constrain us more than any other Religious. I saw a table spread and adorned, and knew that it was not the table of poor men who go from door to door'...

7.5   FRANCIS AND ALL CREATED THINGS

The most blessed father Francis was journeying through the valley of Spoleto, and came to a spot near Bevagna where a very great number of birds of different sorts were gathered together; doves, rooks and those other birds that are called jackdaws.

When he saw then, being a man of the most fervent temper and also very tender and affectionate toward all the lower and irrational creatures, Francis the most blessed servant of God left his companions in the way and ran eagerly toward the birds. When he was come close to them and saw that they were awaiting him, he gave them his accustomed greeting. But, not a little surprised that the birds did not fly away (as they are wont to do) he was filled with exceeding joy and humbly begged them to hear the word of God. After saying many things to them he added:

'My brother birds, much ought you to praise your Creator, and ever to love him who has given you feathers for clothing, wings for flight, and all that you had need of. God has made you noble among his creatures, for he has given you a habitation in the purity of the air, and, whereas you neither sow nor reap, he himself doth still protect and govern you without any care of your own.'

On this (as he himself and the brethren who had been with him used to say) those little birds rejoicing in wondrous fashion, after their nature, began to stretch out their necks, to spread their wings, to open their beaks and to gaze on him. And then he went to and fro amidst them, touching their heads and bodies with his tunic. At length he blessed them, and, having made the sign of the cross, gave them leave to fly away to another place.

7.6   THE CANTICLE OF THE SUN   *c.* 1225

This canticle was composed by Francis during an illness at San Damiano in the last years of his life. It is in Italian and was at once set to music. English church-goers will recognize it in the hymn, 'All creatures of our Lord and King'. This is a translation of the earliest version.

O most high, almighty, good Lord God, to thee belong praise, glory, honour and all blessing!

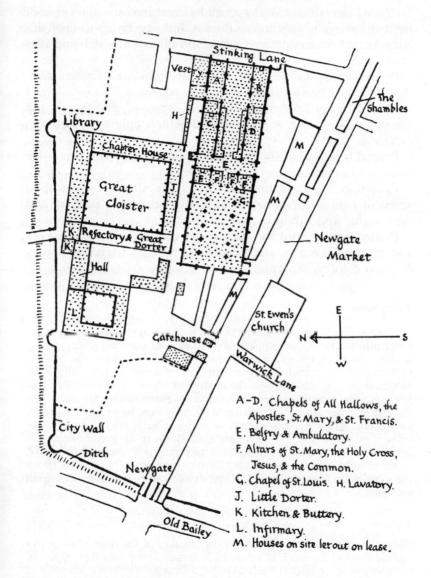

A–D. Chapels of All Hallows, the
    Apostles, St. Mary, & St. Francis.
E. Belfry & Ambulatory.
F. Altars of St. Mary, the Holy Cross,
    Jesus, & the Common.
G. Chapel of St. Louis. H. Lavatory.
J. Little Dorter.
K. Kitchen & Buttery.
L. Infirmary.
M. Houses on site let out on lease.

Plan of the Grey Friars in London

Praised be my Lord God with all his creatures, and specially our brother the sun, who brings us the day and who brings us the light; fair is he and shines with a very great splendour: O Lord, he signifies to us thee!

Praised be my Lord for our sister the moon, and for the stars, the which he has set clear and lovely in heaven.

Praised be my Lord for our brother the wind, and for air and cloud, calms, and all weather by which thou upholdest life in all creatures.

Praised be my Lord for our sister water, who is very serviceable to us, and humble and precious and clean.

Praised be my Lord for our brother fire, through whom thou givest us light in the darkness; and he is bright and pleasant and very mighty and strong.

Praised be my Lord for our mother the earth, the which doth sustain us and keep us, and bringeth forth divers fruits and flowers of many colours, and grass.

Franciscans

Already during Francis's life-time the tensions which were soon to split the order into fractions were apparent. On one wing were the purists whose devotion to Lady Poverty was absolute; on the other those who wanted to assimilate the order to the normal pattern of a monk's life with certain modifications. In between were the moderates whose views prevailed. Differences were sometimes carried to extremes. Some of the 'Spirituals' left the parent order altogether, and some of them were burned as heretics in Languedoc. These rivalries cannot be followed here; but, without taking sides, it may be noted that again and again down to the present men have been found who have tried to get back to primitive Franciscan simplicity, in the same way that every fertile Christian generation tries to recapture the spirit of the apostolic church. These extracts show the Franciscan spirit surviving.

7.7   THE LOVER AND THE BELOVED   *c.* 1275

There is no mistaking the Franciscan spirituality of the *Book of the Lover and the Beloved*, Ramon Lull's disordered masterpiece of mystical reflection. (The following isolated extracts have been arranged to form a sequence of thought.) Lull had been born in Majorca about the year 1235. He became a courtier, lived a gay life, wrote love poems and was very much a man of this world until the year 1266. Then on five successive nights he had a vision of the crucified Christ. His whole life-style changed. He devoted himself to the conversion of Moslems, learning Arabic himself from a Moslem slave. He founded a Franciscan convent at Miramar in Majorca where he himself taught Arabic, although he remained a layman. In 1291, the year that the Crusaders were driven out of their last Palestinian stronghold, Lull made his first missionary journey to North Africa. He divided his time thereafter between work in North Africa and Europe, where he planned a thorough education for future missionaries. Thanks to him, the Council of Vienne in 1311 called for the establishment of Oriental studies in Paris, Oxford and other universities. In 1315 he was stoned to death on the sea shore at Bugia in North Africa. There is an extract from his *Book of the Order of Chivalry* in 5.21.

The lover had to journey long over roads that were rough and hard; and the time came when he should set out, carrying the heavy burden that love makes his lovers to bear. So the lover unburdened his soul of the cares and pleasures of this world, that his heart may bear the weight with more ease, and his soul journey along those roads in its Beloved's company.

The lover longed for solitude, and went away to live alone, that he might gain the companionship of his Beloved, for amid many people he was lonely. The lover was all alone in the shade of a great tree. Men passed by that place and asked him why he was alone. And the lover replied, 'I am alone, now that I have seen you and heard you. Until now, I was in the company of the Beloved.'

The heart of the lover soared to the heights of the Beloved's abode, so that he might not lose his love for him in the deep places of the world. And when he reached his Beloved he contemplated him with joy and delight. But the Beloved led him down again to this world to make trial of him with tribulations and adversities.

The lover saw himself taken and bound, wounded and killed, for the love of his Beloved. And those who tortured him asked him, 'Where is thy Beloved?' He answered, 'See him here in the increase of my love and the strength which it gives me to bear my torments.'

'Say, O lover,' asked the Beloved, 'if I double thy trials, wilt thou still be patient?' 'Yea,' answered the lover, 'so that thou double also my love.'

The lover said, 'The secrets of my Beloved torture me, for my deeds reveal them not and my tongue keeps silence and reveals them to none.'

The lover reproached Christian people because in their hearts they put not first the name of his Beloved, Jesus Christ, to do the same honour that the Saracens do to the false prophet Mahomet, when they honour him by naming him before everything in their letters.

They asked the lover, 'What thing is farthest from thy heart?' He answered, 'Indifference.' 'And why so?' 'Because nearest to my heart is love, which is contrary to indifference.'

'Say, O lover, hast thou riches?' 'Yea,' he replied, 'I have love.' 'Hast thou poverty?' 'Yea, I have love.' 'How then is this?' 'I am poor because my love is no greater, and because it fills so few others with love for the honour of my Beloved.'

Far above love is the Beloved; far beneath it is the lover. And love, which lies between these two, made the Beloved to descend to the lover, and the lover to rise toward the Beloved. And this ascending and descending is the being and life of love.

'What meanest thou by love?' said the Beloved. And the lover answered, 'It is to bear on one's heart the sacred marks and the sweet words of the Beloved. It is to long for him with desire and with tears. It is boldness. It is fervour. It is fear. It is the desire for the Beloved above all things. It is that which causes the Lover to grow faint when he hears the Beloved's praises. It is that in which I die daily, and in which is all my will.'

Source: Ramon Lull, *The Book of the Lover and the Beloved*, nos. 337, 45, 46, 56, 52, 8, 31, 149, 193, 195.

7.8   BROTHER JUNIPER'S PORRIDGE

Francis would not be Francis without his followers, a truly comprehensive school of men who had to learn to live together in the unstreamed community which Francis called the society of Lesser Brothers (*Fratres Minores*). Gaiety and child-like candour marked them all. This story of Brother Juniper—'I could do with a whole forest of Junipers,' Francis once remarked—is set about the year 1235. It formed part of the *Little Flowers of St. Francis*, a collection of the oral tradition of Francis and the early Franciscans, probably first written down in the early fourteenth century.

One day at Assisi Brother Juniper was meditating in front of the altar of the convent just before Christmas. Now this altar was sumptuously adorned, and the sacristan asked him to keep an eye upon it while he went to get something to eat. But as Brother Juniper continued to meditate a poor woman came and begged for alms for the love of God.... There was a fringe of gold on the altar, richly worked, and a row of costly little silver bells. 'Quite superfluous!' said Brother Juniper and he cut them all off with a knife and gave them to the poor woman out of compassion.

The sacristan had scarcely eaten three or four mouthfuls when he remembered Brother Juniper's ways and began to fear for the altar ornaments. There was no knowing what he might not do out of excess of charity. He left the table in haste, returned to the church, and saw that the fringe had been cut about and all the bells were missing. He was scandalized and very angry.

'Don't trouble yourself about those bells,' said Brother Juniper. 'I gave them to a poor woman who had the greatest need of them. Here they are useless and only a bit of worldly vanity and pomp.'

The sacristan ran through the church and out into the city, but found no bells, nor anyone who had seen them. Returning in a rage he took the fringe to the General who was then in Assisi, saying, 'I crave justice against Brother Juniper who has spoilt my fringe, the best in the sacristy . . .'

Calling all the brothers to a chapter meeting, the General rebuked Brother Juniper in the presence of the whole community for the loss of the silver bells and became so furious that he raised his voice too high and grew quite hoarse. Brother Juniper cared little or nothing for his words, for he was delighted when he was reproached and abused, but he began to think how he could find a remedy for his General's hoarseness. When the lecture was over, he went off to the city and had a porridge of flour and butter prepared for him. When much of the night was spent, he goes with his porridge and a lighted candle to the cell of the General and knocks. The General opens and sees him with a lighted candle in one hand and a dish of porridge in the other.

'What is this?' he asks softly.

Brother Juniper replies: 'My Father, when you chid me for my faults today, I noticed your voice was growing hoarse—from overwork, I guessed. So I thought of a remedy and had this porridge made for you. Please eat it, for it will ease your chest and throat.'

Brother William, an English companion of Francis, drawn by Matthew Paris c.1250 in his *Chronica Majora.*
MS at Corpus Chr. Coll. Camb.

'What an hour to disturb people!'

'Look you now, it's made for you. Please eat it without more ado, for 'twill do you a lot of good.'

But the General, angry at the lateness of the hour and his importunity, bade him be gone, for at such an hour he had no desire to eat, and he called him a rogue and a rascal. Seeing that neither prayers nor coaxing would move him Brother Juniper said,

'My Father, since you will not eat, though the porridge was made for you, do this much for me. Hold the candle and I will eat it.'

The General, who was a good and pious man, recognised the simplicity and sanctity of Brother Juniper, and that he had done all this out of pure devotion. 'Well,' he said, 'since you insist, you and I will eat it together.' And together, with a warm friendliness each towards the other, they ate the porridge.

7.9   TWO SINGING FRIARS

This and the following extract come from Brother Salimbene of Parma's *Chronicle*, a largely autobiographical work written about 1285. It shows how Franciscan liveliness was still abundant long after the founder's death.

Friar Henry of Pisa was handsome, of medium height, generous and courteous.... He was a powerful preacher, popular with both clergy and people. He had great skill in writing, illuminating, and composing music, making the sweetest and most lovely songs, both in harmony and plainsong. He was a wonderful singer. He had a loud and resonant voice, so that he filled the whole choir, but he also had a flute-like treble, very high and clear, sweet, soft, and very delightful....

He heard a maid-servant, tripping through the cathedral of Pisa, singing in Italian,

> If thou carest not for me,
> I will care no more for thee.

He then composed words and music of this hymn, keeping to the pattern of the song:

> Christ divine, O Christ of mine,
> Christ the king and Lord of all.

Once when he was Custos [Guardian], he lay sick in the infirmary of the convent in Siena and because he could not write his music, he summoned me and I was the first to record one of his airs as he sang it.

[Salimbene mentions another of friar Henry's songs and continues:]

The music of these words was composed by friar Vita of Lucca, a Franciscan, the best singer in the world then, both in harmony and plainsong. He had a pure, delicate voice, lovely to hear, and even the strictest listened with pleasure. If any talked while friar Vita sang, the others would immediately cry out with the Preacher (Ecclesiasticus 32, 3): 'Hinder not music!'

When a nightingale sang in a hedge or spinney, it would cease at the sound of his singing and listen intently as if transfixed, renewing its own strain when he had finished. So bird and friar would sing antiphonally each carolling his own sweet airs.

He composed the sequence [sung before the gospel at mass] *Ave mundi*, both words and tune and, what the secular clergy particularly enjoy, many hymns in harmony. He was song-master in his own city of Lucca. When Thomas of Capua wrote that sequence *Let the Virgin Mother rejoice*, he begged friar Henry to write a melody for it and he composed a very lovely one. Then friar Vita composed a secondary part in harmony for it, because whenever he found a plain-chant of friar Henry he loved to compose a harmony for it. Philip, archbishop of Ravenna, took friar Vita into his household. He was thin and taller than friar Henry and his voice was fitter for a house than a church.

Vita often left the Franciscans and returned. But he left only to enter a Benedictine house. When he wished to return pope Gregory IX always indulged him, both for St. Francis' sake and for the sweetness of his singing. Once he sang so enchantingly that a certain nun threw herself down from a window to follow him, but could not because she broke her leg with the fall....

Friar Henry of Pisa was my close friend and said he loved me far more than his own brother....

7.10 THE GREAT ALLELUIA 1233

This Alleluia, which lasted for some time, was a period of peace and quiet, when all weapons of war were laid aside, a time of joy and gladness, of merriment and rejoicing, of praise and exultation. And men sang songs of praise to God together, gentle folk and peasants, townsmen and countrymen, young men and maidens, old and young. This devotion was held in all the cities of Italy, and crowds of people came from the villages with banners, men and women, boys and girls together, to hear the preaching and to praise God. And they sang God's songs, not man's and all walked in the way of salvation. They carried branches of trees and lighted tapers, and sermons were made at evening, in the morning, and at noon. They could not cease praising God, so drunk were they with his love....

First came brother Benedict of Parma, called Brother of the Horn.... He was like John the Baptist. He wore an Armenian cap, his beard was long and black, and he had a little horn of brass on which he trumpeted. Terribly could he make it bray at times, and at other times it would make sweet melody. He wore a belt of skin and a black robe of hair-cloth falling to his feet. His rough cloak, like a soldier's was decorated on the front and back with a red cross.... A great crowd of children followed him, many carrying branches of trees and lighted tapers.

'Praised and blessed and glorified be the Father,' he cried, and the children shouted the words after him.

'Praised and blessed and glorified be the Son.

Praised and blessed and glorified be the Holy Spirit.

Alleluia, Alleluia, Alleluia!'

Then he would sound his trumpet . . . I myself saw him preaching.

7.11   A FRIAR PREACHES   *c.* 1260

These three snatches are from sermons by the Franciscan, Berthold of Regensburg. Roger Bacon described him as 'one who by his single efforts has more success from preaching than almost all the other friars of Francis and Dominic together.'

A.

Some people are too bored to stand decently in church for a short hour, while God is served with singing and reading. They laugh and chatter as if they were at a fair.... And you women, you never let your tongues rest from futile gossip. One tells another of her maidservant, how glad she is to sleep, how loath to work. Another complains of her husband, a third grumbles about her children, what a nuisance they are and their ailments.

Yes, brother Berthold, but we don't understand the Mass, and therefore we can't pray as we need to, nor worship properly. The sermon we can follow, every word, but not the Mass. We don't know what is being sung or read, we just can't understand it.'

B.

Fie, penny-preacher, murderer of all the world! With your filthy lucre you cast so many souls from God's own sunlight to the bottom of hell, where there is no more hope for them! You promise so much indulgence for a single halfpenny or penny that many thousands trust you, and falsely dream that they have done penance for all their sins with that penny or halfpenny, as you tell them in your patter. So they will do no proper penance and go straight to hell, where there is no more help for them. . . .

You murderer of proper penitence! One of the seven holy things of the best that belongs to God—you have murdered it among us! It has been so murdered now by penny-preachers that there are few of us who still do penance for their sins, because they rely upon your false promises!

C.

One of the crowd: Brother Berthold, you keep speaking of these devils and of all their tricks, yet we never hear or see or touch or feel a single devil.

Berthold: Look, that is just the worst harm they can do you! For if you had once seen a single devil in his true form, I know for certain that you would never sin again. . . . If the devil were to come out of this forest hard by at this moment, and this city that we see before us were a burning fiery furnace heated through and through, then you would see such a mass of people as you never saw before, and as will never be seen in this world, and all streaming headlong into that burning fiery furnace.

7.12   FRANCISCAN POETS

Dies Irae (Day of wrath, O day of mourning) and *Stabat Mater* (By the Cross her station keeping, Stood the Virgin Mother weeping), two of the supreme Latin poems of the Middle Ages, are the work of Franciscans. They are attributed uncertainly to Thomas of Celano (*c.* 1200–1255), the biographer of Francis, and to Jacopone da Todi (*c.* 1230–1306) respectively. Both are to be found in translation in most English hymn books. Jacopone was undoubtedly the author of many religious songs in Italian. Until forty he had been a lawyer. Then his wife died and he gave up his profession, became a Franciscan Tertiary and took to a roving life, wandering round the Umbrian countryside, making and singing songs of the love of Christ.

At fifty he became a fully professed friar and threw in his lot with the 'Spirituals' or purists. He disliked recent tendencies such as the entry into university life—'Paris has destroyed Assisi,' he said.

Two extracts from his *Laude* show Franciscan courage, gaiety, and imagination at its best. *A* is Evelyn Underhill's translation of lines written after Boniface VIII had imprisoned Jacopone. The opening couplet of *B* refers to the seven seals (Rev. 5.1) and the five wounds of Christ. The translation is by Mrs. Theodore Beck.

A.

O pope Boniface,
  You're merry in your day,
But will it quite so merry be,
  When it comes to going away?
....
Is all your cleverness enough,
  The world to dominate?
What this year brings triumphant in,
  Next year will dissipate.
You may with bit and bridle
  Make a restive horse stand still:
But the world's course is not guided
  According to your will.

B.

I am the book of life with seven seals;
Mine open page five miniatures reveals
Emblazoned with my blood to all displayed...
This is the scripture all can make their own,
So plain to read, yet never wholly known;
Here elephants can swim and lambs can wade.

Waldensians

Many people, when they hear the name Waldensians, will think first of Milton's sonnet,

> Avenge, O Lord, thy slaughtered saints, whose bones
> Lie scattered on the Alpine mountains cold...

This suggests a community of simple hill folk in remote, inaccessible valleys. Nothing could be further from the truth about the origins of the body which still, after centuries of persecution, is the strong church of a tiny minority in Italy. Peter Waldo, the founder, was a rich merchant of Lyons, then as now the busy metropolis of South-East France. He was converted nine years before Francis of Assisi was born. It was among townspeople, spiritually aroused by the ferment of the Crusades and spiritually neglected by a rich church, that he found his followers, mainly in South-East France but also in North Italy. He was excommunicated when Francis was two.

  We know their teaching and their practice only from the writing of enemies, men like Walter Map, archdeacon of Oxford (who described them as 'possessing nothing, having all things in common like the apostles, naked following the naked Christ'); the French Dominican, Etienne de Bourbon; the anonymous chronicler of Laon; and the judicial records of the Inquisition. Reading them, one is tempted to say, there but for the grace of God and the protection of Cardinal Ugolino (Pope Gregory IX) goes Francis of Assisi.

7.13 THE CONVERSION OF PETER WALDO

The Premonstratensian Canon of Laon who wrote the monastery chronicle was strictly orthodox, but he tells the story of Peter Waldo's conversion with sympathy:

This man had made a pile of money by the sin of usury. One Sunday he stepped aside to join a crowd around a jongleur [minstrel], and was so pierced to the heart by the man's recital that he took him home and hung upon his words. Now that passage in the man's story described how St. Alexis had met his happy end in his father's house. Next morning Waldo hurried to the school of theology to enquire after the good of his soul and was told of many ways of coming to God. Then he asked the master what was the surest and most perfect way of all. The master showed him that sentence of our Lord: 'If thou wilt be perfect go and sell all that thou hast and give to the poor...' [Matt. 19, 21. So Waldo provided for his wife, repaid his unjust gains, and gave the greater part of his fortune to the poor.]

7.14 THE DOMINICAN'S TESTIMONY

The French Dominican, Etienne de Bourbon, who as an inquisitor had seen much of the Waldensians, wrote in the thirteenth century.

These men are also called 'Poor Men of Lyons', because they there began their profession of poverty. But they call themselves 'The Poor in Spirit', because the Lord said 'Blessed are the poor in spirit'; but these men are truly poor in spirit, poor in spiritual goods and in the Holy Spirit....

They know the Apostles' Creed excellently in the vulgar tongue and learn by heart the gospels of the New Testament in the vulgar tongue, and repeat them aloud to each other.... I have seen a young cowherd who had lived for only one year in the house of a Waldensian heretic, yet had attended so diligently and repeated so carefully all he had heard there, that he had learnt by heart 40 Sunday Gospels, not counting those for feast days—all learnt word for word in his native tongue. I have seen some laymen, so versed in their teaching that they could repeat by heart a great part of the evangelists such as Matthew or Luke, especially all they contained of the Lord's teaching.... Many Catholics are so neglectful of their own and their family's salvation, that they scarcely know their Pater or their Creed, nor teach it to their servants.

7.15   THE INQUISITOR'S FINDINGS   1319

You, John Chauoat, dwelling at Vienne ... have been found to be of the sect and heresy of those called Waldenses or Poor Men of Lyons, which the holy Roman Church has many years ago condemned as heretics. . . .

They teach that every oath, without exception, is prohibited by God, and is a sin; and we have heard from your own mouth, that you believe this by applying to this purpose (though in a mad and mistaken sense) the words against swearing in the holy gospel (Matt. 5, 34) and of St. James the Apostle (James 5, 12). According to the sound doctine of the saints and doctors of the Church, and the tradition of the said holy Catholic Church, it is not only lawful but necessary to swear for attesting the truth in judgment. . . .

From the same fountain of error and misunderstanding, they assert that all judgment is prohibited by God, and that it is consequently a sin and against the divine prohibition for any judge, in any case or for any cause, to condemn any man to bodily punishment or death. Without a proper exposition, they quote the words of the holy gospel, 'Judge not, that ye be not judged,' (Matt. 7, 1), 'Thou shalt not kill,' (Exodus 20, 13 and see Matt. 5, 21–22), not understanding them or receiving them as the holy Roman Church understands and delivers them. . . .

They persistently err about the sacrament of true penance and the keys of the Church, for they hold that they have power from God, as the Apostles had, to hear confessions of all those who wish to confess, to give absolution and order penances, which they do (see James 5, 16), although they have not been ordained priests by any bishop of the Roman Church, but are mere laymen. . . .

The Waldensians make a jest of the indulgences granted by the prelates of the Church, asserting they are useless. They deny that there is any purgatory for souls after this life, and consequently no prayers, alms, masses, or other pious vows, made by the faithful for the dead, can profit them at all.

They criticise the prelates of the Church of Rome, saying they are blind leaders of the blind (see Matt. 15, 14), and do not preserve the Gospel truth, nor follow apostolic poverty. . . .

Whereas the preaching and exposition of the sacred scriptures is totally forbidden to the laity, they preach from the gospels and epistles and other sacred writings and, by expounding them, they corrupt them.

Source: The Book of Sentences, quoted in Limborch's *History of the Inquisition*, 1693.

Albigensians

If the Waldensians were pushed protesting into heresy, the Albigensians (so-called from the town of Albi in south-west France) were from the start right outside the orthodox Christian faith. They were in no sense marginal heretics. What cut them right off from the main stream was their belief that there was not one Creator but two eternal powers, one good, one evil; and that the visible world was the creation of the evil power, the spiritual world that of the good. This is akin to the teaching of the Manichees (see Vol. I p. 280) and Zoroaster, but it is not clear that there was any direct connection. There were in the eleventh and twelfth centuries similar heresies in Eastern Europe, notably in Bulgaria, and in Constantinople there were both Greek and Latin congregations. The main Albigensian centres were, however, in the south of France, North Spain and North Italy.

There were two grades of Albigensians—Believers, who might marry and behave outwardly as Catholics, though holding Albigensian beliefs and worshipping with them; and 'The Perfect', who had entered into the kingdom of the good power through receiving forgiveness of sins in the spiritual baptism known as *consolamentum*. 'The perfect must remain continent.... They were never to eat meat, milk, or eggs, since these were the fruits of reproduction. They were not to engage in war or to own property' (Latourette: History of Christianity p. 454). Some of 'The Perfect' provided a ministry for the Albigensians; others received the *consolamentum* only as a preparation for death, which might properly be hastened by the *endura* or fast unto death. These ascetic practices, based on the belief that the material world was evil, is reflected by the name by which the Albigensians were best known to themselves, Cathari, 'The Pure', from the Greek word for clean.

7.16   ALBIGENSIAN BELIEFS   20 September 1313

This is the record in the *Book of Sentences* of the examination of an Albigensian heretic in 1313. Note the date. It is more than a hundred years after active repression started. The Albigensians had great moral and physical courage; and, although eventually the sect disappeared, the Church never fully regained its spiritual hold in the south-west of France, which remains a land where anti-clericalism is strong.

You Peter Raymund of Hugones, an inhabitant of Toulouse ... have said, and assert and maintain before us, that you believe and maintain the following errors and horrors:

That carnal matrimony between man and woman is not true

matrimony, nor good, nor lawful, nor instituted by God, and you maintain another spiritual matrimony. . . .

That baptism performed in material water, as the Roman church performs and teaches, is altogether worthless.

That in the Sacrament of the altar, there is not the body of Christ, but only mere bread.

That there will not be a resurrection of human bodies, nor will any one rise in the judgment with his visible and material body.

That a benevolent God made all invisible and incorruptible things, and that an evil ruler, namely Lucifer, made all visible and corruptible things, and even human bodies.

That confession made to the priests of the Roman Church, and absolution given by them to those who confess are absolutely worthless.

That every oath, whether for truth or falsehood, is a sin and unlawful, and you yourself, when we have frequently judicially required you to swear, have persistently refused to do so.

That the sign of the holy cross avails nothing, nor will you sign yourself with that sign, but altogether object and refuse. . . .

Impiously blaspheming the sacrament of the incarnation of the Son of God, you assert that God never entered into the womb of the blessed Virgin Mary, and that the mother, brother, and sister of God are only those who keep the commandments of God the Father (see Mark 3, 35).

You yourself voluntarily take away your own bodily life and kill yourself, because you have put yourself into that abstinence you heretics call *endura*. You have already remained six days without meat and drink; nor would you eat, nor will you now, though many times invited, and thus you hasten to eternal death with the damned.

7.17   ALBIGENSIAN RITUALS

Rituals for the ordination of Believers (credentes) and the Perfect or Good Men survive in a MS in the University of Lyons, a document preserved by the Inquisition. In the Lord's Prayer they used the version which appears in many Vulgate MSS in Matt. 6, 11: 'Give us this day our supersubstantial bread', which they identified with the Bread of Heaven (John 6, 32–35). The Good Men were the Body of Christ (see 1 Cor. 12, 27 and 6, 19) and Believers bowed to them as such; so sacramental bread could not become the body of Christ. The adoremus was, 'Let us adore the Father, the Son, and the Holy Spirit'; the gratia, 'May the grace of the Lord Jesus Christ be with you all'; the parcias, 'Bless us, spare us'.

A. The Bestowal of the Lord's Prayer on a Believer
[The Elder closes a long homily with the words:]
For which cause we pray the good Lord, who gave to the disciples of Jesus Christ virtue to receive that holy prayer in strength, to give you also grace to receive it with strength and with reverence for him, for your salvation.

Then shall the Elder repeat the prayer and the Believer shall follow it. Then the Elder shall say,

This holy prayer we deliver unto you, that you may receive it from God and from us and from the Church; and that you may have power to say it all the time of your life, by day and by night, alone and in company; and that you may never eat or drink without first saying this prayer. And if you omit to do so then you must bear penance for the same.

And he must say, I receive it from God and from you and from the Church.

B. The Consolamentum
[After a long homily, quoting the New Testament texts about the gift of the Spirit, and the power of the Spirit, and some of Christ's rules for the Christian life.]

Then let one of the Good Men say,

Spare us, Lord. Good Christians, we pray you for the love of God that you give of that good which God has given you to this our friend.

Then let the Believer perform his melioramentum [act of contrition] *and say,*

Spare us, Lord. For all the sins which I have done, in word or thought or deed, I come for pardon to God and to the Church and to you all.

And the Christians shall say, By God and by us and by the Church may they be pardoned you, and we pray God that he may pardon you them.

And then shall they console him. The Elder shall take the book [of the Gospels] *and place it on his head and the other Good Men each place their right hand there and say the parcias and three adoremus and then,*

Holy Father, sustain thy servant in thy justice and pour thy grace and Holy Spirit over him.

And let them pray to God with the Prayer, and he that guides the ministration say in low tone the double [eight repetitions of the Lord's Prayer doubled] *and three adoremus and the Prayer once out loud and the gospel* [for Christmas Day, St. John 1, 1–17]. *After the gospel they*

*must say the adoremus three times and the gratia and the parcias. And
then they must give the kiss of peace one with another and with the book.*

The War Against Heretics

The Church's reaction against Waldensians and Albigensians was prompt
and strong. It took four forms: diocesan action by the method of inquisition;
missions; crusade; papal inquisition.

7.18   THE METHOD OF INQUISITION   1184

No sooner was Peter Waldo excommunicated than a hue and cry was set in
foot against his followers and all other heretics. This was automatic. The
papal decree of Lucius III, reproduced in part here, really does no more than
tell the diocesan authorities to do their duty. This needed saying since, for
instance, Innocent III a little later (in 1200) had occasion to remark that
archbishop Bérenger of Narbonne, one of the affected areas, had not visited
his diocese once in ten years.

It is important to distinguish the procedure by the method of inquisition,
which is described here, from the later establishment of the inquisition as an
institution. Inquisition was a procedure derived from Roman law. It is
described in the second paragraph below. Its essence is that a person
suspected of heresy is called on to prove his innocence, not tried to see if he is
guilty.

We lay under a perpetual anathema the Cathari, Patarini, those who
falsely call themselves Humiliati or Poor Men of Lyons, Passagini,
Josepini, and Arnaldistae . . . and all who presume to preach, publicly
or privately, whether actually forbidden, or not sent, not having the
licence of the Apostolic See or the diocesan bishop. . . .

Every Archbishop or bishop shall personally, or through his
archdeacon or by other trustworthy and suitable persons, once or
twice a year, go round any parish where heretics are said to live. They
shall summon three or more persons of good credit—or the whole
neighbourhood if expedient—and require them to take on oath that
they will make it their business to indicate any one in that place
known by them to be a heretic, any persons holding secret gatherings
or leading a different sort of life from that of the faithful. Then the
bishop or archdeacon shall summon the accused before him, and
unless they can satisfactorily clear themselves from the charges
brought against them, or if, after such clearance, they relapse into
error, they shall be punished by the judgment of the bishop. If any
of them, through damnable superstition, shall refuse to swear,
denying the lawfulness of oaths, they are, from that very circum-

stance, convicted heretics, to be subjected to the punishment aforesaid....

Since it sometimes happens, however, that the severity of ecclesiastical discipline required for these offences may be condemned by those who do not understand its benefits, we further decree that whosoever shall be convicted of these errors, shall be stripped of all the prerogatives and privileges of his ecclesiastical office and left to the discretion of the secular power to receive due punishment....

7.19   MASSACRE AT BEZIERS   1209

The second method of dealing with the Albigensians—by mission to bring them back to the Catholic Church—was vigorously pursued. In this work Dominic excelled (see 7.22). But there was a shorter way of dealing with such dissenters, extermination. The papal legate was murdered in 1208. Next year Innocent III launched a crusade against Albigensians. One of their strongholds was the town of Béziers. It was stormed and the inhabitants indiscriminately massacred, although there were many good Catholics among them. Whether the papal legate really said, as Caesarius of Heisterbach reports, 'Kill them for God knows his own,' is uncertain. Caesarius was not there, but far away in his Rhineland monastery. Like the legate, he was a Cistercian, and he does not seem especially astonished or ashamed.

The preacher and chief (of this crusade against the Albigensians) was Arnold, abbot of Citeaux, afterwards archbishop of Narbonne. The crusaders, therefore, came and laid siege to a great city called Béziers, where there were said to be more than 100,000 men. So these heretics, in the sight of the besiegers, defiled the volume of the holy Gospels in such a way as may not be repeated, and threw it from the wall against the Christians.

Then they shot their arrows, crying, 'Behold your law, you wretches!'

But Christ, the author of the Gospels, did not suffer this injury inflicted on him to go unavenged. For certain camp-followers, kindled with the zeal of faith, like lions, even as they of whom it is written in the book of Maccabees (see 1 Mac. 3, 4 and 2 Mac. 11, 11), laid their ladders to the wall and went up fearlessly. The heretics were struck with terror from God and fell away from the walls, and those first, opening the doors to them who followed, took possession of the city.

Learning from their own confession that catholics were mingled with heretics in the city, the crusaders said then to the abbot,

'What shall we do, lord? We cannot tell the good from the evil.'

The abbot feared, like the rest, that the heretics would pretend to be catholics from fear of death, and return to their faithlessness after his departure. So he is said to have answered,

'Kill them, for God knows his own.'

So they were slaughtered in countless multitudes in that city.

7.20   THE COUNCIL OF TOULOUSE ON HERETICS   1229

At the end of the crusade the Council of Toulouse put repression by inquisition on a more systematic basis, but it is still too early to speak of the Inquisition as an institution. That came a little later. Perhaps the best date to give is 1233 when Gregory IX told the French bishops that he was going to employ the Dominicans as his own commissioners for the discovery and repression of heresy. About the same time the Holy Roman Emperor, Frederick II, who was doubtfully a Christian, brought in death as the secular punishment for heresy. It would be wrong to exaggerate the numbers. Between 1308 and 1323 Bernard Guy only handed over 42 persons for execution out of 930 convicted. The use of torture to secure confessions had been legalised by Innocent IV in 1252.

Canon 1. We appoint Archbishops and bishops to swear in one priest, and two or three laymen of good report, or more if they think fit, in every parish both in and out of cities, who shall diligently, faithfully and frequently, seek out the heretics in those parishes by searching all houses and subterranean rooms which lie under any suspicion.

Canon 6. The house in which any heretics are found shall be destroyed.

Canon 10. Those former heretics who voluntarily abandon their heresy and return to the Catholic faith, acknowledging their error, shall not remain in the town in which they previously dwelt, if that town be suspected of heresy, but shall be placed in a catholic town which lies under no suspicion of heresy. Moreover, in detestation of their ancient error, they shall thenceforth wear two conspicuous crosses, of a different colour from their garments, nor shall any one discontinue wearing these crosses without letters testimonial of his reconciliation from his bishop.

Canon 14. We prohibit the laity from having the books of the Old or New Testament, unless, from motives of devotion, one should wish to have the Psalter, or the Breviary for divine offices, or the hours of the blessed Virgin. But we most strictly forbid their having any translation of these books.

7.21   AQUINAS ON HERESY   *c.* 1270

So far we have been concerned with how the Church dealt with heresy. But why, and what did men think about it? This is how Thomas Aquinas put it in his *Summa Theologica* II, Q. 11.

Heretics must be considered from two points of view: themselves and the Church. In the first case there is the sin, whereby a heretic not only deserves to be cut off from the Church by excommunication, but also to be cut off from the world by death. For it is a much more serious crime to corrupt faith, through which comes the life of the soul, than to forge money, by which temporal life is supported. So if forgers of money and other such criminals are immediately and justly put to death by secular princes, heretics may far more justly, immediately they are convicted, be not only excommunicated but also put to death.

In the case of the Church there is mercy aiming at the conversion of those in error. Therefore the Church delays condemnation until after a first and second admonition, as the apostle teaches (Titus 3, 10). After that, if the heretic is still stubborn, the Church gives up hope of conversion and takes thought for the safety of others, by separating him from the Church by excommunication, leaving him to the secular court to be separated from the world by death.

7.22   Dominic: A Friend's Portrait

The Dominicans, the second of the Orders of Friars, sprang out of the mission designed to bring the Albigensians back to the Catholic faith. Dominic (1170–1221) was a canon regular (i.e. a monk) of the cathedral of Osma in the north of Spain. In 1205 Pope Innocent III sent the bishop on a mission to Languedoc. Dominic went with him and stayed behind. He had found his life work there, preaching to the people and debating with the heretics. He gradually built up his irregular band of followers into a new order which the Pope recognized in 1216. When Dominic died at Bologna five years later it had spread throughout western Europe. Dominic was not himself an inquisitor nor did he take part in the crusade against the Albigensians, one of the most ferocious medieval wars. But he was on friendly terms with its leaders, and did not dissociate himself from it. Dominicans were, as we have seen, the first Papal Inquisitors. They were also active above all other Orders in the universities. Thomas of Aquinas, the greatest of the medieval philosophers, was a member of the Order.

This portrait of Dominic is part of the testimony of Brother John of Spain, one of his early companions, given at the proceedings for his canonization at Bologna. It is translated by C. M. Hoinacki, O.P.

Both night and day, Brother Dominic was constant in his prayer. He prayed more than the other brothers who lived with him, kept longer vigils; he used the discipline on his body with greater severity and frequency than the others. [The witness] knows these facts inasmuch as he very often saw [Dominic] doing these things. Some of the brethren also told him that Master Dominic used the discipline on himself and had others administer it; it was an iron chain with three branches. All this was common knowledge among the brethren, but [the witness] heard it from the brothers who had actually used this discipline on [Brother Dominic].

When the brethren were guilty of violations, he punished them according to the Rule. Yet he suffered deeply with the offenders, and was very sorrowful whenever he had to penance anyone for a transgression.

Filled with compassion, he most ardently desired his neighbour's salvation. He himself preached constantly and frequently, and, in every way he could, exhorted the brethren to preach. He sent them out to preach, begging and urging them to be solicitous for the salvation of souls. Confiding greatly in God, he sent even the ungifted ones to preach, saying: 'Go confidently, for the Lord will give you the word of preaching and be with you, and nothing shall be wanting to you.' They went out and it happened to them just as he had said.

And he testified that, when he was with the said Brother Dominic at the monastery of the Church of St. Romanus in Toulouse, Brother Dominic, acting against the admonitions of the Count of Montfort, the Archbishop of Narbonne, the Bishop of Toulouse and certain other prelates, sent the reluctant witness to Paris with five clerical brethren and one laybrother. They were to study, preach and found a priory there. They should not fear, since everything would prosper for them. To the prelates, the Count, and the brethren, he said: 'Do not oppose me, since I know very well what I am doing.' Then he sent others to Spain, giving them a similar reply and set of instructions.

During this same period, many buildings and much property were given to the Order in the country around Toulouse and Albi. Since the Order of Preachers had all this property and wealth in that area, the brethren used to carry money on their journeys, go by horse, and wear surplices. For this reason Brother Dominic worked hard to convince them of the need for relinquishing and contemning all temporal goods—they should embrace poverty, live on alms, not carry money with them nor ride horses. Thus the property in France was given to Cistercian nuns and, in other countries, to nuns there.

Brother Dominic was friendly to all, rich and poor, Jews and pagans (who were very numerous in Spain). As [the witness] noted, he was also loved by all men, with the exception of heretics and enemies of the Church. He used to pursue these persons and refute them in debates and sermons. However, when he argued with them, he lovingly exhorted them to repent and return to the faith—as [the witness] saw and heard.

He often noticed that Dominic slept at night as he was dressed during the day, except that he took off his shoes. When he travelled from one place to another, he also took off his shoes and walked barefoot until he reached his destination. Whenever he got into the country, he again took off his shoes and carried them; he would not let anyone else carry them for him. Asked how he knew, he replied that he heard it from the brethren and had often seen it himself. If he stumbled on a rock, Dominic bore it cheerfully. As a man who always rejoiced in his troubles, he was not disturbed, but used to say: 'This is penance.' He loved poverty very much, and zealously incited the brethren to have a similar love. Asked how he knew this, he answered that Brother Dominic gloried in the poorest clothing, and that, having given up all temporal things, he often exhorted the brethren to love poverty, and this in the presence of the witness.

He was also frugal in eating and drinking, but particularly as regards any special dish. He readily dispensed others, but never himself; rather, he strictly observed the entire Rule.

He did not have a bed of his own, like the other brethren. Asked how he knew this, he replied that if he had possessed his own bed, he certainly would have known about it, for he had gone to great trouble searching for it.

[Dominic] rarely spoke, except with God, that is, in prayer, or of God; further, he urged the brethren to act similarly. [The witness] also said that he was always joyful with others, but he frequently wept while praying and he knew this because he saw and heard his weeping. During and after Brother Dominic's lifetime, the witness heard that he perservered in virginity till his death—a fact well known among the brethren. He once heard Dominic say that he desired to be tortured, cut to pieces and die for the faith of Christ.

Both by word and letter, he often instructed and urged the brethren of the Order to make a constant study of the Old and New Testament. The witness heard him say this and saw the letters. He always carried Matthew's Gospel and Paul's Epistles with him. From studying them so much, he almost knew them from memory.

7.23 Mercenary Mendicants: Chaucer's Friar

A hundred years is a long time in the life of any institution. It is not surprising that in the fourteenth century there were many protests against the corruption which had overtaken many of the friars. There were, of course, many good and humble men still to be found among them, but the predominant impression is of decay.

Lordings, there is in Yorkshire, as I guess,
A marshy county callëd Holderness,
In which there went a limiter[1] about
To preach and eke to beg, it is no doubt.
And so befell that on a day this friar
Had preachëd in a church in his mannère,
And specially, aboven every thing,
He did excite the people by preaching
For trentals.[2] 'Give,' he ṣaid, 'for Goddës sake
Money that men might holy houses make
Where the divine Lord's service is honoùred,
And not where it is wasted and devoured
By those to whom there is no need to give,
Such as possessioners[3] who richly live.
Trentals will save your friends' souls from the pit...
Full hard it is with flesh-hook or with spit
To be a-clawed and then to burn or bake.
Now speed you hastily for Christës sake!'
And when this friar had said all his intent,
With *Qui cum patre*[4] forth his way he went...
    When folk in church had given what they list
He went his way—no longer would he rest—
With scrip and tippëd staff stuck up on high.
In every house he gan to pore and pry,
And beggeth meal and cheese or else some corn.
His fellow had a staff tippëd with horn,
A pair of tablets all of ivory,
Also a stylus polished prettily,
Who always wrote the names down, as he stood,
Of all the folk who gave him any good,
Assurances that he would for them pray.
    'Give us a bushel of wheat or malt or rye,
A little cake for God's sake, crumb of cheese,
Or else whatever you like, we may not choose.

A penny to say mass or half a penny?
Or give us of your brawn if you have any;
A strip off your own blanket, dearest dame,
Our sister dear—lo! here I write your name—
Bacon or beef, or such thing as you find.'
   A sturdy varlet went with them behind,
The servant to their guests,[5] and bore a sack,
And what men gave them laid it on his back.
And when that he was out of door anon,
He planed away the names of every one
That he before had written in his tables.
He'd served them all with fairytales and fables.

[1]: Limiters were licensed to beg in a limited area. [2]: Trentals were sequences of 30 masses to shorten a soul's stay in purgatory. [3]: Possessioners were beneficed clergy. [4]: The first words of doxology at the close of a sermon. [5]: Convent guests.

CHAPTER EIGHT

THE SCHOLAR'S FAITH

In the twelfth century there was a memorable quickening and sharpening of men's minds. Schools with a more than local reputation grew up at monasteries, like Bec in Normandy under its two famous North Italian abbots, Lanfranc and Anselm, both of whom became archbishops of Canterbury. More important perhaps were the cathedral schools which drew students from all over Europe—German once so rang in the streets of Orléans that one would have thought oneself in the Fatherland, as a fourteenth century writer quoted by Helen Waddell put it. Men came for many reasons. Some simply delighted in the pleasures of student life—much the same then as now though without the benefit of student grants. Some hoped to qualify for professional employment in the law—canon (church) law or civil—or to get preferment in the church. All the work now done by civil servants fell to men with this background. Others wished to steep themselves in the Latin classics and write like their favourite authors. Increasing numbers were caught by sheer intellectual delight as they followed wherever the argument led as it swayed to and fro in the dialectic of the schools. Most no doubt had mixed motives which changed imperceptibly in the long years as they moved from master to master and from place to place.

By the beginning of the thirteenth century the major schools were crystallizing into universities. All, of course, were not only Christian but church-based. Students and masters were all clerks under church law, though this does not mean that all or even most of them were priests. Theology was the 'queen of the sciences'; its doctors had precedence in university status, as they still do in the older universities. There was a certain element of specialization. Bologna had a special eminence in law; Salerno and Montpellier were the places for medicine; Oxford and Paris for philosophy and theology. Paris indeed stood supreme among the universities of Christendom.

At this time, too, the philosophical works of Aristotle which had been lost (the twelfth century knew only his logic) became available in Christendom through translations of translations—Greek into Arabic or Hebrew into Latin. Henceforward Aristotle became 'The Philosopher', an authority of almost equal authority with Moses. It is fair to say that never have men's minds been sharper; what was still lacking was empirical observation and experiment.

8.1 A Student's Progress

Giraldus Cambrensis (Gerald the Welshman, *c*. 1145–1220) was an indefatigable traveller who wrote first-rate books on Wales and Ireland. He combined a genuine love of learning with a strong eye to his own career. He failed to become bishop of St. David's, but at least he was an archdeacon. He called his autobiography *Things I have done*.

As a child he was hampered by the·companionship of his brothers, who would play together on holidays, glorifying the deeds of the knights they wished to become. So his progress was far slower than it should have been. But then he was scolded and corrected by his uncle David, of blessed memory, then bishop of Menevia [St. David's] and was also helped to amend through the mockery of two of the bishop's clerks. One teased him by repeating the degrees of comparison of *durus* (hard); *durior, durissimus*, while the other cried '*stultus* (stupid), *stultior, stultissimus!*' So he began to make progress, spurred by conscience rather than the rod, by shame rather than by fear, and not because of the teaching from his masters. He began to study with such fury that he quite out-stripped the schoolmates of his own age [at St. Peter's, Gloucester].

In due course, anxious to acquire greater learning, he thrice crossed the sea to France, and spent three periods of several years at Paris in the study of the liberal arts, becoming one of the greatest teachers of the *Trivium* [the three 'Liberal Arts': Grammar, Rhetoric, Dialectic]. He won especial fame in the art of rhetoric. He was so devoted to his studies, so free from all frivolity both in word and deed, that when the teachers of arts wished to produce a model of excellence from among their best scholars they unanimously selected Giraldus. Thus in early youth his virtues made him fit not only to seek a standard of excellence for scholars, but also to set one. . . .

Giraldus, collecting his treasure-store of books, resolved to cross the sea to France yet again to study the liberal arts at Paris, and on this foundation he hoped to raise high the walls of civil and canon law and finally add the sacred roof of theology. He would bind this threefold edifice with bands that time could not destroy. So for many years he applied himself to the study first of the Imperial and then the Pontifical Constitutions and finally to the Holy Scriptures. He won great popularity by his exposition of the Decretals, which were usually debated on Sundays, and when it was known in the city that he intended to speak, almost all the teachers with their pupils gathered to have the pleasure of hearing his voice, so that even the

largest hall could scarcely contain his audience. For he discussed civil
and canon law in a most lively way, enriching his discourse with all
the persuations of rhetoric, adorning it with figures and flowers of
speech as well as profound arguments, using apt quotations of
philsophers and other authors and applying them with wonderful
artistry to appropriate subjects. Therefore the more learned and
expert his audience the more eagerly they opened their ears and minds
to drink in his words and fix them in their memory.... Numbers of
students wrote down his lectures word for word and tried most
earnestly to take them to heart; and once when a great crowd had
come to hear him as soon as he stopped speaking a chorus of praise
and applause rose from all the assembly.

8.2   From Scholar to Pope

The Church really did provide a career open to talent. It was even possible for
a charity boy to become pope as happened to Nicholas Breakspear, the only
English pope, who reigned as Adrian IV from 1154 to 1159. This account of
how it happened is from the history of England written by William of
Newburg, a monk of Rievaulx (see 6.18). He is a first-rate authority for the
years 1154–1197.

When pope Anastasius died after only one year as pope, in the first
year of the reign of Henry II, he was succeeded by Nicholas, bishop of
Albano, who changed his name with his fortune and was called
Adrian. It must be told how he was raised as if from dust to sit among
princes on the throne of apostolic glory.

He was born an Englishman; his father was a clerk of small means
who with his little son forsook the world to become a monk at St.
Albans. When the son grew to adolescence he was too poor to go to
school and hung about the monastery for the daily dole of charity.
His father was ashamed by this, slated him bitterly for his idleness
and drove him out in high dudgeon.

Alone, impelled by dire necessity and honourably ashamed to dig
or beg in England, he ventured into France [and was a student first in
Paris then at Arles]. Not prospering there he wandered further,
crossing the Rhone into Provence, where there was a fine monastery
of regular canons named after St. Rufus. Here [at Avignon] he found
an opportunity to stay, taking trouble to commend himself to the
brethren by rendering them such services as he could, and as he was
an attractive young man, good looking, wise in speech and keen to
obey, he found favour with them all. They begged him to adopt the

habit of a canon-regular and he settled there for many years, competing with the best in the discipline of the rule. Keenly intelligent and a fluent speaker, he advanced in knowledge and eloquence by constant hard study. So when the abbot died, the brethren unanimously and canonically elected him as their father [1137].

When he had presided over them for some time the monks changed their minds and were angry at raising a foreigner to rule them. They became faithless and hostile towards him and they grew to regard with violent hatred him who had formerly found favour in their sight. Finally they concocted charges against him and summoned him before the apostolic see. Eugenius of pious memory was then pope. He heard the complaints of these rebellious sons against their father, noted the wise and modest way the abbot defended himself, and tried hard to restore peace between both parties. He strongly reproved them for their fratricidal strife and urged them again and again to keep the unity of the Spirit in the bond of peace (Eph. 4, 3). Then he sent them back to their abbey, reconciled.

But never-resting malice could not be silenced for long and the storm broke out again with double violence. A second appeal was made by the brethren to the same venerable pope, whose ears still rang with the rancours of the first. Surveying both parties with eyes both kind and shrewd, he said:

'Brethren, I know where the seat of Satan lies, I know what raises this strife among you. Go, choose a father under whom you may, or rather will abide in peace, for this man shall be a burden to you no longer.'

So he sent the monks away but kept the abbot in the service of St. Peter. He consecrated him bishop of Albano and soon afterwards when he had proved his devotion he sent him as his legate with plenary powers, to work among the wild and savage races in Denmark and Norway (1152–4). When he had completed his task wisely and efficiently he very happily returned to Rome and was received by the pope and cardinals honourably and triumphantly. Some days later Anastasius, Eugenius' successor, died and Nicholas was elected pope by a unanimous vote. He changed his name to Adrian and, remembering his early training and especially his father, he endowed the church of the blessed martyr Alban with gifts and perpetual privileges.

8.3 Anselm's Reasonable Faith in God   *c.* 1095

Anselm (1033–1107) was born in Aosta in North Italy. He became prior of the Norman abbey of Bec when he was thirty and abbot fifteen years later. When Anselm was sixty William Rufus made him archbishop of Canterbury, 'a wild, untameable bull yoked to an old and feeble sheep' was Anselm's description of their probable relation. But Anselm too proved untameable and was twice exiled because he could agree neither with Rufus nor Henry I about the respective spheres of church and state. His lasting fame, however, depends on his work as an outstanding teacher in the monastic school and a penetrating Christian thinker. The first two extracts come from his *Proslogion*:

A.

I do not seek, O Lord, to penetrate your sublimity, as I in no way compare my understanding with it; but I desire to some extent to understand your truth, which my heart believes and loves. That is to say, I do not seek to understand so that I may believe, but I believe so that I may understand.

B.

The non-existence of God is inconceivable. This is so true that its negation is inconceivable. For it is quite conceivable that there is something whose non-existence is inconceivable, and this must therefore be greater than that whose non-existence is conceivable. Therefore if that object, than which no greater thing is conceivable, can be conceived as non-existent, then that very thing, than which a greater is inconceivable, is not that thing which a greater is inconceivable; which is a contradiction.

It is so true that there exists something than which a greater is inconceivable, that its non-existence is inconceivable. And, Lord our God, thou art this thing!

So certainly do you exist, O Lord my God, that your non-existence is inconceivable, and with good reason. For if a man's mind could conceive anything better than you, the creature would rise above the Creator and judge him; which is utterly absurd.

8.4 Anselm on the Atonement   *c.* 1097

The Church has never defined the doctrine of the Atonement though no Christian has ever doubted its reality. Anselm's approach was worked out in his book *Cur Deus Homo* (Why God became man) which he wrote in exile:

We must ask why God can forgive man's sins; and it will make it clearer if we first see what it is to sin and what to make satisfaction for sin. Sin is failure to render to God what is his due. The entire will of a rational creature ought to be subject to the will of God. He who does not render this honour to God, robs God of what belongs to him and dishonours God. This is sin. It is not enough simply to restore what has been taken away, but in return for the insult offered he ought to restore more than he took away (Bk. 1, 11).

Let us see whether God could properly remit sins by mercy alone without reparation. To remit sin in this way is the same as not to punish it. But the only possible way of correcting sin for which no satisfaction has been made is to punish it. Not to punish it is to let it go without correction. But God cannot leave anything uncorrected in his kingdom. Also, to leave sin unpunished would be to treat the sinners and the sinless alike, a thing unbefitting to God (1, 12).

It is necessary, therefore, that either the honour taken away should be repaid, or punishment follow. Otherwise either God will be unjust to himself or he will be powerless to secure either alternative—a thing wicked even to imagine (1, 13). Satisfaction or punishment must follow every sin (1, 14). The satisfaction must be made according to the measure of the sin (1, 20).

Have you considered the heavy weight of sin? Suppose you were in the presence of God and someone said to you, 'Look over there,' and God said, 'I wish you on no account to look'; ask yourself whether there is anything in the whole of existence for the sake of which you ought to take that look contrary to the will of God. Perish the whole world and all that is not God rather than do the least act against his will! But suppose it happened that you did take that look against the will of God, what could you pay for that sin? You cannot make satisfaction for it unless you pay more than what you were prepared to lose for it—the whole creation (1, 21).

With regard to human nature it is necessary that God should make perfect what he has begun; and this cannot be done except by a complete satisfaction for sin, which no sinner can make (Bk. 2, 4). Someone must pay to God in compensation for man's sin something greater than everything that exists except God. Nothing is greater than all that is not God, except God himself. Therefore no one can make this satisfaction except God himself. But no one ought to make it except man. Then if only God *can*, and only man *should* make this satisfaction, one must make it who is both God and man (2, 6).

The mercy of God, which seemed to be 'clean gone' (Psa. 77, 8), when we were looking at the justice of God and the sin of man, is so great and in such harmony with his justice, that nothing greater or more just can be imagined. For what greater mercy can be conceived than that God the Father should say to the sinner—condemned to eternal torments and unable to redeem himself from them—'Accept my only Son and offer him for thyself', while the Son himself says, 'Take me and redeem thyself'? And what is more just than that he who receives a payment, far more valuable than all the debt, if given with the right intention, should forgive the whole debt? (2, 20).

Peter Abelard

Peter Abelard (1079–1142) is remembered today, as he has been in every generation since his own, as a partner in one of the world's great love stories. But we are not concerned here with his relation to Héloise, but with him as the most exciting and challenging teacher of the middle ages. Others were to carry on his work and, a hundred years later, Thomas Aquinas perfected a philosophical and theological system comparable in its articulation and influence with Aristotle's. Abelard left no such monument but, as these extracts show, he set men thinking and arguing with a passion, a freedom, and an honesty which can still be felt. His, too, was a deeply religious mind. It is perhaps easier today to enter into the intellectual ferment of the middle ages by reading Abelard than in any other way.

8.5   ON HOW TO STUDY

In an early work, *Sic et Non* (Yes and No) Peter Abelard confronted his students with contradictory opinions on 168 topics ranging from non-Christian marriage to the relation of the Father and the Son. The opinions came from sources which all carried almost the authority of Holy Writ—indeed the Bible amongst them. Abelard did not tell his young men what to think, but how to think and how to set about the work which his provocative collection invited:

We must be careful not to be led astray by attributing views to the Fathers which they did not hold. This may happen if a wrong author's name is given to a book 'or if a text is corrupt. For many works are falsely attributed to one of the Fathers to give them authority, and some passages, even in the Bible, are corrupt through the errors of copyists.... We must be equally careful to make sure that an opinion quoted from a Father was not withdrawn or corrected by him in the light of later and better knowledge (as, for instance, blessed Augustine often did [especially in one of his last books, *Retractiones*]). Again the passage in question may not give the

Father's own opinion, but that of some other writer whom he is quoting. . . .

We must also make a thorough inquiry when different decisions are given on the same matter under canon law. We must discover the underlying purpose of the opinion, whether it is meant to grant an indulgence or exhort to some perfection. In this way we may clear up the apparent contradiction. . . . If the opinion is a definitive judgment, we must determine whether it is of general application or directed to a particular case. . . . The when and why of the order must also be considered because what is allowed at one time is often forbidden at another, and what is often laid down as the strict letter of the law may be sometimes moderated by a dispensation. . . .

Furthermore we customarily talk of things as they appear to our bodily senses and not as they are in actual fact. So judging by what we see we say it is a starry sky or it is not, and that the sun is hot or has no heat at all, when these things though variable in appearance are ever constant. Can we be surprised, then, that some matters have been stated by the Fathers as opinions rather than the truth? Then again many controversies would be quickly settled if we could be on our guard against a particular word used in different senses by different authors. . . .

A careful reader will employ all these ways of reconciling contradictions in the writings of the Fathers. But if the contradictions are so glaring that they cannot be reconciled, then the rival authorities must be compared and the view that has the heaviest backing be adopted. . . .

By collecting contrasting divergent opinions I hope to provoke young readers to push themselves to the limit in the search for truth, so that their wits may be sharpened by their investigation. It is by doubting that we come to investigate, and by investigating that we recognise the truth.

8.6   ON THE AUTHORITY OF THE CHURCH

I think that these words of Jerome make it clear that Christ's mandate to Peter or to the rest of the apostles [see Matt. 16, 18–19; 18, 19] on binding and loosing the chains of sin, must be understood to refer to these particular apostles and not to all bishops in general. However, we may accept that it applies to all priests, as Jerome does, if we take the binding and releasing to mean the ability to distinguish guilt and innocence. So priests can decide who deserve to be bound by God and who can be released. They can discriminate between clean and unclean. Origen, dealing with this text, distinguishes between the elect bishops who deserve the privilege given to Peter, and other bishops. He quotes the text in defence of episcopacy. It was applied to Peter who is said to have received the keys of the kingdom of heaven from Christ. Those bound with these keys are bound in heaven. Those loosed by them, those who obtain forgiveness, are loosed in heaven.

This argument is good provided that the bishops justify in practice the commendation of Peter when he was given this authority. The bishops must be men on whom the Church of Christ may be built without 'the gates of hell prevailing against them'. Otherwise it is absurd to hold that a man who is bound by a chain of his own sins, dragging behind him a long rope of his sins, bearing guilt as oxen bear the yoke, should, just because he is a bishop, bind and loose people on earth and claim the right of having them bound or loosed in heaven. Let the bishop who would bind or loose another be himself 'above reproach, married only once, temperate, sensible, dignified ... no lover of money. He must manage his own household well, keeping his children submissive and respectful in every way' (1 Tim. 3, 2–4). Such a man can justly bind on earth and justly loose.... If anyone is a 'Peter' and does not possess the character attributed to him in this passage, and yet claims the authority to bind and to loose as it is in heaven, he deceives himself. He does not understand the meaning of Scripture and his conceit will receive the devil's sentence.

Source: Abelard, *Ethics.*

8.7   ON THE ATONEMENT

Abelard, like Anselm in the preceding generation, thought deeply about the mystery of the redeeming love which he had experienced. His teaching, expressed here in a passage from his commentary on Romans and (8.8) in a hymn for the nuns of the Paraclete where Héloise was abbess, has a psychological insight which has a greater appeal today than Anselm's logic. The translation of the hymn is by Helen Waddell.

Men's sins were forgiven them long before the Passion: Mary Magdalen, for instance, and the paralytic to whom Our Lord said, 'Son, thy sins are forgiven thee.' What necessity, what reason, what need was there for the Son of God to endure such intolerable anguish, when the divine compassion was able to deliver a man from the evil one by the sole vision of Himself? When it seems to us both cruel and unjust to demand the blood of the innocent in any kind of bargain, or to find any kind of pleasure that the innocent should be slain, how should God find the death of His Son so agreeable, that thereby He should be reconciled to the world? These, and other points like them, seem to me to raise no small question as to our redemption by the death of Our Lord....

What then is our redemption? We are justified in the blood of Christ and reconciled to God, because by the life and death of His Son He has so bound us to Himself that love so kindled will shrink from nothing for His sake. Our redemption is that supreme devotion kindled in us by the Passion of Christ: this it is that frees us from the tyranny of sin and gives us the liberty of the sons of God, so that we do His will from love and not from fear. This is that fire which Our Lord said He had come to kindle upon earth. It is the goodness of God that leads us to repentance: we grieve to have sinned against God, from love, and not from fear; less because He is just than because He is merciful. We are reconciled to God in that grief: in whatsoever hour the sinner shall grieve, says Ezekiel, he shall be saved: that is, he is made fit to be saved (Ezek. 18, 21–28).

8.8   GOOD FRIDAY: THE THIRD NOCTURN   *c.* 1135

Alone to sacrifice thou goest, Lord,
    Giving thyself to death whom thou hast slain.
For us thy wretched folk is any word,
    Who know that for our sins this is thy pain?

For they are ours, O Lord, our deeds, our deeds,
    Why must thou suffer torture for our sin?
Let our hearts suffer for thy passion, Lord,
    That sheer compassion may thy mercy win.

This is that night of tears, the three days' space,
    Sorrow abiding of the eventide,
Until the day break with the risen Christ,
    And hearts that sorrowed shall be satisfied.

So may our hearts have pity on thee, Lord,
    That they may sharers of thy glory be:
Heavy with weeping may the three days pass,
    To win the laughter of thine Easter Day.

8.9   BERNARD ON ABELARD

Abelard inevitably made many enemies. The most powerful was Bernard of Clairvaux. They were two great men whose minds could never meet.

We have in France an old teacher turned into a new theologian, who in his early days amused himself with dialectics, and now pours out wild baseless speculations about the Bible. He is trying to revive false ideas long since condemned and buried—his own and other people's; and he is adding fresh errors. I can think of nothing in heaven above or on earth beneath which he will admit that he does not understand. He looks up to heaven and explores the deep things of God. Coming back to us he reports things which cannot be expressed, words which it is not lawful for a man to speak. He has the temerity to give a reason for everything, even for those things which are above reason; he makes unwarranted assertions against reason and against faith—for what is more unreasonable than to try by reason to transcend reason? And what is more against faith then to be unwilling to believe what reason cannot reach? . . . But our theologian says: 'What is the use of speaking of doctrine unless what we wish to teach can be explained in an intelligible way?' And so he promises that his hearers will understand even those most sublime and sacred truths which lie hidden in the bosom itself of our faith. . . . On the very threshold of his theology, or rather of his 'foolology', he defines faith as private judgment.

[Bernard ignored, or failed to grasp, the distinction Abelard drew between comprehension and understanding. Man cannot, he held, comprehend God —know God as God knows; but he can understand, reach a limited knowledge of truths which are not perceptible to man's senses. The word which Bernard took to mean opinion really stands for mental apprehension.] . . .

Is not our hope baseless if our faith is subject to change? Surely our martyrs were fools if they accepted such cruel tortures for an uncertainty, and entered without hesitation on an eternal exile by bitter death, if there was a doubt about the reward that awaited them. But far be it from us to think—with him—that anything in our faith or hope depends on an individual's judgment, when the whole of it rests upon sure, solid truth, certified by miracles and revelations from heaven, founded and consecrated by the Son of the Virgin, by the Blood of the Redeemer, by the glory of the risen Christ. . . . 'I know in whom I have believed, and I am confident' (2 Tim. 1, 12) the Apostle proclaims; you mutter in my ear that faith is only an opinion. . . .

But now notice other points. I pass over his saying . . . that the Holy Spirit is the world-soul; . . . Here, while he exhausts himself to make Plato a Christian, he proves himself a heathen. All these things and his numerous other silly stories I leave on one side and come to graver matters.

[Bernard went on to attack Abelard's teaching on the Atonement and especially his rejection of the idea of a ransom paid to the devil.]

8.10 ABELARD CONDEMNED 1140

The campaign by Bernard and others led to Abelard's condemnation as a heretic by a Council at Sens. Abelard, who had been expected to defend himself there vigorously, decided that there was no hope of success as things stood, kept quiet, and appealed to Rome. What his impetuous followers thought of the proceedings is clear from this open letter from Berengar, one of them.

You set up Peter Abelard as a mark for your arrows, to vomit forth the venom of your bitterness against him, to carry him from the land of the living and set him among the dead. You gathered bishops from all directions and condemned him as a heretic in the Council of Sens. . . . When the bishops had dined, Peter's book was produced and a reader chosen to read it in a loud voice. But he, out of hatred for Peter, and well-wetted from the wine (not him who said, 'I am the true vine', but that vine which stretched the patriarch Noah naked on the ground), bawled even louder than required. Soon the bishops could be seen leaping from their seats and stamping their feet, laughing and joking, so that all could note that their vows had been paid not to Christ, but Bacchus. Toasts were raised, goblets honoured, wines are praised, the prelates' throats well-washed. . . .

Then the heat of the wine went to their heads and all eyelids drooped in the heaviness of sleep. Still the reader bawls, but his hearers snore. One leans on his elbow and sleeps, another nods and blinks on his soft cushion, a third dozes with his head on his knees. Then, when the reader stumbled in a rather knotty passage, he would cry to these deaf ears, 'Damnatis? Do you condemn it?' And a few, roused by the sound of this last word, murmured in a sleepy voice with nodding head, 'Damnamus, we condemn it,' while others, aroused by this chorus of their fellows, droned out, 'Namus, namus!'

8.11 ABELARD AT PEACE 1142

After Sens Abelard retired from public life and found a welcome, peace, and affection at Cluny. Peter the Venerable looked after him tenderly, even managed something of a reconciliation with Bernard and, when Abelard died, wrote a letter to Héloise, part of which we quote here. Abelard's body was taken to the Paraclete for burial.

I do not remember to have known a man whose appearance and bearing manifested such humility. St. Germain cannot have seemed humbler or St. Martin poorer. I set him among the first of this great flock of brethren, but by the carelessness of his apparel he seemed the least of all. When in our processions he walked before me with the community I have often marvelled that a man so famous should be able thus to despise and abase himself....

Beloved sister in Christ, he to whom you were first united by the bonds of the flesh and then by the stronger and more sacred bonds of divine love, he with whom and under whose guidance you have long served the Lord is now cherished in his bosom. God keeps him for you....

8.12　Roger Bacon's Wistful Thinking　　　　　　　　1272

Compare this outburst by a frustrated Franciscan, Roger Bacon, with Abelard's advice to his students given 150 years before (8.5). Abelard put his hearers on the right path; Bacon shows that they had not taken it. Of course there had been a great philosophical flowering, and powerful, self-governing universities had grown up in place of the collection of cathedral and monastic schools in which Abelard had taught. But men's minds had been diverted to metaphysics, and shied away from asking those questions about literary and historical evidence which are akin to work in the empirical sciences. Note that both Roger Bacon (1214–1294) and Robert Grosseteste (d. 1253), to whom Bacon refers in this passage, were not only literary scholars but also writers and workers in the natural sciences. Both worked at Paris and in Oxford; both were Franciscans. Grosseteste became bishop of Lincoln, but Bacon twice fell into disgrace with his order because of the direction of his thought. He was silenced and confined from 1257 to 1267 and from 1278 to 1292. He owed the ten years' interval to the intervention of Pope Clement IV for whom he wrote his *Opus Majus*, a study of grammar, logic, mathematics, physics and philosophy.

There has never been a greater appearance of wisdom nor a busier pursuit of learning, in so many subjects and in so many parts of the world, as in the last 40 years. Doctors, especially Doctors of Divinity, are scattered through all cities, towns and boroughs, chiefly by the two student orders during the last 40 years approximately. In reality, however, there has never been more ignorance, nor such deep error, as I shall prove quite clearly in this thesis....

Consider the religious orders—I exclude none from my comments. See how low they have sunk from their first dignity. All the clergy pursue pride, lechery and avarice; and wherever clerks are gathered together, as at Paris and Oxford, they shock all the laity with their wars and quarrels and vices....

Compare our condition with that of the ancient philosophers. Though they lacked that saving grace which makes man worthy of eternal life and which we receive at baptism, yet they lived far better lives than we live: in decency, scorning the world with all its pleasures and riches and honours, as all may read in the works of Aristotle, Seneca, Cicero, Al-Farabi, Avicenna, Alfarabius, Plato, Socrates, and others. So they have discovered nothing worthy of those philosophers and cannot even understand their wisdom. . . .

If you would pride yourself on Aristotle's science, you must learn it in his native tongue, because false translations are everywhere—in theology as well as in philosophy. . . . We have very few good books of philosophy in Latin; for though Aristotle wrote a hundred books (as we read in his life), we possess only three of any importance: his *Logic*, his *Natural History*, and his *Metaphysics*. . . .

In the same way innumerable works of God's wisdom are still lacking. Many books of holy writ have not been translated:—both books of the Maccabees, which I know exist in Greek, and many books of many prophets cited in the *Books of Kings* and *Chronicles*. . . . The Latins also lack innumerable books of the Hebrew and Greek commentators, such as Origen, Basil, Gregory Nazianzus, Damascenus, Dionysius, Chrysostom, and other noble doctors who wrote in Hebrew as well as in Greek. So the Church sleeps, for she has done no translating for 70 years, except that the lord bishop of Lincoln, Robert Grosseteste of holy memory, translated into Latin some of the books of St. Dionysius, Damascenus, and a few other holy teachers. . . . The Bible has been corrupted. A detailed examination would show that there is scarcely a sentence without a falsehood or at least some uncertainty. . . . Therefore all theologians nowadays, whether they are reading or preaching, use false texts.
Source: Roger Bacon, *Compendium Studii Philosophiae.*

8.13 Moralising Animals

For every reader of the *Opus Majus* there must have been thousands of the *Physiologus*, a fanciful handbook of zoology first produced in Alexandria about the year 150. The common medieval view was that everything must have a moral, and a reference to man's good in this world or the next. Every plant was a medicine or a poison; every animal pious or impious. The *Physiologus* admittedly met this need. Few monastic libraries can have been without a copy. There are, for instance, translations in Ethiopian, Armenian, Syriac, Arabic, Old High German, Icelandic, Provencal, and Old French. It need hardly be said that the mixture, though palatable, was good neither for science nor theology. But to understand the carvings and stained glass in medieval churches one needs the *Physiologus* as a guide. The Pelican, reviving her young by her blood, became a symbol of the Holy Communion, and the feast of Corpus Christi.

A. The Panther

The prophet prophesied and said: 'I will be to Ephraim as a panther' (Hos. 5, 14).

Physiologus relates of the panther that he has the following attribute: He is the friendliest of all beasts, but he is an enemy to dragons. He is as many-coloured as Joseph's coat. He is very quiet and gentle. When he has eaten and satisfied himself, he goes to sleep in his cavern. And on the third day he awakes out of his sleep, and cries with a loud voice. And the animals both far and near hear his voice. And after the cry a very pleasant odour proceeds out of his mouth, and the animals follow the pleasant odour, and run to be near him.

So also, when Christ awoke the third day and rose from the dead, he spread a pleasant odour of peace both far and near. Very manifold is the true wisdom of God. The psalmist says: 'The Queen stands at thy right hand clothed in a garment of gold and many colours' (Psa. 45, 9–14), which is the Church. Very manifold is Christ, because he himself is chastity, temperance, charity, faith, virtue, patience, harmony, and peace.

Finely spoke *Physiologus* of the Panther.

Panther: on Norman arch, Alne, N. Yorks

B. The Pelican

The holy prophet David sings: 'I am like a pelican in the wilderness' (Psa. 102, 7).

Physiologus relates of the pelican that he loves his young very much. When the young are born, and as soon as they are a little grown, they strike their parents in the face. Then the parents strike back again, and kill them. But presently the parents begin to have compassion on them and, after they have mourned three whole days over the children they killed, the mother comes at the end of the third day and opens her side and drops her blood on the dead bodies of the young and arouses the life in them.

So also said our Lord by the prophet Isaiah: 'I have raised up sons, but they have fallen away from me.' (Isa. 1, 2). God has created us, and we have fought against him. We, the creatures, have set ourselves against the Creator. Yet, when he came to the height of the Cross he opened his side and dropped blood and water to our redemption and eternal life—the blood because he said: 'He took the cup and gave thanks', and the water because of the baptism of penitence.

The Pelican in her Piety
From a misericord at Wells, c.1330

8.14 Architectural Daring

The universities turned away from the natural sciences, and no progress was made until the Renaissance. Technology was different, though it was never part of the university curriculum and there were no technical colleges. It should be mentioned, however, that the educational blindness to science was not accompanied by a neglect of mathematics. Almost every generation brought radical changes in architecture, and especially in the design of churches. These changes were made by daring experimenters. Something of the magnitude of their technical achievement can be seen in this drawing of a section of Reims Cathedral, built in the first half of the thirteenth century. How to counteract the outward thrust of the high roof of the nave without sacrificing the aisles was solved by flying buttresses, and that necessity was turned into ornament and further beauty.

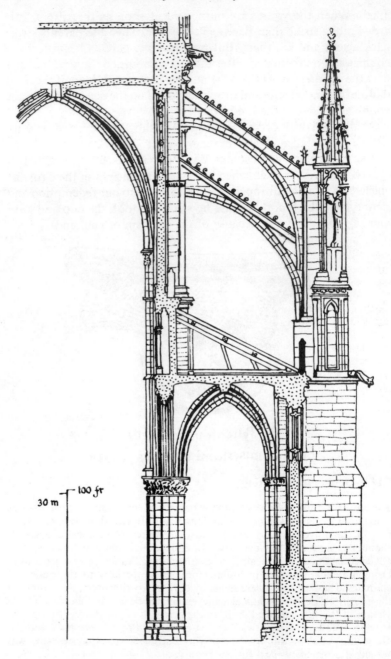

30 m — 100 fr

8.15   Aquinas on Predestination

Nothing could be more alien from the *Physiologus* than the mind of Aquinas (*c.* 1225–1274) who accepted the material creation as a rational universe, governed by law and explicable by the light of reason. In him the medieval scholar's faith reached its culmination. He was born in Aquino in South Italy, a nobleman's youngest son. At the age of five he was sent to school at Monte Cassino, but at fifteen he took himself off from the religious seclusion of Benedict's famous monastery to the exciting life of Naples, the university recently founded by the highly secular emperor, Frederick II. There he encountered and rapidly absorbed the full impact of Aristotle, who was then for the first time available to western scholars in his entirety. He also met and was captured by the enthusiasm of the new mendicant orders. When he was nineteen he joined the Dominicans against his family's wishes—his brothers kidnapped him and held him prisoner for a year. Then the Order sent him to Paris. For nearly thirty years he lived the life of one who was both a scholar and a friar. He taught at Cologne, at Paris, in Orvieto, in Rome, in Naples, in Viterbo and once again in Paris. His journeys were made on foot in strict fulfilment of his devotion to voluntary poverty. Intellectually his care was to integrate philosophical rigour with Christian revelation, to hold (as Josef Pieper says) 'Bible' and 'Aristotle' together in a world in which others were splitting them apart. His works are so closely argued, each part leading relentlessly to the next, and so lengthy, filling many bookshelves, that no single extract can indicate the majestic, unified structure of the whole. The following extract is however characteristic of a thinker who in our own time, five hundred years after his death, has gained a new importance. Other extracts are given in 7.21, 9.11, 9.18, 9.19, 9.31, 14.15.

If divine Providence be the direct cause of everything that happens in this world, at least of the good things, does it not then seem that everything must come about of necessity? Take God's knowledge first: that cannot fail, and, therefore, if he knows an event, is it not bound to happen? . . .

The difficulty comes about when the activity of God's mind is reduced to the condition of our own mental processes. With regard to knowledge, note that events in time stand in a different relation to a mind that is inside the time-series and to a mind that is entirely outside. *Before* and *after* in magnitude apply also to motion, and consequently to time [Aristotle: *Ethics* viii]. Accordingly, we may draw a useful analogy from locations in space. Imagine many people marching in column along a road. Each of them knows the men in front of and behind him by reference to his own position. But an observer high above, while he sees how one precedes another, takes in the column as a whole without having to work from a position inside it. Human thoughts, however, are qualified by time . . . for it takes time for the mind to combine or divide parts [Aristotle: *De Anima* iii]. We know events as past, present, or future. Past events we remember; present events we perceive actually existing somehow through our senses; future events we know, not in themselves, for they are not yet in existence, but in their causes with certitude if the causal system is governed by determinism, with shrewd suspicion if we know how the causes usually act, but not at all if the causes are indeterminate. What can be is known only from what is; potentiality is discovered only from actuality [Aristotle: *Metaphysics* ix].

Now God is wholly outside any system measured by time. He dwells at the summit of eternity in a duration entire and complete all at once. The whole stream of things below him falls under his single and simple regard. With one glance he sees all the events that take place in time, and he sees them just as they are in themselves. The causal order is appreciated, but events are not seen as past or future to him. They are eternally in his presence, and he sees them, to whatever period they may belong, as we see a man actually sitting down, not merely going to sit down.

Because we see somebody actually seated, it does not follow that the sitting down was a necessary (inevitable) event, not a free choice. For contingency [an event liable but not certain to occur] and necessity is defined by reference of effect to cause. Past all doubt the man is actually sitting down, and in that sense the event is settled and beyond recall: what is is. God most certainly and unmistakably always knows everything that takes place in time: but on that account it does not follow that they are thereby necessary, and not contingent. *Source:* Aquinas, Perihermenias I, Lect. 14.

CHAPTER NINE

SALVATION
AND THE SACRAMENTS

The Last Things

9.1 DEATH

When a man came to die the Church was with him to hear his last confession, give him absolution and Christian burial, and speed him on his way with the triumphant commendation of the Roman Church:

Go forth, Christian soul, from this world: in the name of the Father Almighty who created thee: in the name of our Lord Jesus Christ, the Son of the living God, who died for thee: in the name of the Holy Spirit who was shed upon thee: in the name of angels and archangels, in the name of thrones and dominations, in the name of principalities and powers, in the name of Cherubim and Seraphim, in the name of patriarchs and prophets, in the name of holy apostles and evangelists, in the name of holy martyrs and confessors, in the name of monks and hermits, in the name of holy virgins and all the saints of God. Today in the heavenly Jerusalem let thy peace and habitation be, through Jesus Christ our Lord.

9.2 THE CASE OF HAMO BLUND 1197

Because a man's last will was closely associated in the middle ages with his last confession, it fell to the Church to supervise its making and its carrying out.

Relatives with the help of a complaisant priest might conspire to persuade a dying man to leave his money in a way that offended the current sense of what was right. But if there was a strong man in the position of the man's parish priest he might intervene, even after the man's death, to see that what he regarded as justice was done. Abbot Samson of St. Edmundsbury was such a man, as Jocelyn of Brakelond tells in his *Chronicle*:

Hamo Blund, one of the richest men of the town, was at the point of death, and would hardly be persuaded to make any testament. At length, when nobody but his brother, his wife, and the chaplain could hear, he made a testament to the paltry amount of three marks. And when after his death the abbot heard this, he summoned those three persons before him and sharply reproved them, because the brother, who was heir, and the wife, wishing to have all, would not allow anyone to have access to the sick man. And then in their presence the abbot said: 'I was his bishop and had the cure of his soul, and, lest his ignorance should imperil me, his priest and confessor,—for not being present I could not counsel him—I will now do my duty, albeit at the eleventh hour. I order that all his chattels and the debts due to him, which it is said are worth two hundred marks, be set down in writing and that one share be given to the heir, and another to the wife, and a third to his poor cousins and other poor folk. As to his horse which was led before the bier and offered to St. Edmund, I order that it be remitted and returned, for it is not fit that our church be polluted by the gift of one who died intestate, and who is commonly accused of having habitually lent his money at usury. By the face of God! if anything of this sort happens again in my days, the delinquent shall not be buried in the churchyard.' When they heard this they retired in confusion.

9.3   HELL AND PURGATORY EXPLAINED   *c.* 1220

Caesarius of Heisterbach, novice master at a Cistercian monastery in the Rhineland, was a born story-teller. These are extracts from his *Dialogue on Miracles*. The mouth of Hell, identified here with the crater of a volcano, was a universal terror to medieval man. It was pictured in most churches and many manuscripts such as that shown in Plate 6.

There are two places God has prepared as an eternal reward for man's daily work: heaven and hell, heaven for the good and hell for the wicked. The judge at the end shall say to the good, 'Come O blessed of my Father inherit the kingdom prepared for you from the foundation of the world' (Matt. 25, 34); but to the others he shall say, 'Depart from me you cursed, into the eternal fire prepared for the devil and his angels' (Matt. 25, 41). How great is the reward of the good, how indescribable, how wonderful is summed up by Isaiah in these few words: 'Eye has not seen, nor ear heard, what thou hast prepared for those that love thee' (Isaiah 64, 4 as quoted in 1 Cor. 2, 9 A.V.).

Of the pains of hell, which are countless, nine are specially noted: pitch, snow, darkness, the worm, scourging, chains, festering, shame, terror. These nine torments have no end.

There is still a third place after this life, appointed for some chosen for purging, called purgatory. This lasts until the day of judgment.

How great is the glory of the good, or the punishment of the wicked, or how those in purgatory may be given help, you may reckon from the following examples.

Of the punishment of a steward of Kolmere who was sent into Stromboli
Once upon a time some Swedes were returning from a pilgrimage to Jerusalem. As they sailed near the ever-burning fires of Stromboli words sounded from it:

'Welcome, welcome, our friend the steward of Kolmere. It is cold; stoke up the fire for him.'

They knew the man, noted the day and the hour and when they returned home found that that steward had died just at that time. They went to his wife and told her what they had heard.

'If that's the state of affairs,' she said, 'I had better go to his aid.'

And she left all and went on a pilgrimage to the shrines of the saints, beseeching God with alms and prayers to save his soul.

Of the Purgatory of the monk William
Twelve years ago a monk of ours named William died. He entered our Order as a boy, a young boy for he was really pure. He was of noble birth, but his virtuous character ennobled him more. When the year of his probation was completed, he fell ill the next day and died a few days later, making a holy end.

Immediately after his death he appeared to one of the brothers and, questioned about his condition, said he was in pain. The other wept in terror at these words.

'If you who never sinned are in pain, what will become of me a sinner and others like me?'

The dead man comforted him thus: 'Do not weep, for the only pain I suffer is that I have not yet seen God.'

He was right to think that glory deferred is painful. 'Hope deferred maketh the heart sick.' And he added:

'How glorious shall be one who comes immediately into the presence of God! Ask our lord abbot to order prayers for me at the chapter and to say a collect for me himself, that I may be freed.'

'Which collect?'

'That of St. Michael.'

When the vision was told to our lord abbot Henry, he himself at once celebrated the mass of archangel Michael, and in the chapter ordered psalm 42, *As the hart panteth after the waterbrooks*, to be said for seven days by all. Oh the wonderful power of their prayers! When

Conrad, now prior of Marienstatt, was standing in the choir and in a light sleep, he saw, at the verse of the psalm, *My God, early will I seek thee*, William standing under the cloak of the blessed Mother of God. He was saying most thankfully:

'Now I am completely freed.'

Then, appearing again to the monk, he testified that he had only been in purgatory for seven days, absent from the face of God. And he told him much about the condition of souls.

Novice: Then purgatory is an earthly paradise.

Monk: Well if in fact souls are freed from their bodies there and the sight of God denied them, that delightful place is to them a purgatory.

9.4   A VISION OF HEAVEN   *c.* 1100

This vision of the heavenly Jerusalem comes from a poem by Hildebert of Lavardin (1056–1133), bishop of Le Mans, and was probably written during a period of exile in England. The translation is by William Crashaw (father of the poet Richard) and was first published in his *Manuell for True Catholics* in 1611.

In Sion, lodge me, Lord, for pity—
Sion, David's kingly city,
Built by Him that's only good;
Whose gates be of the Cross's wood;
Whose keys are Christ's undoubted word;
Whose dwellers fear none but the Lord.
Whose walls are stone, strong, quick and bright,
Whose keeper is the Lord of Light:
Here the light doth never cease,
Endless Spring and endless peace;
Here is music, heaven filling,
Sweetness evermore distilling;
Here is neither spot nor taint,
No defect, nor no complaint;
No man crookèd, great nor small,
But to Christ conformèd all.
Blessed town, divinely gracèd
On a rock so strongly placèd,
Thee I see and thee I long for,
Thee I seek and thee I groan for,
O what joy thy dwellers taste
All in pleasure first and last!

What full enjoying bliss divine;
What jewels on thy walls do shine!
Ruby, jacinth, chalcedon,
Known to them within alone.
In this glorious company
In the streets of Sion, I
With Job, Moses, and Eliah
Will sing the heavenly Alleluia.

Amen.

9.5   HEAVEN WELL LOST   *c.* 1200

It is well to hold the balance. A modern note, or perhaps an antique echo, can be heard a little later in the simple romantic love story of *Aucassin and Nicolette*. The story comes from Provence. In this extract Aucassin says what he thinks of the warning he had just been given that, if he took Nicolette to bed, he would never go to heaven. The 'vair and the grey' refers to precious furs as named in heraldry.

What have I to do in heaven? I have no wish to go there unless I have Nicolette, my very sweet friend whom I love so deeply. For to heaven go only such people as these: doddering old priests and lamed and maimed old dotards who grovel all day and all night before the altars and in ancient crypts, and those in old rags and tatters and old worn-out cloaks, who are naked and barefooted and barearsed, and die of hunger and thirst and cold and misery. Those are they who go to heaven and with them I'll have nothing to do.

But to hell will I go. For to hell go fair clerks and handsome knights killed in tournaments and glorious battles, good soldiers and noble men. With these I wish to go. And there go the lovely ladies of gentle birth who have two lovers, or three, besides their lords. And there go the gold and the silver, the vair and the grey; and there go the harpers and the jongleurs and the kings of the world. With these I want to go, so long as I have Nicolette, my very sweet friend, with me.

The Seven Sacraments

By the eleventh century the Church recognized seven sacraments, as it exalted seven virtues and warned against seven deadly sins. Each of the seven sacraments are here introduced by the relevant passage from the metrical catechism issued both in Latin and English by John Thoresby archbishop of York on November 25th, 1357. As the order of the seven varies, we follow that of Thoresby. He, in 1361, laid the first stone of the choir of York Minster, in cubic capacity the largest in Christendom.

9.6 Baptism

The first sacrament of seven is our baptism
That we take the first time that we become Christian,
In which both the first sin that we are born with
And allkind other sin is washed away
That we are defiled with ere we take it.
And the truth of holy church is taken therein
Without which no sinful man's soul may be saved.

9.7   THE FATE OF THE UNBAPTIZED   *c.* 1150

The official doctrine on the fate of the unbaptized according to Canon Law,
the law of the church, is given by Gratian, greatest of Church lawyers:

Hold fast to this truth, that not only men of rational age, but even
babes who, having begun to live in the mother's womb, either die
there, or die after birth unbaptized in the name of Father, Son, and
Holy Spirit, pass from this world to be punished in eternal fire.

9.8   SOULS IN LIMBO   *c.* 1314

But Gratian's formulation proved too hard to bear. It was no doubt taught
from many pulpits, but more thoughtful and imaginative minds puzzled until
they found at least a partial way out. Aquinas developed a theory that the
pain unbaptized infants suffered was purely the negative one of deprivation
of the vision of God. Dante, following his teaching, placed them, along with
the great and good men of antiquity, in Limbo, the first circle of hell. Dante's
guide through hell in the Divine Comedy was Virgil, himself one of these
men.

Here was no noise, no cry of agony,
    Only the susurration of a sigh
    That shivered through the everlasting air.

No torment was the cause of such a sorrow,
    Though suffered by this world's vast multitudes,
    The little children with the men and women.

My good guide spoke to me: 'Do you not wish
    To know about these spirits that you see?
    Before you go further, learn—for fear you wrong them—

That they were blameless, for they merited
    Nothing but praise, yet none had been baptised,
    That gateway to the faith which you profess.

They lived before the time of Christendom,
  Not knowing how to love God as they should,
  And I myself, alas, am one of them.

For this defect and not for other evils
  We suffer loss, afflicted only thus:
  That here we live, and long, but have no hope.

9.9   BAPTISM AND THE PARISH PRIEST   *c.* 1400

At the end of the fourteenth century John Myrc, prior of a monastery at Lilleshall in Shropshire, wrote *Instructions for Parish Priests* in English. The incurably legal outlook of the middle ages is conspicuous here. It was important that a baptism should be valid as the terrible precision of 9.7 showed. Myrc did well to be careful.

If any child mischance at home
And is baptized and given his name,
When it is brought to church to thee,
As it later ought to be,
Then must thou full subtilly
Ask of them that were thereby
How they did then in that case
When the child baptizèd was,
Whether the words were said aright
And not disordered in that plight ...
English or Latin, whichever is saith,
It is sufficient to the faith
If the words are said in order.
'I christen thee or baptise thee
In the name of the Father, and the Son, and the Holy Spirit,
In nomine patris et filii et spiritus sancti.'

And though, I say, they often use
Sorry Latin in this wise:
'In nomina patria et filia spiritus sanctia'
Of these words take thou no heed;
The christening is good, no dread,
If their intention and their wit
Was for to baptize it.
So that they hold the first syllàble
The baptism is good, no fable.
Pa of patris, fi of filii, spi of spiritus sancti ...
But if they said the words amiss—

In nomine filii et patris
Et spiritus sancti—
Then must thou, to make it true,
Say the service all anew.

9.10   Confirmation

The Synod of Exeter, 1287, ordered children 'to receive the sacrament of confirmation within three years of their birth, if they have the opportunity of being brought to a bishop.' There are some 30 'seven sacrament fonts' in East Anglia whose panels all portray confirmation of infants in arms, but in practice the villagers waited until the bishop came their way.

The second sacrament is Confirming
That the bishop gives to them that are baptized,
Gives through his power to them that take it
The grace and the gifts of the Holy Ghost,
To make them more stalwart than they were before
To stand against the fiend and deadly sin,
Which none has power to do but the bishop alone,
Who has the state and the stead of Christ's apostles.

9.11   AQUINAS ON CONFIRMATION

The sacraments of the New Law are instituted to produce special effects of grace. Accordingly, where a special occasion occurs, there a special sacrament is provided. Things of sense bear the likeness of things of mind, and turning points in the life of the body have their equivalents in the life of the spirit. Coming of age ends a definite period; after that a man is capable of acting for himself: 'When I was a child, I spoke as a child, I understood as a child, I thought as a child; but when I became a man I put away childish things' (1 Cor. 13, 11). By the process of being born we receive bodily life, by the process of growing up we become adult. So it is in the life of the spirit. Born by baptism, we reach our full stature by confirmation.
Source: Thomas Aquinas, *Summa Theologica*, 3a, 62.

9.12   Penance

The third sacrament is called penance,
That is soothfast forethinking we have of our sin,
Without will or thought to turn again to it.

And this must have three things if it be steadfast:
One is sorrow of heart that we have sinned;
Another is open shrift of our mouth, how we have sinned;
And the third is right making amends for what we have sinned.
These three with good will to forsake our sin,
Cleanses and washes us of all kinds of sin.

Penance; the devil departing.
14th century misericord in
New College chapel, Oxford.

9.13 THE PRIEST IN THE CONFESSIONAL

This was the first duty of the parish priest according to Myrc. He gave it most
space in his *Instructions*. Housel means receiving Communion.

When a man hath done a sin,
Look he lie not long therein,
But anon that he him shrive
Be it husband, be it wife,
Lest he forget by Easter Day
And out of mind it go away.

Women that be with child also,
Thou must teach them what to do.
When their time is nearly come,
Bid them do thus, all and some.
Teach them to come and shrive them clean
And also housel themselves at e'en,

For dread of peril that may befall
In their travailing that come shall...

And first when any shriven would be,
Teach him to kneel down on his knee.
The first thing thou must ask him then
Is whether he be thy parishen.
And if he answer and say nay
Teach him to fare home on his way
Unless he hath leave of his priest
To be a-shriven where he list...

For causes such as these, no nay,
He may have leave to go his way:
[i.e. go to a priest outside his parish]
If he knew by ready token
That his shrift would be made open,
Or if himself had done a sin
With the priest's own sibling kin...
Their shrift lawfully you may hear
Of scholar, sailor, or passenger...

Teach him to kneel down on his knee,
Poor man or rich man whether he be;
Over your eyes then pull your hood,
And hear his shrift with mild mood.
But when a woman cometh to thee
Be sure her face thou dost not see,
But teach her to kneel down thee by,
And thy face somewhat from her wry.

Still as stone do thou sit,
And be careful not to spit
Nor cough at hearing of the sins,
Nor twist about with thy shins,
Lest she suppose you make that stir
For loathing what you hear from her...

9.14   THE PERSISTENCE OF MAGIC

At confession the priest was likely to discover the survival of many
pre-Christian religions and magical practices. Berthold of Regensburg, the
noted Franciscan preacher, believed that the salvation of many villagers was
imperilled by the village witch:

'One woman baptizes a waxen image, another a piece of wood, another a dead man's bone, all for working some charm. One bewitches with herbs, another with holy chrism, another with God's body.... She conjures to get a husband, she conjures when she has got him; she conjures before her child is born, conjures before it is baptized, conjures after its baptism.'

Earlier, Burchardt, bishop of Worms, had produced a long list of questions to be asked of penitents to find out how far they indulged in these survivals of the old religions.

c. 1020

Have you kept the New Year's Day with pagan rites by doing anything more on that day than you usually do on the day before or after?

Have you sat on the roof of your house, having drawn a circle round you with a sword, so that you might see and know what was going to happen to you in the coming year?

Have you sat on a bull's hide at the cross-roads, so that there too you may learn your future?

Have you caused loaves to be made in your name on New Year's Eve, so that you might foresee a year of prosperity for yourself, if the loaves rose high and were close-textured?

Have you done what some do on the first of January, the octave of Christmas Day, spin, weave, and sew on that holy night so that whatever task they begin on that New Year is begun on the devil's instigation?

Have you done as some women do at certain times of the year, prepared a table in your house with food and drink and three extra knives, so that those three sisters whom ancient ignorance and folly called the Fates should get refreshment there?

Have you taken the power and Name of divine piety and handed it over to the devil? I mean, have you believed that those you call the sisters can be of any help to you now or in the future?

9.15   ABELARD'S ADVICE TO PENITENTS

There are doctors so unskilled that it is dangerous or useless to entrust sick people to them. Similarly many priests may be found who, without faith or discretion, will lightly reveal sins confessed to them. To confess to such men is not only useless: it may be dangerous.

They do not pray with intention and are not worthy to have their petitions heard. They do not know the canon law and prescribe excessive penances. They often promise, as a consequence of those penances, a false security. The hopes they instil are disappointed. To quote the scriptures they are blind leading the blind and both will fall into a pit (Matt. 15, 14). Also, as we said, by turning confidences into gossip they arouse the indignation of their penitents. Instead of healing sin they cause it to break out afresh and those who hear them blabbing resolve to abstain from confession. The priest's betrayals of his vows, whether from anger or frivolity, is a serious sin against the Church. It also causes serious danger to the penitents.

On account of these dangers some penitents decide to go to others whom they consider better fitted to deal with their case, and you cannot blame them. Their resort to an abler physician is entirely reasonable. And if they can get their own priests to agree to the change it is even more commendable, for they make the change in a spirit of humble obedience. On the other hand arrogant priests may forbid it, feeling that it is an insult to their own competence if a better physician is asked for. But let the sick man who cares for his health insist on receiving the medicine he believes is the best, and the wiser counsel. If one is given a guide who turns out to be blind, one is not obliged to follow him into the pit. It is far better to choose a guide who can see.

Source: Abelard, *Ethics.*

9.16   The Sacrament of the Altar

Archbishop Thoresby insisted in his catechism that every layman should communicate once a year at Easter. Clearly he did not expect that many would communicate more frequently. 'Pasque' is Easter, 'skilwise' means 'reasonable'.

The fourth is the sacrament of the altar,
Christ's own body in likeness of bread,
As whole as he took it of that blessed maiden,
Which each man and woman that is of age
Ought for to receive once in the year,
That is to say at Pasque as holy church uses,
When they are cleansed of sin through penance,
On pain of being cast out of holy church.
But if they forbear for skilwise cause
That ought to be known to him that shall give it.
For he that takes it worthily takes his salvation,
And whoso unworthily takes his damnation.

9.17 THE LAYMAN AT MASS

The mass was essential. Like baptism everybody needed it; but not once for good, like baptism, but many times over. Alive or dead, you could not have too many masses said for you. Every layman's fate was literally in the priest's hands. He alone could offer the sacrifice of the mass for the living and the dead. Compared with earlier and later times the layman's part, the congregation's part, in the thirteenth and fourteenth centuries, was passive. In the earlier part of the middle ages there had been what would now be called a dialogue mass, but the decay of Latin as a spoken tongue and the refusal to allow the language which people spoke to be used in the mass combined to confine laymen to 'hearing mass'. There thus came to be a dichotomy between the laity and the clergy in the way in which they worshipped at mass.

The English metrical aid to devotion usually known as the Lay-Folk's Mass-book faithfully reproduces English fourteenth century practice. The laity carry on with their private devotions while the priest celebrates. The moments picked out for their special attention are the reading of the Gospel and the Elevation, when after the consecration the host was raised by the priest. The accent is on the sacrifice of the mass offered by the priest and not on the communion—there was no general communion.

Laymen who had mastered the suggestions in the Lay-Folk's Mass-book and followed them would have been able to worship profitably. But they must have been a minority. Many simply did not understand what was going on, and gossiped happily to their neighbours: 'The sermon we can follow every word, but not the Mass. We don't know what is being sung or read, we just can't understand it.' These words from a sermon by Berthold of Regensburg ring true.

And then when thou hast this all done
Kneel down on thy knees anon;
If they sing Mass or if they say,
Thy pater-noster rehearse alway,
Till deacon or priest the gospel read.
Stand up then and take good heed
For then the priest flitteth his book
North to that other altar nook,
And makes a cross upon the letter
With his thumb—he speeds the better—
And such another on his face
For he has mickle need of grace...
At the beginning heed thou take,
A large cross on thee thou make,
Stand and say on this manère
As thou mayst see is written here:
  In the name of Father, Son & Holy Ghost
  A steadfast God of mights the most,

Be God's word welcome unto me
Joy and Love, Lord, be to thee.
Whilst it is read, speak thou nought
But think on him that dear thee bought,
Saying thus in thy mind
As thou shalt after written find:
  Jesu, mine, grant me thy grace
  And of amendment might and space,
  Thy word to keep and do thy will,
  The good to choose and leave the ill...
Repeat this often in thy thought
Till gospel be done forget it not.
When the time is near of sacring
A little bell is wont to ring.
Then shalt thou do reverence
To Jesus Christ's own presence
That may loose all baleful bands.
Kneeling hold up both thy hands
And so the Elevation thou behold,
For this is he whom Judas sold,
And then was scourged and killed on rood,
And there for mankind shed his blood,
And died and rose and went to heaven,
And yet he'll come with justice even
To every man for what he's done:
That same is he you look upon.
....
Such prayer then thou make
As likes best thee to take...

9.18 THE BODY AND BLOOD OF CHRIST

The authoritative definition of the nature of the presence of Christ in the Eucharist came with the Third Lateran Council in 1215 during Innocent III's pontificate. The almost equally authoritative explanation, satisfying in terms of the current philosophy, came from Thomas Aquinas a generation later—probably about 1270.

On whether bread can be converted into the body of Christ: I reply that this conversion is not like natural conversions, but is wholly supernatural, effected solely by the power of God. All conversion which takes place according to the laws of nature is a change in form.... But God can produce not only a formal conversion, i.e. the superseding of one form by another in the same subject, but the conversion of the whole being, i.e. the conversion of the whole 'substance' of A into the whole 'substance' of B. And this is done in this sacrament by the power of God, for the whole 'substance' of bread is converted into the whole 'substance' of Christ's body.... Hence this conversion is properly called transubstantiation.

On whether in this sacrament the 'accidents' of bread and wine remain after the conversion: I reply that it is apparent to sense that after consecration all the 'accidents' of bread and wine remain. And this indeed happens with reason, by divine providence. First, because it is not customary but abhorrent for men to eat man's flesh and to drink man's blood. Therefore Christ's flesh and blood are set before us to be taken under the appearances of those things which are of frequent use, namely bread and wine. Secondly, lest this sacrament should be mocked at by the infidels, if we ate our Lord under his proper appearance. Thirdly, in order that, while we take the Lord's body and blood invisibly, this fact may avail towards the merit of faith.

Source: Thomas Aquinas, *Summa Theologica,* III, Q. 75, Articles 4, 5.

9.19   A PRAYER OF PREPARATION

The Eucharistic theology of Aquinas naturally found its expression in worship. The immensely popular feast of Corpus Christi (Thursday after Trinity Sunday) was proclaimed by the pope in 1264, largely as a result of the influence of a nun from Liège. Thomas Aquinas wrote for it the well-known hymn, *Pange lingua gloriosi corporis mysterium,* 'Now my tongue the mystery telling of the glorious body sing'. Though he treated the mass in daunting academic fashion in his *Summa Theologica,* what it really meant to him is best shown in that hymn and in his beautiful prayer of preparation.

Almighty and everlasting God, I approach the sacrament of thy only-begotten Son, our Lord Jesus Christ. As sick I come to the physician of life, as unclean to the fountain of mercy, as blind to the light of eternal splendour, as needy to the Lord of heaven and earth, as naked to the King of glory, as a lost sheep to the Good Shepherd....

I therefore pray thee of the abundance of thine infinite mercy to heal my sickness, to wash my foulness, to lighten my darkness, to enrich my poverty, to clothe my nakedness; that I may receive the Bread of angels, the King of kings and Lord of lords, with such reverence and fear, such contrition and love, such faith and purity, such devotion and humility, as is expedient for the welfare of my soul.

And grant me, merciful God, so to receive the body of thy only-begotten Son our Lord Jesus Christ, which he took of the Virgin Mary, that I may be incorporated into his mystical body and ever reckoned among his members. And O most loving Father, grant that he whom I now purpose to receive under a veil I may at length behold with open face, even thy beloved Son, who with thee and the Holy Spirit liveth and reigneth ever one God, world without end.

9.20   FAITH ENOUGH FOR TWO

The doctrine of transubstantiation was not easy for some devout and willing minds to accept. There is pastoral wisdom in Bernard of Clairvaux's handling of this problem with one of this monks. No doubt he knew his man.

A certain monk insisted that the bread and wine mixed with water on the altar could not possibly be transubstantiated into the real body and blood of our Lord Jesus Christ. So he scorned to take the life-giving sacrament as useless for his soul. At last the brothers noticed that he never partook of the sacrament ... and reported it to the venerable abbot, who summoned him and reasoned against his disbelief with all the wisdom he possessed.

But the monk said: 'No words can bring me to believe that the bread and wine on the altar are the real body and blood of Christ, so I know that I must go to hell.'

At this the man of God, who always showed a wonderful strength of authority in extreme difficulties, cried aloud:

'What! a monk of mine go to hell? God forbid! If you have no faith of your own, yet in virtue of your vow of obedience I order you to go and take the communion with *my* faith!'

So the monk, as he was bound to obey, though seemingly utterly without faith, came to the altar and communicated, and he was immediately enlightened by the holy father's merit and received a faith in the sacraments which he kept untarnished to the day of his death.

Source: John the Hermit, *Life of St. Bernard.*

9.21   FAITH INTO SUPERSTITION   *c.* 1220

Caesarius of Heisterbach had improving stories to tell his novices about the superstitious uses to which uninstructed lay folk would put the Blessed Sacrament. They were not surprising perhaps in view of the general ignorance and of the wide persistence of magical rites (see 9.14). And while Caesarius himself thought these abuses very wrong, he did not question their physical effectiveness.

A certain woman kept many bees, which did not thrive, but died in great numbers. As she sought everywhere for a remedy, she was told that if she placed the Lord's body among them this plague would soon cease. So she went to church and, seeming to communicate, took the Lord's body; but she took it from her mouth as soon as the priest had gone and laid it in one of her hives.

Mark the marvellous power of God! These little insects, recognising the might of their creator, built for their sweetest guest out of their sweetest honeycombs a tiny chapel of marvellous workmanship, and there they built an altar of the same material and laid upon it this most holy body. And God blessed their labours.

In process of time the woman opened this hive and noticed this chapel. Then she hastened to the priest and confessed all she had done and seen. Taking his parishioners with him he came to the hive and they drove away the bees that hovered around and buzzed in praise of their creator. Marvelling at the little chapel with its walls and windows, roof and tower, door and altar, they brought back the Lord's body with praise and glory to the church. For though God be marvellous in the saints, yet these his smallest creatures preached him yet more marvellously.

9.22 Unction

'Extreme Unction' is the last sacrament given to a dying person. His eyes, mouth, nose, ears, hands and feet are anointed with consecrated olive oil.

The fifth sacrament is the last anointing,
With oil that is hallowed and handled by priest,
To them that he wots are of reasonable age
And that he sees certainly in peril of death.
It lightens and alleviates their sickness
If God wills that they turn again to health,
Gives also forgiveness of venial sins
And lessens the pain if they pass from hence.

9.23 Ordination

The sixth sacrament of holy church is Order
That gives power to them that rightwisely take it
To serve in holy church according to status,

And to those that take the order of priest
To serve and administer the sacraments of church
That fall to those of their state and degree.

9.24   THE STRUGGLE FOR CLERICAL CELIBACY

The marriage of priests was common in the Dark Ages, and has always been
the practice for parish priests in the Orthodox Church. The first extract shows
how Gregory VII, one of the strongest popes, tried to stamp it out in Catholic
countries. He insisted on celibacy for sub-deacons and deacons as well as
priests. The second extract shows that Gregory was unsuccessful—probably
because he was in effect trying to impose celibacy on a quite impracticably
high proportion of educated people. For the nature of sex and its place in
Christian morals see 9.31–32 and Vol I pp. 280–5.

A. To Bishop Otto of Constance   1074

The body of the Catholic Church consists wholly of virgins, married
people, or those who hold themselves in restraint. Therefore all
outside those three classes can not be counted among the sons of the
Church or inside the bounds of the Christian religion. So if we know
for certain that even one of the lowest laymen is living with a
concubine, we should cut him off completely from the Lord's body
and blood until he has done due penance. Then how can any one be a
distributor or server of the holy sacrament if he cannot possibly be a
partaker of them? Furthermore we are impelled to this course by
order of the blessed pope Leo who forbad subdeacons to marry; and
his successors in the holy Roman Church, especially that famous
doctor Gregory, have given that decree such legal force that the
marriage bond has been absolutely forbidden to the three orders of
priests, deacons, and subdeacons.

B. Innocent III to the Bishop of Winchester   1205

It has reached our hearing that many sons of priests in the diocese of
Winchester have churches where their fathers ministered immediately
before them, to the dishonour of ecclesiastical dignity and canon
law.... Where you know of any persons in your diocese who have
succeeded their fathers in churches, we command you by apostolic
letter to remove them completely without appeal. Then you should
diligently institute other suitable persons at the presentation of those
who own it. But if these refuse, from favour to those whom they have
already presented there, or from malice or wilfulness, though often
warned, then rely on our authority and obedience to God and
proceed with institutions in these churches.

9.25   THE STRUGGLE FOR CLERICAL LITERACY

One of the major problems the Church had to face was the inadequacy of the educational system to provide enough priests to staff the parishes who really knew what they were doing. The illiteracy of many clergy was a root cause of the failure of the Church to live up to what the Church preached.

1222

Acts of the Chapter held by William, dean of Salisbury, at Sonning, in the year of our Lord 1222, on the Friday before the feast of St. Martin....

Vitalis, a priest, perpetual vicar of Sonning presented the chaplain (his curate) Simon whom he had recently engaged until Michaelmas. When examined as to his orders, he said he was ordained subdeacon at Oxford by a certain Irish bishop named Albin, then suffragan to the bishop of Lincoln, from whom he also received deacon's orders. He received priest's orders from Hugh (of Wells), now bishop of Lincoln, four years ago.

He was examined in the Gospel for the first Sunday in Advent (Matt. 21, 1f) and was found incapable of understanding what he was reading. Then he was tried in the canon of the Mass: *Te igitur, clementissime Pater* ... *rogamus* (Thee, therefore, most merciful Father   we pray). He knew not the case of *te* (accusative), nor by what word it was governed (*rogamus*, we pray). When we asked him to concentrate and see which word could most fittingly govern it, he answered,

'*Pater*, for he governs all things.'

We asked him what *clementissime* was, its case, and how it was declined; he did not know. We asked him what *clemens* was; he did not know. Further, he could not tell one antiphon from another, nor the tunes of the hymns, not even the hymn *Nocte surgentes*. He did not know by heart any part of the services or the psalter. He said it was not proper to be examined before the Dean as he was already in holy orders. We asked him where he was when he had been ordained priest: he said he had forgotten. He is practically illiterate.

Source: Sarum Registers.

9.26   THE RIGHT TO A LIVING   1202

Clerks in holy orders without means of support were liable to get into trouble. They should not be ordained unless there was provision for them—not necessarily a parish but some office or patron to support them.

Innocent III to the Archbishop of Canterbury (Hubert Walter)

According to the Apostle, he who serves the altar should live from the altar and he who is chosen for a task should not be denied the reward (1 Cor. 9, 13).... Our beloved son Adam, the bearer of this letter, maintains that he was ordained deacon by you, but has not obtained any ecclesiastical benefice. Therefore we command you by apostolic letter that, if those to whom we have committed his examination find him to be a suitable person not unworthy of an ecclesiastical benefice, you should provide for him the necessities of life until, through you, he has secured an adequate benefice. If you ordained him on the presentation of some patron who can provide a suitable benefice for him, see that he (or if he be dead his successor) provides for him in the same way. If after examination he is found to be a proper person and if you have failed to provide for him, assuredly we will compel you to do so by ecclesiastical discipline as soon as we receive such a report. We do not wish to order what is unjust, but when we order what is just we wish to be effectively obeyed.

Source: Muniments of Canterbury Cathedral.

9.27   AN ORDINATION AT EXETER   1315

Walter Stapledon was bishop of Exeter from 1307 to 1326, when he was murdered by a London mob. When not busy on the king's affairs abroad or founding his college at Oxford (Exeter College), he was busy in his diocese as his Register shows. It includes this entry.

September 20 *Exeter*   Ordination held in Exeter Cathedral. Examiners for sub-deacons, deacons, and priests Masters R. de Coletone, then Official of the Lord Bishop; and N. de Hele; for the acolytes, J. de Lancestone; for those to receive the first tonsure, W. de Wolleghe.

> *Numbers Ordained:*
> Boys given the first tonsure—71
> Acolytes 25 (including 1 with dispensation for his illegitimacy; 2 Dominican friars)
> Coristes 6 (including 1 Franciscan, 1 Canon Regular)
> Sub-deacons 28 (including 1 Dominican; 3 Canons Regular; 3 Rectors)
> Deacons 31 (including 3 Canons Regular; 1 Rector)
> Priests 44 (including 2 Monks of Ford; 3 Rectors; 1 Vicar)

The examining chaplains found their task more straightforward than at a good many of Stapledon's ordinations at which several candidates for the various grades were marked 'not ordained because he could not sing', or 'not to be ordained to higher orders until he can sing'. Two years later three of the men ordained priests had to take an oath not to hear confessions, except in danger of death, until they had received the bishop's special licence, without which too they were not to receive a cure of souls.

9.28 DISORDERLY CLERKS 15 October 1330

The disadvantage of having clerks who would not sing the service properly is shown by an entry in the Register of Bishop Grandisson, Stapledon's successor:

We are gravely displeased to learn from reliable witnesses that certain vicars and other ministers of our cathedral church—to the offence of God, the notable hindrance of divine service, their own damnation, and the scandal of our cathedral church—are not afraid to indulge in irreverent and damnable disorders, laughings, gigglings, and other breaches of discipline during the solemn services. This is shameful to tell and horrible to hear.

To specify some out of many cases: those who stand in the upper stalls of the choir, with lights in reach at matins, deliberately pour the drippings or snuffings of the candles upon the heads or hair of those standing in the lower stalls. This is to raise laughter or start a quarrel, or at least create ill-will and silent hate among the ministers, which God forbid! . . .

Item: when some ministers sometimes (too often, we are sorry to say) make mistakes in singing or reading, others who know better (and should pity the ignorant and deplore their brethren's defects) give vent in the vulgar tongue to this response, in condemnation and derision:

'Cursed be he who told the last lie!'

9.29 THE GOOD PRIEST

Chaucer's priest was the rector (parson) of a widespread parish, not a congested city district. To confine 'town' to big urban communities is a modern usage. Chaucer's priest avoided the lure of London and the money to be made out of charities and guild chaplaincies. The last of these lines is a reference to St. John 10, 12. This version, though clarified for modern readers, keeps as close as possible to Chaucer's text.

A good man was there of religioun,
And was a poor parson of a town;
But rich he was of holy thought and work.
He was also a learned man, a clerk,
That Christes gospel trewely would preach;
His parishners devoutly would he teach.

Benign he was and wonder diligent,
And in adversity full patient,...

Wide was his parish, houses far asunder,
But he neglected not, for rain or thunder,
In sickness or in mischief, to visit
The furthest in his parish, much and lit,
Upon his feet and in his hand a stave.
This noble ensample to his sheep he gave,
That first he wrought, and afterwards he taught;
Out of the gospel he those words had caught
And this figure he added eke thereto,
That if gold rusts, what shall the iron do?
For if a priest be foul, on whom we trust,
No wonder that a simple man should rust.
And shame it is—let any priest take keep—
To see a shitten shepherd but clean sheep.
Well ought a priest ensample for to give
By his cleanness how that his sheep should live.
He did not set his benefice to hire
And leave his sheep encumbered in the mire,
And run away to London to St. Paul's
To seek him out a chantery for souls
Or with a Brotherhood to be enrolled,
But dwelt at home and tended well his fold,
So that the wolf would not make it miscarry.
He was a shepherd and no mercenary.

9.30 Matrimony

The seventh sacrament is Matrimony,
A lawful fastening betwixt man and woman
At their both assent to live together
Without any loosing while their lives last,
A remedy of sin and a getting of grace
If taken in good intent and cleanness of life.

9.31   AQUINAS ON MARRIAGE

Married friendship is useful, delightful, and honourable. It serves to provide for domestic life. It brings the delight of sex, and the physical pleasure animals have. And if husband and wife are fair to one another, their friendship is expressed in virtue proper to them both, rendering it mutually agreeable.

9.32   THE VIRTUE AND DELIGHT OF SEX

Abelard strikes both a modern and an antique note in this discussion on sex in his *Ethics*, written after his seduction of Héloise, his marriage to her and his castration by his enemies. It is certainly not typical medieval teaching, but it put into words what many, perhaps most, of his hearers felt. For Abelard see also 8.5–11.

The mere desire to do something immoral is never to be called a sin, but only the consent to it is sinful. We consent to the immorality when we do not draw ourselves back from such a deed, and are prepared to complete it should opportunity offer. He who is discovered in this intention, though he has not completed the deed, is already guilty in the eyes of God, for he is trying hard to sin and, as the blessed Augustine reminds us, he performs as much in his own mind as if he were caught in the act.

Some are highly indignant when we assert that the act of sinning adds no further to the guilt in God's eyes. They argue that in this act a certain delight accrues which increases the sin, as in sexual intercourse or indulgence in food. Their statement is absurd unless they can prove that physical pleasure of this kind is a sin in itself, and that such pleasure cannot be taken without committing a sin. If it is as they say, then no one is permitted to enjoy physical pleasure. Married couples do not avoid sin when they take their physical rights, nor does a man who eats his own fruits with relish. . . .

God, the creator of food and of the bodies that receive it, would be guilty for having instilled flavours which must involve the ignorant tasters in sin. Yet why did he supply such things for our consumption or let them be consumed, if it is impossible for us to eat them without sinning? How can there be sin in doing what is allowed? If things which were once unlawful and forbidden are later made lawful and allowed, they can be done entirely without sin. For instance, eating pork and much else which was once forbidden to Jews are now allowed to Christians. When Jews become Christians they gladly eat of these foods their law had prohibited, and we can only defend the rightness of their act by affirming that this freedom has been given to them by God. . . . Who then shall say that a man sins in a matter which has been made lawful for him by divine permission? If the marriage-bed or the eating of delicious foods was permitted from the first day of our creation, when we lived in Paradise without sin, who can prove that we sin in these pleasures so long as we do not pass the permitted limits?

Another objection is that sexual intercourse in marriage and the eating of delicious food are only allowed if they are done without pleasure. If this is so, they are allowed to be done in a way in which they never can be done. Such a concession is not reasonable. By what reasoning did the ancient law enforce marriage so that each should leave his seed to Israel? Or how did the apostle order wives to fulfil the mutual debt (1 Cor. 7, 3–5) if these acts could not be done without sinning?... I think it is clear that no natural physical delight can be accounted a sin, nor can man be guilty to delight in what, when it is done, must involve the feeling of pleasure.

CHAPTER TEN

MARY AND THE SAINTS

Mary

From the eleventh century onwards the age-old cult of Mary, the Mother of God, began to develop with remarkable acceleration so that she became our Lady as truly as Jesus was our Lord. A rich vein of apochryphal material was worked to provide a fuller life of Mary than the New Testament provides, complete with the Seven Sorrows and the Seven Joys, the Assumption and her Coronation as Queen of Heaven. The West fronts of many cathedrals

Coronation of the Virgin,
St. Mary's Church, Black Bourton, Oxford.
A 13th century fresco in a village church.

were hymns in sculptured stone to Mary the Queen. Plate 7 shows part of the carvings at Notre Dame, Paris, where many of the scenes are legends of Anne, Mary's mother. The Assumption is simply represented on the lintel of the West door of Senlis cathedral by six angels tenderly lifting Mary's body out of the tomb. Probably nearly every parish church had a coronation of the Virgin in a fresco on its walls. We reproduce that at Black Bourton, Oxfordshire. The ordinary medieval layman had no means by which to distinguish apocryphal from biblical material. Both came to him with the authority of priests in precious manuscripts and rich wall decorations. They met a real psychological need. The cult of Mary played a notable part in civilising manners (it had links with the development of courtly love). No doubt it fed on, but also helped to sublimate, the sexual desires of that very large number of men on whom the medieval church imposed the obligation of celibacy.

10.1   THE HEAVENLY REAPERS   *c.* 1120

The Cistercian order was to be closely associated with the growing devotion to our Lady in the twelfth century. This vision which came to a Cistercian novice is typical. It comes from the *Exordium Magnum.*

Soon after Renaud was received at Clairvaux he went out into the field with other monks to work at the wheat harvest. And as he stood a little apart from the others he began to rejoice in spirit at the sight of the reapers, marvelling to see so many learned, noble and delicately reared men undertaking such toil and trouble for Christ's sake. They suffered the burning sun as cheerfully as if they were picking apples of heavenly fragrance in some garden of delight or feasting sumptuously at some table loaded with delicious meats. Raising eyes and hands to heaven, he thanked God for bringing him, unworthy sinner that he was, into so holy and great a fellowship.

Thinking thus and almost bursting with joy, he was suddenly aware of three noble ladies with rosy cheeks and snow-white garments, one walking ahead with brighter robes and fairer form and loftier stature than the others. The three came down the near-by mountain towards the brothers as they toiled on the steep hill-side. Shaken and amazed at this strange sight he exclaimed:

'Lord God, who are these ladies, so fair, so noble, who approach our monastery against the custom of women?'

Even as he spoke he noticed a reverend white-haired man in a long white robe who said:

'The taller lady in front is Mary herself, the Virgin mother of Jesus Christ, and those who follow are Elizabeth and Mary Magdalen.'

As soon as Renaud heard the name of God's mother his heart melted, for he loved her vastly.

'And where O where is our Lady going?'

'To visit her reapers,' the other answered, and vanished.

The man of God marvelled all the more. He looked again at the holy mother of God and her companions. They approached the brethren slowly, one behind the other, then entered in among them, threading their way backwards and forwards among the monks and lay brothers, as though they were directing the work. Then even as they moved they vanished.

10.2   BUILDING CHURCHES FOR MARY   1145

The cult of Mary was reflected in a great outburst of church building in her honour. The fever spread outwards from Chartres. It overwhelmed St. Pierre-sur-Dives whose abbot, Haimon, wrote to the prior of his daughter house of Tutbury in Staffordshire to describe what was happening. The text is in the Bibliothèque de Chartres.

God has drawn to himself those that started away from him, and recalled the wandering, and taught them a new manner of seeking him, a manner new, I say, and unheard-of in all ages. For who ever saw, who ever heard, in all the generations past, that kings, princes, mighty men of this world, puffed up with honours and riches, men and women of noble birth, should bind bridles upon their proud and swollen necks and submit them to waggons which, after the fashion of brute beasts, they dragged with their loads of wine, corn, oil, lime, stones, beams, and other things necessary to sustain life or to build churches, even to Christ's abode? Moreover, as they draw the waggons we may see this miracle that, although sometimes a thousand men and women, or even more, are bound in the traces (so vast indeed is the mass, so great is the engine, and so heavy the load laid upon it), yet they go forward in such silence that no voice, no murmur, is heard; and, unless we saw it with our eyes, no man would dream that so great a multitude is there. . . .

The priests of Christ, set each above his own waggon, exhort all men to confession, to lamentation, to the resolution of better life, while the people fall to the ground, whereon they lie outstretched and kiss the earth again and again; old men and young men, with children of the tenderest age, cry upon the Mother of God, to whom especially they uplift their sobs and sighs from the inmost recesses of their heart with the voice of confession and praise: for this work is known to be specially hers next to her gentle son. She more especially commended herself in this work after him; she adorned first the cathedral of Chartres and then our church dedicated to her with so many and so great signs and wonders that, if I would express all that it hath been vouchsafed to me to see, even in a single night, my memory and tongue would utterly fail me.... When they were come to the church, then the waggons were arrayed around it like a spiritual camp; and all that night following this army of the Lord kept their watches with psalms and hymns; then waxen tapers and lights were kindled in each waggon, then the sick and infirm were set apart, then the relics of the saints were brought to their relief, then mystical processions were made by priests and clergy, and followed with all devotion by the people, who earnestly implored the Lord's mercy and that of his blessed Mother for their restoration to health. If, however, the healing were but a little delayed, nor followed forthwith after their vows, then all might have been seen putting off their clothes—men and women alike, naked from the loins upward, casting away all confusion and lying upon the earth.

Moreover, their example was followed even more devoutly by the children and infants who, grovelling on the ground, not so much crept from the church porch upon their hands and knees, but rather dragged themselves flat upon their bodies first to the high altar and then to all the others, calling upon the Mother of Mercy in this new fashion of prayer....

Truly the Mother of Mercy is moved without delay to pious compassion on those who afflict themselves before her, and showeth by the immediate efficacy of her healing hand how nearly she is touched and how truly she hath heard their cries; for soon all the sick and infirm leap forth healed from waggon after waggon, casting away the staff whereupon they had hitherto leaned their crippled limbs, and hastening without support to render thanks at her altar. Blind men see, and thread their way with ease; the dropsical are relieved of their grievous load and lose their fatal thirst. What say I? Why should I enumerate one healing after another, when they are innumerable and more than man can tell? After each miracle a solemn procession is held to the high altar, the bells are rung, praise and thanks are rendered to the Mother of Mercy.

10.3 BERNARD ON THE IMMACULATE CONCEPTION

At Lyons a new feast was introduced towards the middle of the twelfth century—the feast of the Immaculate Conception of the Virgin Mary. Mary had no more ardent follower than Bernard, but he sternly condemned the new cult for the reasons which he gave in this letter to the cathedral chapter. Even his immense reputation, however, failed to stop the spread of the doctrine. It was not until 1854 that Pius IX made the decision which in the last sentence of this extract Bernard said he would be ready, if necessary, to accept.

The Mother of the Lord, you say, ought greatly to be honoured. You say well, but the honour of a queen loves justice. The royal Virgin does not need false honour since she is amply supplied with true titles to honour and badges of her dignity. Honour indeed the purity of her flesh, the sanctity of her life; wonder at her motherhood as a virgin; adore her divine offspring. Praise the wonder of the way in which without pain she brought into the world the Son, whom she conceived without sexual desire. Proclaim how she is reverenced by the angels, was desired by the nations, foretold by patriarchs and prophets, chosen by God from among all women and raised by him above them all. Magnify her as the means by which grace came, as the instrument of salvation, the restorer of the ages; and finally praise her as the one who has been raised high above the choirs of angels to the heavenly kingdom. These things the Church sings in praise of her, and has taught me to do likewise. What I have learnt from the Church I firmly hold and teach. What I have not received from the Church I admit I should have great difficulty in accepting. I have learnt from the Church that the day when Mary was taken up from sinful earth and entered heaven is a day to be kept with great solemnity, a festival of most honoured joy (August 15: Feast of the Assumption). . . . Beyond doubt the mother of the Lord was holy before birth; and holy Church is not wrong to count the day of her birth a holy day and keep it each year with solemn and thankful joy. I consider also that she was further blessed so that not only was her birth holy but her whole life was free from sin—a gift given to no other person born of woman. . . .

What addition can possibly be made to these honours? Some say that her conception as well as her birth should be honoured since, if the one had not first taken place, neither would the other which we keep as a feast. But what if some one else, arguing in the same way, should declare that festivals should be set apart for both her parents, for her grandparents, and their parents, and so *ad infinitum*? We should have festivals without number. Such abundance is suitable for heaven, not for this exile of ours. It is the happiness of those who live there, not of strangers and pilgrims. . . .

Although it has been given to some, though only to a few, to be born holy, no one has been conceived in that state. This privilege alone belongs to him who makes all holy, and by his coming into the

world without sin makes atonement for sinners. The Lord Jesus alone
was conceived by the Holy Spirit because he alone was holy before he
was conceived. With this exception all the children of Adam are in the
same position as the psalmist who most humbly and truthfully
confessed, 'I was shapen in iniquity, and in sin has my mother
conceived me' (Psalm 51, 6). And since this is so, what ground can
there be for a Feast of the Conception of the Virgin?... But what I
have said is subject to the judgment of whoever is wiser than myself;
and especially I refer the whole of it ... to the authority and decision
of the See of Rome, and I am ready to modify my opinion if in
anything I think otherwise than that See.

10.4   OUR LADY: THE POPULAR IMAGE

These three short passages illustrate the exaggerations and dangers to which
the cult of Mary could and did give rise. The first comes from Caesarius of
Heisterbach, a Cistercian; the second from the *Speculum Historiale* of
Vincent of Beauvais, a French Dominican; and the third from an English
Franciscan in *Fasciculus Morum*.

A.   *c.* 1223
A certain lay-brother of Hemmenrode was rather badly tempted; so
as he stood praying he used these words:

'Truly Lord, if thou dost not deliver me from this temptation I will
complain of thee to thy mother!'

The loving Lord, a lord of humility and lover of simplicity,
prevented the brother's complaint and soon relieved his temptation
as if he feared to be accused before his mother. Another lay-brother
who stood behind the other, smiled at hearing this prayer and
repeated it for the edification of the rest.

B.   *c.* 1250
I advise you to call upon Mary the mother of Jesus before all others
and attend her with perpetual prayers, for she is the only hope of
man's reconciliation, she is the first agent of man's salvation.

C.   *c.* 1320
We ought to copy the man who has incurred the anger of a king.
What does he do? He goes secretly to the queen and promises a gift.
He does the same to the earls and barons, then to the freemen of the
household and lastly to the servants.

So when we offend Christ we should first go to the queen of heaven and offer her, not presents, but prayers, fasts, vigils and alms. Then like a mother she will come between you and Christ, the father who wants to beat us, and throw the cloak of mercy between the rod of punishment and ourselves, allaying the king's anger against us. After that we should go to the earls and barons—the apostles—and ask them to intercede for us, then to the knights and squires—the martyrs and confessors—and then to the ladies of the queen's bedchamber—the women saints. Lastly we should go to the servants—the poor, for even the poor ought to be moved by our alms to pray to Christ for us.

10.5   A CAROL TO THE VIRGIN   13th Century

Of one that is so fair and bright
   Velut maris stella,
Brighter than the day is light,
   Parens et puella;
I cry to thee, thou see to me,
Lady, pray thy Son for me
    Tam pia,
So that I might come to thee,
   Maria!

In care, for counsel thou art best,
   Felix fecundata;
To all the weary thou art rest,
   Mater honorata.
Beseech him with thy mild mood,
That for us all did shed his blood
   In cruce,
So that we might come to him
   In luce.

All the world it was forlorn
   Eva peccatrice,
Till our Lord was y-born
   De te genetrice.
With Ave[1] there went away
Thickest night and came the day
   Salutis;
Out of thee the well doth spring
   Virtutis.

Lady, flower of everything,
  Rosa sine spina,
Thou bearest Jesu, heaven's king,
  Gratia divina;
Of everyone thou bearest the prize,
Lady, queen of Paradise
  Electa,
Maiden mild and mother, *es*
  Effecta.

Well he wots he is thy son
  Ventre quem portasti,
He will not refuse thy boon,
  Parvum quem lactasti.
So kindly and so good he is,
He brings us all into his bliss
  Superni,
He hath shut up the foul pit
  Inferni.

[1] A favourite anagram: Ave reversing the sin of Eva.

Saints

The saints were not in Purgatory but in Paradise. They did not, like the other dead, need our prayers; instead we asked for theirs. Prayers to the saints, to one's patron saint, or to a saint with a special concern for, say, scholars—St. Nicholas—was a regular and important part of religious life.

10.6   RECOGNIZING A SAINT   1202

For the first thousand years of Christianity men were not made saints by formal procedure, but recognized by popular esteem. Innocent III was the first pope to reserve the right of canonisation to Rome. In 1202 Gilbert of Sempringham, who had died in 1189 when he was over a hundred years old, was canonised. The decision conveyed in this letter by Innocent III to Hubert Walter, archbishop of Canterbury, sets out the reasons for the decision and how it was reached. The Order which Gilbert founded was made up of double houses for nuns and canons regular all in or near Lincolnshire.

To be accepted as a saint among those in the church militant, two things are essential: merits and miracles, each bearing witness to the other. Merits without miracles or miracles without merits are not enough to certify sainthood in this world because sometimes even Satan is transformed into an angel of light (2 Cor. 11, 14) and there are

Pharisees who do their works to be seen by men (Matt. 23, 5). Even the magicians of Pharaoh once worked wonders, as will Antichrist in the future so as to deceive if possible even the elect (Matt. 24, 24). So the evidence of works is sometimes deceptive, as in hypocrites, as is the evidence of miracles in the case of magicians. But the real proof of a saint is when genuine merits come first and are followed by notable miracles ... as can be inferred from the words of the gospel writer speaking of the Apostles: 'They went forth and preached everywhere, the Lord working with them and confirming the word with signs following' (Mark 16, 20).

Beloved sons, the prior and monastery of Sempringham petitioned us long ago to inscribe the founder of their Order, master Gilbert of pious memory, on the roll of saints, as one worthy of veneration. They affirm that he abounded in good works before his death and now shines forth with irrefutable miracles. But we refused to grant their request immediately and decided to examine the facts about the holiness of his life and his miracles more fully, though these had been faithfully reported to us by our well-beloved son in Christ, John, illustrious king of the English, his nobles, you and your suffragans, the prior and monastery of Sempringham and many abbots and priors. As we wished to exercise the greatest caution in so important a matter, we wrote to you and our venerable brother the bishop of Ely, and our beloved sons the abbots of Peterborough and Wardon directing you—trusting in our authority—to go together to Sempringham and there proclaim a three days' fast for the whole community of the Order so that the brothers and sisters might beseech Him who is the way, the truth, and the life (John 14, 6) to reveal a way of finding the truth that leads to life. Then from the evidence of witnesses, by common report and authentic documents, you were to search for absolute certainty about the holiness of his life and his mighty signs, that is, his merits and his miracles.

You carefully examined the witnesses on oath (monastic and secular, clergy and laity, men and women) about the mighty signs claimed to have been wrought by the virtues of master Gilbert, and you have honestly put the statements of these witnesses in writing and sent them to us enclosed under your seals. These proofs were clear and certain but so many and diverse that it has seemed unnecessary to describe them in this letter. Concerning the integrity of his life, which is a matter of common knowledge, you carefully questioned the canons who used to wait upon him and so were familiar with his private life; and they all invariably and steadily testified to his spotless and holy life.

... Among the many works which made his life famous, one was outstanding: he chose poverty and devoted all the worldly wealth that God had given him to the needs of the brothers and sisters whom he skilfully organised and carefully protected as a regular Order. In time God greatly increased his grace and holiness, so that he built nine houses for nuns and four for regular canons where at his death there were many canons and 1,500 nuns continually serving God....

Wherefore, being assured of his merits and miracles, we have inscribed the blessed Gilbert on the roll of saints.... You will ensure that his festival is solemnly celebrated throughout your province so that by his merits and prayers you may obtain mercy from the most merciful judge.

10.7   VERIFYING A MIRACLE

This is a 'memorandum' from the Register of Walter Stapledon, bishop of Exeter, for July 30, 1315.

A blind man, Thomas Crey, a fuller, from the town of Keynsham in the diocese of Bath and Wells came to the collegiate church of the Holy Cross at Crediton on the Wednesday before the feast of St. Peter ad Vincula and remained there until the feast itself which was on Friday. During High Mass in the presence of Bishop Walter, after the Epistle but before the Gospel, Thomas said that he received his sight as he stood praying before the altar of St. Nicholas. When the bishop was told of this after mass he ordered Thomas to attend in the church so that he might go fully into what had happened because such things ought not to be believed without full proof. Accordingly the bishop sat in the Lady Chapel of the church and Thomas, his wife, some Crediton people and certain members of the Bishop's household appeared before him and were sworn on the Holy Gospels. Thomas told how while he had his sight, he worked as a fuller in the town of Keynsham. On Thursday in Easter week (March 27) he fell asleep after dinner in his house at Keynsham. Up to that time, all his life long, he had had perfectly good eyesight. But when he woke up he could see nothing at all, and this continued until the Friday, St. Peter's Day. The bishop then asked him if he could now see, and he said he could. And, to test him, the Bishop asked him on which hand and on which finger he was wearing his ring. And many other similar questions he asked him, to all of which Thomas replied correctly. He was then asked about his neighbours in Keynsham who knew about what had happened to him. He gave the names of Walter of

Greenway, John Raulfe, Walter Keteford, John Keteford, William le Thechere, Adam le Thechere, who knew that he had been blind from the time he had mentioned until he set out for Crediton. And there were many other neighbours who could speak to this.

He was then asked how he came to know of Crediton. He replied that once, during his blindness, he was told in a dream that he should visit the church of the Holy Cross at Crediton, and that there he would receive his sight. His wife was then questioned and confirmed all that Thomas had said with the exception of his dream. The other witnesses then stated that they had seen that Thomas was blind, with his eyes always closed, while he was in Crediton.

At the conclusion of the hearing the bishop ordered the Canons and Vicars then present to have the bells rung and to give thanks most solemnly and with great devotion to God, to the Blessed Mary, to the Holy Cross, and to All Saints, as is customary in such cases.

10.8   AN AWKWARD SAINT: STEPHEN HARDING

12th Century

In due course Stephen Harding (see 6.13) was recognized as a saint. It is the nature of saints to work miracles and this power continued after their death, chiefly through their relics. Miracles may be troublesome as well as helpful. A quaint and charming story in the *Acta Sanctorum* tells of a complaint made at Citeaux to St. Stephen

Servant of God, you have shown us the path of poverty and taught us with all your might to walk in it. Will you now by your miracles draw us away from the steep and narrow way that leads to life into the broad and easy way that leads to destruction (Matt. 7, 13–14)? We are not curious to see your miracles, we are sufficiently convinced of your sanctity. So beware of continuing to work these miracles which, while they exalt your holiness, make us lose our humility. Be not so anxious for your own glory that you neglect our salvation. Otherwise we tell you and firmly proclaim—through that obedience we promised you—that we will dig up your bones and cast them hence into the river.

10.9   A WARNING ABOUT IMAGES   c. 1360

This warning from a sermon is earlier by some years than the Lollard movement. Compare 4.23–28 on image worship in the East. The

Priory of Bromholm on the Norfolk coast claimed to have a piece of the cross:

Some lewd [unlearned] folk ween that the images do verily the miracles by themselves, and that this image of the crucifix be Christ himself, or the saint is the image there set for likeness. And therefore they say 'the sweet rood of Bromholm', 'the sweet rood of grace', 'the sweet rood at the north door', 'our dear Lady of Walsingham', but not 'our Lady of heaven' nor 'our Lord of heaven'. They leave sadly, stroking and kissing these old stones and stocks, laying down their great offerings and making vows right there to these old images to come the next year again, as if they were Christ and our Lady and John Baptist and Thomas of Canterbury and such other.

Source: B.M. Add. MS. 24202, p. 28.

CHAPTER ELEVEN

THE BIBLE PORTRAYED

Few western Christians outside the monasteries could read the Bible. This was partly because few people could read at all; partly because it was in Latin (the Anglo-Saxon interlining had ceased—see 2.22); and partly because, before printing, Bibles were scarce.

The problem was to make its more important teaching known. This was done, but very imperfectly, in sermons, plays and pictures. Parish churches had their wall paintings but these were as much (or more) concerned with the saints and the apocryphal life of our Lady as with the Bible. It may be doubted whether most laymen clearly distinguished between biblical and non-biblical material.

There was a contrast between East and West in the selection of material.

Judgment of Solomon (1 Kings 3, 16f)
12th Century capital, Westminster Abbey

Emile Male pointed out that while a painter's handbook in the Greek Church dealt with forty parables, the Western Church portrayed only four in the thirteenth century—the Good Samaritan, the Wise and Foolish Virgins, the Prodigal Son, and Dives and Lazarus. Adequate representation of carvings, glass, wall paintings, and mosaics is outside the scope of this book. The following extracts show something of the development of religious drama.

11.1 Easter Ceremonies

Christian religious drama had its origin in the dramatic ceremonies of Holy Week and Easter. In this passage John Myrc explains the symbolic meaning of the unusual things that were done, and the usual things that were not done, in church from Maundy Thursday to Easter Day. He was writing in the fourteenth century, but the ceremonies were much older. Thus Ethelwold, writing about 970, described the way in which the cross is kissed by each of the congregation in turn on Good Friday and then, 'Let the deacons come and wrap it in a cloth in the place where it was adored. Then let them carry it back, singing anthems, until they come to the place of the monument (the Easter Sepulchre), and there having laid down the cross as if it were the body of our Lord Jesus Christ, let them say an anthem. And here let the holy cross be guarded with all reverence until the night of the Lord's resurrection.' This was the practice in many monastic houses, Ethelwold said, and he commended it for general use 'for the strengthening of faith in the unlearned vulgar'.

In holy church it is called our Lord's supperday. . . . It is also called Shear-Thursday, for in the days of the old Fathers men would that day trim themselves and shave their heads and clip their beards and make themselves decent for Easter Day. . . . And a priest shall shave his crown so that there shall be nothing between God Almighty and himself. He shall also shave the hairs of his beard that comes of the superfluity of humours of the stomach, and pare the nails of his hands that comes of the superfluity of humours of the heart. So just as we shave and shear away the superfluity of outward filth, we shall shave and shear away the superfluity of inward sin and vice. . . . This day no pax is given at mass, for Judas betrayed Christ this night with a kiss. . . .

On Easter Eve the Paschal candle is made, which betokens Christ; for as the Paschal candle is the chief taper in the church, so is Christ the chief saint in the church. Also this Paschal betokens the pillar of fire that went before the children of Israel when they went out of Egypt into the land or promise, that is now Jerusalem (Exodus 13, 21). They travelled through the Red Sea, whole and sound, for seven days and thanked God each day for their passage; therefore holy Church all Easter week goes in procession to the font, which is now the Red Sea to all Christian people who had been baptized in the font. For the water in the font betokens the red blood and water that ran down from the wounds of Christ's side (John 19, 34), and in this the power of Pharaoh (that is, the very Fiend) is drowned and all his might is lost and all Christian people saved.

The font is hallowed on Easter Eve and Whitsun Eve.... And the Paschal candle is hallowed and lit with new fire, and from it all other tapers are lit. For all light and holiness of good works come from Christ's lore, and holy Church is lit with the burning charity of his commands.

Five pips of incense are stuck in the Paschal candle in the form of a cross. That, Bede says, betokens the wounds that Christ suffered in his body, and shall be kept fresh and sweet as incense till the day of doom....

In the font-hallowing the priest pours water into the four quarters of the font; for Christ bade his disciples to go into the four quarters of the world and preach and teach the four gospels, and baptize in the name of the Father, and of the Son, and of the Holy Ghost. After this the priest breathes on the water; for the Holy Ghost, in the making of the world, was borne by the waters (Gen. 1, 2). Wherefore when God for Adam's sin cursed the earth, he spared the water.

11.2 The Easter Play

The other element needed in addition to dramatic action in order to produce a play is the use of dialogue. Already in the ninth century at the monastery of St. Gall there was at Easter (and also at other major festivals) a seasonal extra or 'trope' in dialogue form introduced into the regular liturgical services. This first form of what was to become the developed Easter play is very brief and forms part of the Introit at mass. The women come to the tomb and there meet the angels (Luke 24, 4):

'Whom seek you in the sepulchre, O followers of Christ?'
'Jesus of Nazareth, the crucified, celestial ones.'
'He is not here; he is risen, just as he foretold.
Go and proclaim that he is risen from the tomb.'

A hundred years later this had been developed into something much more elaborate. Ethelwold about the year 970 described what was said and done at

Winchester, no longer as part of the Introit at mass but at Matins on Easter morning:

While the third lesson is chanted, four brethren invest themselves, of whom one, vested in an alb, enters as if to take part in the service, and approaches the sepulchre without attracting attention and sits there quietly with a palm in his hand. While the third responsory is sung the remaining three follow, all vested in copes and carrying censers in their hands, and stepping delicately, as if seeking something, they come to the place of the sepulchre. These things are done in imitation of the angel sitting in the monument and the women coming with spices to anoint the body of Jesus. When therefore he that sits there shall see the three approach him, as if straying about and seeking something, let him begin in a dulcet voice of medium pitch to sing:
'Whom seek you....'
When he has sung this to the end, let the three respond in unison:
'Jesus of Nazareth....'
To whom that one 'He is not here...'
At the word of this bidding, those three turn to the choir and say:
'Alleluia! The Lord is risen today,
Strong lion, the Christ, God's Son!
Give thanks to God, hurrah!'
This said, the one still sitting there, as if recalling them, shall say the anthem:
'Come, see the place where the Lord was laid.
Alleluia! Alleluia!'
And saying this, he rises and lifts the veil and shows them the place bare of the cross, but only the cloths laid there in which the cross was wrapped. Seeing this, they set down the censers which they carried into that same sepulchre, and lift the cloth and spread it out before the clergy; and, as if to show that the Lord had risen and is no longer wrapped therein, let them sing this anthem:
'The Lord is risen from the sepulchre
Who for us hung upon the cross.'
... Then they lay the cloth upon the altar. The anthem ended, the prior, rejoicing with them at the triumph of our King who conquered death and rose again, begins the hymn, *Te Deum laudamus*, We Praise Thee O God, and all the bells ring out together.
Source: Ethelwold, *Regularis Concordia.*

11.3   The Play of Mary and the Shepherds   10th–11th Century

This early dramatic insertion in the liturgy, a parallel to the Easter play
(11.2), comes from Rouen in Normandy. Many churches today use nativity
plays which differ little from its closely biblical form. But already, when the
shepherds worship at the manger, rather more of their devotion is directed to
the mother than there is precedent for in Luke.

When the 'Te Deum laudamus' is finished, let the Office of the
Shepherds be performed in this way, according to the usage of
Rouen.

Let a manger be prepared at the back of the altar and a figure of the
holy Mary placed in it. First, a boy, like an angel, from a lofty place in
front of the choir, announces the birth of the Lord ... and the
shepherds enter by the main door of the choir, pass through the
middle of the choir, vested in tunics and amices, and sing this verse:

'Fear not: for behold I bring you good tidings of great joy, which
shall be to all people. For unto you is born this day in the city of
David a Saviour which is Christ the Lord. And this shall be a sign
unto you: you shall find the babe wrapped in swaddling clothes and
lying in a manger.'

Let there be many boys in the roof of the church like angels who
shall begin in a loud voice,

'Glory to God in the highest, and on earth peace, good will to men.'

Hearing this, the shepherds approach the place where the manger
has been prepared, singing this verse:

> Peace on earth, proclaim it!
>   Glory in the highest!
> Earth is joined to heaven
>   By the means of grace.
>
> God-man, mediator,
>   Comes down to his own,
> Guilty man may rise to
>   Unforbidden joys.   Eya! Eya!
>
> Let us go and see there
>   What has come to pass,
> Let us go and learn there
>   What has been announced.

In Judea a boy cries,
    Saviour-boy of man,
Whom our ancient foe knew
    Must be conqueror.

Let us draw near, near the
    Manger of the Lord,
Joying all together,
    Virgin, mother, hail!

When they enter this place two priests of the upper row, clothed in dalmatics, like midwives who had served at the manger, say:

'Whom seek you in the manger, shepherds, say.'

The shepherds reply:

'The Saviour Christ, the infant Lord, wrapped in swaddling clothes, according to the message of the angel.'

Whereupon the midwives draw aside the curtain and show the boy, saying:

'The little one is here with Mary his mother, whom the prophet Isaiah spoke of long ago' [Isa. 7, 14].

—and here he shall reveal the mother of the child, saying—

'"Behold a virgin shall conceive and bear a son." And now as you go forth announce that he is born.'

Then having seen him they worship the boy, with bowed heads, and salute him, saying:

Hail, virgin unparalleled!
Ever virgin, bride of God!

Him, ere time began, begotten
In the heart of God the Father,
Let us worship now as offspring
Of a mother's flesh.

Purge us, Mary, through thy prayers,
From the taint of sin;
So direct our life on earth here
That thy Son may let us see
The Vision of thyself.

Then they leave and return to the choir, saying:

'Alleluia! Alleluia! Now we know the truth that Christ is born into the world, of whom let all sing, saying with the prophet....'

[The words of the hymn or anthem which followed here are not given in the Rouen MS. Such a text as Isaiah 9, 6: 'Unto us a child is born' etc. would have been used.]

This ended, the Mass is begun and the Shepherds rule the choir. *Source:* Rouen MS. y.110.

11.4 Growth of the Guild Plays

The Easter and Christmas liturgical dramas developed into a great cycle of plays illuminating man's fall and final redemption or damnation. The plays were taken out of the churches into the churchyards and then into various stations in the town, especially the galleried courtyards of the principal inns. They were acted on wagon stages by the craft guilds and spoken in the vernacular, not in Latin.

There are records of such performances from all over England, from Cornwall to Newcastle, but only four sets of the texts have survived, for York (48 plays), Chester (25), Wakefield (30) and Coventry (42). In these we find that the Old Testament scenes were chiefly confined to the Creation and Fall, Cain and Abel, Noah and the Flood, Abraham and Isaac, and Moses. These were followed by the New Testament scenes which, like the Apostles Creed, tend to jump\from 'born of the Virgin Mary' to 'suffered under Pontius Pilate'. The exceptions are plays about Christ's baptism, temptation, the woman taken in adultery, and the raising of Lazarus. Often the plays helped to advertise the skills of the guilds: the Deluge was acted by the 'Waterleaders and Drawers of the Dee' at Chester, the Magi and their offerings were portrayed by the Goldsmiths at York.

The whole cycle was put together about 1300 and performed during the long June light of Corpus Christi day (see E. K. Chambers, *Medieval Stage*, Vol. 2).

A   THE WAKEFIELD SHEPHERDS

Non-biblical and apocryphal material invaded the texts. Noah's wife becomes a prototype of the pantomime comic dame. The Wakefield play of the Shepherds opens with the men complaining about the bad weather, how the poor serfs cannot get on with their ploughing because they are 'lord-fast', bound to a lord, or are obliged to lend their plough and wagon to some 'proud peacock' of a man. Then a notorious sheep-stealer called Mak joins the three shepherds on their night vigil, steals a sheep as the others sleep, slips it home to his wife and returns to the sleepers. Soon the sheep is missed, Mak accused, and his home searched. The sheep is swaddled in a cradle and Mak's wife is groaning in bed from the pains of childbirth.

> *Wife* Ah, my middle!
> I pray to God so mild,
> If ever I you beguiled,
> That I eat this child
> That lies in this cradle.

[Later, the third and youngest shepherd says:]

Mak, with your leave
Let me give your bairn
But sixpence.

   Mak Nay, do way! He sleepys.
 3rd Shepherd Methinks he peepys.
   Mak When he wakens he weepys.
     I pray you go hence.
 3rd Shepherd Give me leave him to kiss, and lift up the clout.
     What the devil is this? He has a long snout!

The shepherds take their sheep, toss Mak in a blanket, return to their flock, go to sleep again and are roused by the *Gloria in excelsis* of the angels: 648 lines of comic invention give way at last to 117 lines on the Nativity.

B   THE YORK DAY OF JUDGMENT

The final scene of the Guild Cycle of plays was the Day of Judgment, acted in York by the Mercers. The surviving manuscript is early fifteenth century, but it is stated to be a transcript of the 'originals', and directions were given in 1390 for the performances to take place 'at the stations anciently assigned'. The forty-seven and a half stanzas of the manuscript have here been reduced to eleven and a half. Note how closely the plot follows Matt. 25, 31–46. For a typical portrayal of the mouth of Hell see Plate 6.

[God first appears, talks of the creation, man's fall, his Son's redemption]

Men see the world but vanity,
Yet will no man be ware thereby;
Each day their mirror may they see,
Yet think they not that they shall die.
All that ever I said should be
Is now fulfilled through prophecy.
Therefore now is it time to me
To make ending of man's folly.

[*He commands his angels to sound the trumpets*]

 2nd Angel Every creature, old and ying,
     Betimes I bid you that ye rise!
     Body and soul with you ye bring,
     And come before the high justice!

For I am sent from heaven's king
To call you to this great assise
Therefore rise up and give reckoning
How ye him served in several wise.

2nd Good Soul Ah! Lovèd be thou, Lord of all,
That heaven and earth and all has wrought,
That with thine angels would us call
Out of our graves, hither to be brought.
Oft have we grieved thee, great and small;
Thereafter, Lord, thou doom us not;
Nor suffer us never to fiends to be thrall,
That oft in earth with sin us sought!

1st Evil Soul Alas! alas! that we were born!
So may we sinful caitiffs say.
I hear well by this hideous horn
It draws full near to doomesday.
Alas! we wretches that are for-lorn,
That never yet served God to pay,
But oft we have his flesh forsworn.
Alas! alas! and wellaway!

Jesus [descends] My apostles and my darlings dear,
The dreadful doom this day is dight [prepared]
Both heaven and earth and hell shall hear
How I shall hold what I have hight, [promised]
That ye shall sit on seatès sere [several thrones]
Beside myself to see that sight,
And for to doom folk far and near
After their working wrong or right.

Here he goes to the judgment seat with the singing of angels.

3rd Devil He shall do right to foe and friend,
For now shall all the sooth be sought.
All wicked wights with us shall wend;
To endless pain they shall be brought.

Jesus [*to his 'blessed children' on his right hand*]
When I was hungry, ye me fed;
To slake my thirst your heart was free;
When I was clotheless, ye me cled;
Ye would no sorrow upon me see;

'Doom painting': South Leigh, Oxfordshire.
Paintings of the Day of Judgment, generally over
the chancel arch, were as common in village churches as stone carvings of it on the greater churches.

Venite benedicti Patris mei

Discedite maledicti

ASTF

In hard prison when I was sted,
Of my pains ye had pity;
Full sick when I was brought to bed,
Kindly ye came to comfort me.

When I was weak and weariest,
Ye harboured me full heartily;
Full glad then were ye of your guest,
Had pity for my poverty;
Betimes ye brought me of the best
And made my bed full easily.
Therefore in heaven shall be your rest
In joy and bliss to be by me.

1st Good Soul When had we, Lord that all has wrought,
Meat and drink thee with to feed?
Since we in earth had never naught
But through the grace of thy godhead.

2nd Good Soul When was it that we clothing brought?
Or visited thee in any need?
Or in thy sickness we thee sought?
Lord, when to thee did we this deed?

Jesus My blessed children I shall say
What time this deed was to me done:
When any need had, night or day,
And asked your help and had it soon;
Your free hearts said they never nay,
Early or late mid-day or noon;
But as oftimes as they would pray,
They had but to bid and have their boon.

[*Jesus then addresses the Evil Souls.*]
Clotheless when I was ofte and cold,
At need of you, went I full naked;
House nor harbour, help nor hold
Had I none of you, though I quakèd.
My mischief saw you manifold.
Not one of you my sorrow slakèd,
But ever forsook me, young and old.
Therefore shall ye now be forsakèd.

[The Evil Souls answer, 'When saw we thee' etc. and receive the answer,
What they had failed to do 'for least or most' they had failed to do for him.]

My chosen children come to me!
With me to dwell now shall ye wend;
There joy and bliss, shall ever be,
Your life in liking shall ye spend.

Ye cursed caitiffs from me flee,
In hell to dwell without an end.
There ye shall never but sorrow see
And sit by Satanas the fiend.

And thus he makes an end, with the melodies of angels crossing from place to place.

11.5 The Guild of the Lord's Prayer

Sometimes special guilds, which were not apparently trade-based, were formed for the express purpose of presenting each year a revival of a play that had been a marked success. Such was the Guild of the Lord's Prayer at York. This account comes from the Public Record Office: 308 no. 109.

As for the beginning of this guild, be it known that once upon a time a play, setting forth the goodness of the Lord's Prayer, was played in the city of York, in which all kinds of vices were held up to scorn and the virtues praised. This play was so popular that many said, 'Would that this play could be kept up in this city, for the good of souls and comfort of the citizens!' So the keeping up of this play was the sole cause of the beginning of the fellowship of this brotherhood. And the main charge of the guild is to keep up this play, to the glory of God the maker of the said prayer and to the scorn of sins.

And because those who remain in their sins are unable to call God their father, the brothers of the guild are bound first of all to shun company and businesses that are unworthy and keep to good and worthy businesses. And they are bound to pray for the brothers and sisters of the guild both alive and dead, that the living may be able to keep the guild in such a way that they may deserve to win God's fatherhood, and that the dead may have their torments lightened. . . .

Also they are bound to find one candle-holder with seven lights, in token of the seven petitions in the Lord's Prayer, and this shall hang in the cathedral church of York and be lighted on Sundays and feast days, to the glory and honour of God Almighty, the maker of that prayer. . . .

Also they are bound to make, and to renew when necessary, a tablet showing the whole meaning and form of the Lord's Prayer, and to keep this hanging against a pillar in the said cathedral church near the aforesaid candle-holder.

CHAPTER TWELVE

CHRISTIANS AND JEWS

In the Dark Ages

This chapter, which covers the whole eight centuries with which this volume is concerned, starts in the Mediterranean area among the remnants of the old Roman Empire. There had been widespread Jewish colonies here long before there had been any Christians. They were in general peaceable, law-abiding, industrious—and valuable to the state. They were therefore protected against the riots to which as an unpopular, unassimilable minority they were often exposed.

12.1   THEODORIC PROTECTS THE JEWS   *c.* 520

Theodoric, the greatest of the Gothic kings in Italy, was a man to whom the Jews could and did appeal for protection. These two extracts come from the collection of his official letters which his minister Cassiodorus made. In his Edicts, collection of laws, Theodoric recognized the Jews' right to control their own internal affairs according to the Law of Moses. For Cassiodorus see introduction to 1.9.

A. King Theodoric to the Roman Senate

The good manners which are characteristic of the City of Rome must be maintained. To fall to rioting and the burning of their own city is quite un-Roman.

But we are informed by Count Arigern that the people of Rome, enraged at the punishment inflicted on some Christian servants who had murdered their Jewish masters, have risen in fury and burned their synagogue to the ground. . . .

Be pleased to enquire into this matter and severely punish the ringleaders of the riot, who are probably few in number. At the same time enquire into the complaints which are brought against the Jews, and if you find any grounds for them, punish accordingly.

B. King Theodoric to the Jews of Milan

For the preservation of good manners the benefits of justice are not to be denied even to those who are recognised as wandering from the right way in matters of faith.

You complain that you are often victims of unprovoked attacks, and that the rights pertaining to your synagogue are ignored. We therefore give you the needed protection of our Mildness, and give orders that no member of the Church shall infringe the privileges of your synagogue, nor mix himself up in your affairs. But let the two communities keep apart, as their faiths are different, you on your part not attempting to do anything unmannerly against the rights of the said Church....

But why, O Jew, petition for peace and quiet upon earth when you cannot find that rest which is eternal?

12.2   APOSTACY OR CONVERSION?   576

This story of apostacy or conversion (according to one's standpoint) and its consequences comes from Gregory of Tours, who had close contacts in Clermont and wrote about the time of the event. For Gregory, see introduction to 1.1.

Since our God always gives glory to his bishops, I shall tell what happened to the Jews in Clermont this year. The blessed bishop Avitus had often urged them to remove the veil of the Mosaic Law, to realise the spirit of their Scriptures and with pure hearts to recognise in those sacred texts the Christ, the son of the living God promised by the authority of law and prophets. But there remained upon their hearts not the veil which covered Moses' face (Exodus 34, 33–35) but what I call a wall.

The bishop prayed that they might be converted to the Lord and that the veil of the letter might be rent from them (see 2 Cor. 3, 6 and Matt. 27, 51), and at last one of them asked to be baptised on holy Easter. Born again in God by the sacrament of baptism, he joined the white-robed procession himself in white. But as they entered the gate of the city, a Jew, prompted by the devil, poured rancid oil on the head of the Jewish convert. When all the people, horrified at this, wanted to stone him, the bishop would not allow it. But on that blessed day when our Lord ascends to heaven in glory after redeeming us, while the bishop was walking in procession from the cathedral to the basilica, a crowd of those who followed rushed to the Jewish synagogue and smashing it at the foundations levelled it to the ground.

Another day the bishop sent the Jews this message: 'I am not forcing you to confess the Son of God, but I preach him and season your hearts with the salt of wisdom. For I am appointed shepherd over the Lord's sheep, and the true Shepherd who suffered for us was

speaking of you when he said that he had other sheep which were not
of his fold but which he must bring in, so that there may be one flock
and one shepherd (John 10, 16). Therefore, if you will believe as I,
become flock with me as your guardian; but if not, leave this place.'

For a long time they wavered and were full of doubt, but on the
third day—through the prayers of the bishop as I believe—they met
together and sent this answer: 'We believe that Jesus is the Son of the
living God, promised us by the mouths of the prophets'... The
bishop rejoiced at the news and after Vigils on the eve of Pentecost he
went out to the baptistry beyond the walls, and there the whole
multitude prostrated themselves and begged for baptism. With tears
of joy he washed them all with water, anointed them with oil and
gathered them into the bosom of mother Church. Candles were lit,
lamps gleamed, the city was silvered by the white-robed throng, and
the joy was as great as the joy that Jerusalem saw when the Holy
Spirit descended upon the apostles.

The baptized were more than 500; but those who refused baptism
left the city and returned to Marseilles.

12.3   GREGORY THE GREAT'S SCRUPULOUS CARE   *c.* 600

The first of these extracts from Gregory the Great's letters shows the pope
over-ruling another bishop's action in seizing a synagogue. The second shows
Gregory accepting slavery, but rejecting the idea of a Christian being a slave
to a Jew. But even so he is scrupulous in his respect for Jewish legal rights. For
Gregory see introduction to 1.11. A Defensor was a magistrate who provided protection against oppression by the governors.

A. Synagogues in Sicily: Gregory to Fautinus, 'Defensor' of Palermo
Recently we wrote to Victor, our brother and fellow-bishop, because
certain Jews have presented a petition to us complaining that he has
unreasonably taken possession of synagogues and their guest-rooms
in the city of Panormus, and we advised him to keep aloof from their
congregation until it could be determined whether this action had
been taken justly....

We find from the report of Salarius our notary that there had been
no reasonable cause for seizing these synagogues, and that they have
since been unwisely and rashly consecrated. Since what has once been
consecrated cannot be restored to the Jews again, we enjoin your
Experience to take care to see that our said brother and fellow-bishop
pays the price at which our sons, the glorious Venantius the Patrician
and Urbicus the Abbot, may value the synagogues themselves, with
the guest-rooms under them or adjoining their walls and the gardens

belonging to them. So what he has seized may belong to the church and the Jews neither oppressed nor made to suffer injustice.

B. Christian Slaves to Jews: Gregory to Fortunatus, bishop of Naples
Having learnt what zeal inflames your Fraternity on behalf of Christian slaves whom Jews buy from the territories of Gaul, we inform you that your solicitude has so pleased us that it is also our own deliberate judgment that they should be prohibited from traffic of this kind. But we find from Basilius the Hebrew, who has come here with other Jews, that such purchase is enjoined on them by various judges of the republic, and that Christians along with pagans come to be procured this way....

Accordingly let your Fraternity with watchful care provide for this being observed and kept to: that when the purchasers return from the aforesaid province any Christian slave who may happen to be brought by them should either be handed over to those who gave the order or sold to Christian purchasers within 40 days.

Atrocities Against Jews

The pilgrimages of the tenth century reflected and magnified popular sentiment about the Holy Land where Jesus was crucified. What the Orthodox call the Church of the Resurrection is to Catholics the Church of the Holy Sepulchre. This concentration on the scene and events of the Passion misled unsophisticated minds and inflamed barbarian tempers so that they were more liable than before to violent outbursts against the Jews of the West. Crusades against Moslems in the Holy Land were paralleled by pogroms against Jews at home.

12.4   POGROMS   1009
Ralph the Bald, a Cluniac chronicler, explained one serious anti-Jewish outbreak. No doubt the reason he gave was the one generally believed in the West. In fact, however, Caliph Hakim's campaign against non-Moslems (1004–1014) was specifically directed against Jews as well as Christians. But it was the destruction of the Church of the Holy Sepulchre in 1009 which caught the imagination of the West, and was 'of course' put down there to the Jews.

In the ninth year after the thousandth anniversary, the church at Jerusalem which contained the sepulchre of our Lord and Saviour was utterly overthrown at the command of the prince of Babylon.... Within a brief space it became fully evident that this great iniquity had been done by the wickedness of the Jews. When therefore this was spread abroad through the whole world, it was decreed by the common consent of Christian folk that all Jews should be utterly driven forth from their lands or cities.

Thus they were held up to universal hatred and driven out. Some were slain with the sword or killed in many other ways, and some also killed themselves. Consequently, after this well-deserved vengeance had been wreaked, scarcely any Jews could be found in the Roman world.

Then the bishops published decrees forbidding all Christians to associate with Jews in any matter whatever; but whoever would be converted to baptismal grace and completely shun the customs and manners of the Jews, he only should be received. This indeed was done by very many of them, for love of this present life, impelled by fear of death rather than by the joys of the life everlasting; for all those who simulated this conversion very soon returned impudently to their former way of life.

12.5	BIRTH OF AN ATROCITY STORY	1144

William, twelve years old, was seen entering a house in the Norwich Jewry on the Wednesday before Easter (Passover-time). His body was found in Thorpe Wood on Good Friday. There are almost no facts to prove the Jews were his murderers, but the testimony of Theobald, a converted Jew, triggered off a riot and the Norwich Jews took refuge in the castle close by. There seems to be no truth in Theobald's account, and the most reasonable explanations of the boy's death are that Theobald was defending himself or that William was the victim of Jewish horse-play that went too far.

The translation of the relics in 1151, the growth of the cult of St. William, and this account by Thomas of Monmouth led to a spate of child martyrs. A boy Harold was found in the Severn at Gloucester in 1168, accusations of child murder were made against the Jews of Orleans and of Blois in 1171, Richard of Pointoise was killed in 1179 (which led to a persecution of Jews in France), a Robert of Bury St. Edmunds was killed in 1181 and Hugh of Lincoln ('Little St. Hugh') in 1255.

As proof of the truth of this happening we now quote something we have heard from Theobald, once a Jew and afterwards a monk. He related that in the ancient writings of the fathers it was written that the Jews could neither gain their freedom nor ever return to their fatherland without the shedding of human blood. Hence it was decreed in ancient times that every year they must sacrifice a Christian to the most high God in some part of the world, in scorn and contempt of Christ; and they avenge their sufferings thus because it was owing to Christ's death that they had been shut out of their country and were in exile as slaves in a foreign land.

Therefore the chief men and rabbis of the Jews, those who live in Spain around Narbonne..., meet and cast lots for all the countries where Jews are living. And the metropolis of the country chosen by lot has then to repeat the process among its towns and cities, and the place whose lot is drawn then has to fulfil the duty decreed.

Now on that year in which we know that William, God's glorious martyr, was killed, it happened that the lot had fallen upon the Jews of Norwich and all the synagogues of England agreed by letter or message that the crime should be carried out at Norwich.

'I was then at Cambridge,' said Theobald, 'a Jew among Jews, and the commission of the crime was no secret to me. In the process of time, after the glorious display of miracles which the divine power performed through the merits of the blessed martyr William, I became very afraid. So following the counsel of my conscience I forsook Judaism and turned to the Christian faith.'

12.6   THE JEWS IN HOLY WEEK   1152

Holy Week was an especially dangerous time for Jews. It was the time of Passover when Christians, remembering the Bible, expected Jews to sacrifice. It was the time, too, when Christians recalled the Passion and turned their indignation and guilt against the Jews. Sometimes, however, the Jews could buy immunity even from a returning Crusader. This incident comes from Prior Geoffrey's Chronicle of 1152.

When Raymund Trenchaval, viscount of Béziers, returned from Jerusalem in the year 1152, he received money to release the Jews from the persecution they suffered from Christians in the week of our Lord's passion. I will describe the matter at length for those who may not know of it.

Many Jews have lived in the town of Béziers from time immemorial. On Palm Sunday the bishop, after preaching a mystic sermon to the people, used to exhort them in many words to this effect:

'Lo! You see before you the descendants of those who condemned the Messiah, and who still deny that Mary was the Mother of God. Lo! This is the time when our hearts reverberate more often to the injury done to Christ. Lo! These are the days when you have leave from the prince to avenge this great iniquity. Now therefore, taught by the custom of your ancestors and fortified with our blessing after that of the Lord, cast stones against the Jews while yet there is time and, as far as you can, atone manfully for the evil done to our Lord.'

When, therefore, the bishop had blessed them and (as in former days) the prince had given them the customary leave, they would batter the Jews' houses with showers of stones, and very many were often wounded on both sides. This fight was commonly continued from Palm Sunday until Easter Eve, and ended about the fourth hour; but no one was allowed to use any other weapon than stones.

All this, as we have said, was forgiven to the faithless Jews by this Raymund.

12.7   THE EFFECT OF THE CRUSADES   1189

From the time of Peter the Hermit the preaching of a crusade meant trouble for Jews. The news of the fall of Jerusalem after nearly a century of Christian rule made Westerners feel guilty. Jews suffered as Christians prepared for the Third Crusade. What happened in England is told here in the Chronicle of Ralph de Diceto, Dean of St. Paul's (d. 1202) and by Benedict of Peterborough (d. 1193) in *Records of King Richard.*

A.

Many people throughout England, in a hurry to get to Jerusalem, decided to attack the Jews before they attacked the Saracens. So on February 6 at Norwich all Jews found in their homes were slaughtered. Some took refuge in the castle. On March 7 in Stamford on market day many were killed. On March 16 at York nearly 500 are said to have been murdered, though there they killed each other, preferring death from their own people rather than from hands of the uncircumcised. On March 18, Palm Sunday, 57 are reported as killed at St. Edmunds. Wherever Jews were found they were massacred by pilgrims unless rescued by their own fellow-citizens.

Do not suppose that this terrible and wicked slaughter of Jews was approved by sensible people for we often hear that saying of David, 'Slay them not!' (Psa. 59, 11).

B.

Some Jews in the city escaped the massacre by shutting themselves up in the Tower of London and hiding in friends' houses. Next day when the king heard what had happened, he sent officers through the city to arrest some of the culprits and bring them before him. Three were hanged by judgment of the court. . . .

Then King Richard sent letters by his messengers through all the counties of England forbidding anyone to harm the Jews, who were to enjoy his peace. But before this law was proclaimed the Dunstable Jews had become Christians, got baptised and married their wives, and the same thing occurred in many other English towns.

Jews and the Law in England

'That no Israelites had ever dwelt in this country before the year 1066 we dare not say; but if so, they have left no traces of their presence that are of any importance to us. They were brought hither from Normandy, brought hither as the king's dependants and (the word will hardly be too strong) the king's serfs.' Thus Pollock and Maitland in their great *History of English Law*. They were brought here as the king's, and the nobles', financiers. They were as necessary, and as unpopular, as those concerned with money but not with productive industry and agriculture always are in a primitive society. 'Their function in the state was two-fold, to supply the crown at any moment with ready money, and to act as a channel for the conveyance to the king of the property of his subjects.' That is how Bland, Brown and Tawney put it in *English Economic History: Select Documents*.

The first extract shows the conditions which they had to accept if they lived in England—conditions virtually unchanged since they first came here. The second, from the Annals of Osney, records their banishment in 1290. They did not return for three centuries, and it was yet another before Cromwell made their residence legal. In the later middle ages their place in the economy was taken by the great Italian banking houses.

12.8   CONDITIONS OF RESIDENCE   1253

The King (Henry III) has provided and decreed ... that no Jew shall dwell in England unless he do the king service, and that as soon as a Jew shall be born, whether male or female, in some way he shall serve the king.

And that there be no communities of the Jews in England save in those places wherein such communities were in the time of the lord King John, the King's father.

And that in their synagogues the Jews, one and all, worship in subdued tones according to their rite, so that Christians hear it not. And that all Jews answer to the rector of the parish in which they dwell for all parochial dues belonging to their houses.

And that no Christian nurse hereafter suckle or nourish the male child of any Jew, and that no Christian man or woman serve any Jew or Jewess, nor eat with them, nor dwell in their house. And that no Jew or Jewess eat or buy meat in Lent.

And that no Jew disparage the Christian faith, nor publicly dispute concerning the same.

And that no Jew have secret intercourse with any Christian woman, nor any Christian man with a Jewess.

And that every Jew wear on his breast a conspicuous badge.

And that no Jew enter any church or chapel save in passing through, nor stay therein to the dishonour of Christ. And that no Jew

in any wise hinder another Jew willing to be converted to the
Christian faith....

Witness the King at Westminster on the 31st day of January.

By the King and Council.

12.9 THE JEWS BANISHED 1290

A notable event, never to be forgotten but to be commemorated for
ever, took place this year. This last summer about the Nativity of
John the Baptist [June 24] the King [Edward I], acting we may be sure
on the advice of his nobles, published this edict throughout the realm:

All Jews living in the cities and towns of England, of whatever
condition, age or sex ... being enemies of the cross of Christ and
blasphemers against the Christian faith, must leave the borders of this
realm by the feast of All Saints [November 1] and are condemned to
perpetual banishment without hope of return. If any is found in
England after this date he will be executed or hanged.

In great fear of this terrible edict all but a few crossed the sea and
took themselves and what goods they could pack into foreign lands.
And it was common gossip that those who embarked at the Cinque
Ports were robbed of their money when out at sea and barbarously
butchered by the ships' masters and thrown overboard. Others were
marooned on a sandbank uncovered by the retreating tide and so
drowned when the tide returned. When the king heard of this he
condemned very many of the murderers and robbers to be hanged.

A Jewish Traveller and a Jewish Poet

Up to this point we have been looking at Jews through Christian eyes. This
last section is taken from the writings of two notable twelfth century Jewish
writers. Both were born in Tudela at a time when it was just inside the
boundary of Moorish Spain. One was a traveller, the other a poet. In their
time civilization had reached in Moorish Spain a fine flowering to which
Christian Europe was to owe among other debts its recovery of the long-lost
books of Aristotle, a discovery which raised him at once in educated circles to
the dignity of 'The Philosopher'. In this cultured Moorish society the Jews
played a distinctive and welcome part. They made their contributions to the
philosophical revival through the medium of Arabic, but in religion and
poetry they used their own Hebrew.

12.10 ORIENTAL JEWS *c.* 1170

Benjamin of Tudela (d. 1173) wrote a record of his travels which took him
through France, Italy, Greece, the Near East, and well on the way to China.
Everywhere he went he found fellow-Jews, so wide was the Dispersion.

A. In Constantinople

No Jews live in the city, for they have been placed behind an inlet of the sea. An arm of the sea of Marmora shuts them in on one side and they are unable to travel except by sea if they wish to do business with the inhabitants. . . .

No Jew is allowed to ride on horseback except Rabbi Solomon Hamitsri, who is the emperor's physician; through him the Jews enjoy considerable relief from oppression. For their condition is very low and there is much hatred against them; this is fostered by the tanners who throw out their dirty water in the streets in front of the doors of the Jewish houses and defile the Jews' quarter. So the Greeks hate the Jews, good and bad alike, oppress them greatly, beat them up in the streets and treat them roughly in every way. Yet the Jews are rich and good, kindly and charitable, and bear their lot with cheerfulness. The district they inhabit is called Pera.

B. In Bagdad

In Bagdad there are about 40,000 Jews, and they live in security, prosperity, and honour under the great Caliph. Among them are very learned men, the heads of ten Academies engaged in the study of the law. . . .

At the head of them all is Daniel the son of Hisdai, styled 'Our Lord the Head of the Captivity of all Israel.' He possesses a book of pedigrees going back as far as David, king of Israel. . . . The Emir al Muminin, Lord of Islam, has invested him with authority over all the congregations of Israel. . . .

Every fifth day he visits the great Caliph, when horsemen, Gentiles as well as Jews, escort him and heralds proclaim in advance, 'Make way before our Lord, the son of David, as is due to him,' the Arabic being 'Amilu tarik la Saidna ben Daud.' He is on horseback in robes of embroidered silk, with a large turban on his head. From the turban hangs a long white cloth with a chain, upon which the cipher of Mohammed is engraved. Then he appears before the Caliph and kisses his hand, and the Caliph rises and places him on a throne which Mohammed had ordered to be made for him; and all the Mohammedan princes attending the court rise up before him.

C. In Jerusalem

Jerusalem is a small city, fortified by three walls. It is full of people whom the Mohammedans calls Jacobites, Syrians, Greeks, Georgians, and Franks, and people of all languages. It contains a dyeing-house, for which the Jews pay a small yearly rent to the king [Amalric], on condition that only Jews be allowed as dyers in Jerusalem.... About ten cubits (five yards) of the lower part of the walls of the Tower of David is part of the ancient foundation laid by our ancestors; the rest was built by the Mohammedans. There is no structure in the whole city stronger than the Tower of David.

In the Hospital, a building in the city, are 400 knights, and all the sick who go there are lodged and cared for both in life and death. Another building is the Temple of Solomon, the palace built by Solomon, king of Israel. Every day 300 knights, who are quartered there, come out for military exercise, and there are also Franks and others from various parts of Christendom, who have vowed to serve there for a year or two.

In Jerusalem is the great church called the Sepulchre and here is the burial-place of Jesus, to which the Christians make pilgrimages....

On the site of the sanctuary of our ancient Temple, Omar ben al Khataab erected a building with a very large and magnificent Dome. The Gentiles do not bring any image or portrait into it, but they come there just to pray.

In front of this place is the western wall, one of the walls of the Holy of Holies. This is called the Gate of Mercy, and all the Jews come there to pray before the wall of the court of the Temple.

12.11 THE LORD'S SONG IN A STRANGE LAND

Judah Ha-Levi, reckoned the greatest post-Biblical Hebrew poet, probably died in Egypt in 1141 on his way to Palestine. He had lived both in Christian and Moslem Spain, but his heart was always in Israel and he believed that it was there that his people's redemption was to be accomplished. These two poems, taken from David Goldstein's translation, are so thoroughly Biblical in feeling that Christians will find they can make the words their own.

A. The Servant of God

If only I could be the servant of God who made me,
My friends could all desert me, if he would but befriend me.

My maker and shepherd, I, body and soul, am your creation.
You perceive all my thought; you discern my intention.
You measure my journeying, my steps, my relaxation.
If you help me, who can throw me down?
If you confine me, who but you can break my bonds?

My inner heart yearns to be near to you,
But my worldly cares drive me away from you.
My paths have strayed far from the way you pursue.
O God, help me to follow your truth. Give me instruction.
Lead me gently in judgement. Stay your conviction.

I am reluctant to perform your will, in my vigour.
And so in old age what can I hope for? Of what be sure?
O God, heal me; for with you, God, is my cure.
When old age destroys me, and my strength forgets me,
Do not forsake me, my rock, do not reject me.

Broken, despairing, I remain, fearful every minute.
Because of my mocking vanity I go naked, empty-handed.
And I am stained with my iniquity, for it is abundant.
It is sin that makes a division between you and me,
And prevents my eye from seeing the light of your glory.

Incline my heart to serve in your kingdom's service.
Cleanse my thoughts that I may know your divineness.
Do not delay your healing power in the days of my sickness.
Answer, my God. Do not chastise. Do not withhold reply.
Employ me again as your servant. Say: 'Here am I.'

B. Jerusalem
Beautiful heights, joy of the world, city of a great king,
For you my soul yearns from the lands of the West.
My pity collects and is roused when I remember the past,
Your glory in exile, and your temple destroyed.
Would that I were on the wings of an eagle,
So that I could water your dust with my mingling tears.
I have sought you, although your king is away,
And snakes and scorpions oust Gilead's balm.
How I shall kiss and cherish your stones.
Your earth will be sweeter than honey to my taste.

CHAPTER THIRTEEN

THE EAST AGAIN

Rome and Constantinople

These five extracts deal with the worsening relations between the Holy
Roman Empire and the Eastern Empire, between Catholics and Orthodox.
Constantinople, although its empire was contracting—a principal reason for
the Crusades—was still a far greater, more sophisticated and richer city than
any in the West.

13.1   AN ITALIAN VIEW OF GREEK BISHOPS   967

Liutprand, bishop of Cremona (see 14.5) was on his way back from an
embassy to Constantinople from the Holy Roman Emperor, Otto the Great.
His account shows that there were more than theological difficulties in the
way of ecumenical understanding. The ostensible quarrel was about the
'absurd' claim of Greek bishops to wear the pallium, a woollen vestment
worn by the pope and some archbishops to whom he personally gave the
right.

On December 6 we came to Leucas where the bishop, who is a
eunuch, received and treated us very unkindly, as all the other
bishops had done. In all Greece I do not lie I found no hospitable
bishops. They are both poor and rich, rich in gold coin with which
they gamble recklessly, poor in servants and equipment. They sit
alone at a bare little table with a ship's biscuit in front of them and
don't exactly drink their bath water, but sip it from a tiny glass. They
do their own buying and selling, open and shut their own doors, act as
their own stewards, ass-drivers, and capones. Aha! I meant to write
caupones, innkeepers, which is against canon law, but the truth will
out and I wrote capones, eunuchs, which is also uncanonical. It is
true to say of them:
> A lettuce once closed the repast:
> Now 'tis the first course and the last.
If their poverty imitated that of Christ I should say, good for them!
But their reason is sordid gain, the accursed greed for gold. May God
have mercy on them!
   I think they live like this because their churches are taxed by the

state. The bishop of Leucas swore to me that his church had to pay Nicephorus 100 gold pieces a year, and other churches paid at the same rate according to their means. The injustice of this is shown by the laws of the holy patriarch Joseph, who during the famine made all Egypt pay tribute to Pharaoh, but exempted the land of the priests.

13.2   A 'FINAL' BREACH BETWEEN EAST AND WEST   1053

The letter of Leo IX, from which this extract is taken, begins, 'Peace on earth to men of good-will.' It is the pope's answer to the patriarch's order to close all churches using the Latin rite. This marks a formal and, in a sense, a 'final' separation between Catholic and Orthodox (so it is usually regarded) which was completed by an exchange of excommunications the following year. But this did not prevent relatively harmonious relations between the two churches during the First Crusade.

It is said that you have publicly condemned the Apostolic Latin Church, without either a hearing or a conviction. Your chief reason for this condemnation, which reveals an unequalled presumption and an incredible effrontery, is that the Latin Church dares to celebrate the commemoration of the Lord's passion with unleavened bread. What a reckless accusation is this of yours, what a wicked piece of arrogance! . . .

By prejudging the case of the highest See, on which no judgment may be passed by man, you have received the anathema from all the Fathers of the Venerable Councils.

13.3   CONSTANTINOPLE IN 1170

The splendour of the twelfth century city and its great church of St. Sophia shines out of this account by a Jewish rabbi, Benjamin of Tudela (see 12.10).

In Constantinople is the church of St. Sophia, the cathedral of the pope of the Greeks, since the Greeks do not obey the pope of Rome. . . . The like of its wealth is not to be found in any other church in the world. In it are pillars of gold and silver, and lamps of silver and gold more than one can count.

Close to the walls of the palace is a place of amusement belonging to the emperor, called the Hippodrome, and every year on the anniversary of the birth of Jesus the emperor gives a great entertainment there. Men from all the races of the world come before the emperor and queen, either with jugglery or without, and introduce lions, leopards, bears and wild asses, and make them fight one another; and the same is done with birds. Nothing like this entertainment is found in any other country.

13.4   A CRUSADE AGAINST CONSTANTINOPLE

'There was never a greater crime against humanity than the Fourth Crusade.'
That is Steven Runciman's verdict. These two extracts concern this war of
Catholics against Orthodox or, more accurately, this buccaneering expe-
dition of Western nobles and Venetian merchants in search of easy fortunes.
The great pope, Innocent III, blessed it; when he heard what it had done he
bitterly condemned it. It was too late to undo the harm. It was this crusade
rather than theological niceties, which caused the total separation of
Orthodox and Catholic.

A.   A NUBIAN KING'S VISIT   1203

This extract shows the astonishment of a simple foot-soldier from Picardy,
Robert of Clary, at encountering a Christian ruler from Ethiopia. The
African must have been equally bewildered—not only by the richness of the
city but by the behaviour of Robert of Clary's fellow-Crusaders. Runciman
in his *History of the Crusades* writes: 'The sight of the haughty Frankish
knights striding through the streets exasperated the citizens.... Parties of
drunken Western soldiers constantly pillaged the villages in the suburbs, so
that life was no longer safe outside the walls. A disastrous fire swept through
a whole quarter of the city when some Frenchmen in an access of piety
burned down a mosque built for the use of visiting Moslem merchants.'

One day the barons went to the palace for the pleasure of seeing Isaac
(Angelus) and his son the emperor (Alexius IV). While they were
there a king arrived whose skin was all black and he had a cross
branded in the middle of his forehead with a hot iron. This king was
staying in a very rich abbey in the city, where Alexius had asked he
should be put, and he was the lord and squire and guest of it as long as
he wanted to stay. When the emperor saw him coming he rose to meet
him and gave him great honour.
    'Do you know who he is?' he asked the barons.
    'No, Sire.'
    'I'faith he is the king of Nubia, come on pilgrimage to this town.'
    With interpreters they made him talk; they asked him where his
country was. He answered in his own language and through the
interpreters that his country was a hundred days' journey beyond
Jerusalem. He had come from there to Jerusalem on pilgrimage.
When he left his country he had 60 of his people with him and when he
reached Jerusalem only ten were left alive, and when he reached
Constantinople from Jerusalem, only two were left. And he said he
wanted to go on pilgrimage to Rome, and from Rome to St. James'
(Compostella), and then return to Jerusalem, hoping to live and die
there. And he said all the people of his country were Christians, and
when a child was born and baptised, they branded a cross on his

forehead like his. The barons thought this king was a great marvel.
Source: Robert of Clary, *The Conquest of Constantinople*.

B.   THE SACK OF ST. SOPHIA   1204

The political arrangements made by the Crusaders did not last. A Greek
counter-coup turned out the puppet-rulers. The Crusaders then decided to
instal a Frankish noble as emperor and a Venetian as patriarch. They
stormed the city and turned it over for three days of looting. 'Even the
Saracens would have been more merciful,' wrote the Greek historian,
Nicetas. St. Sophia itself was not spared. Far away in Russia the Novgorod
chronicler noted:

The Franks entered the city on the Feast of St. Basil, Monday, April
12th, and pitched camp in the sanctuary of the Holy Redeemer, where
the Greek Emperor had recently stayed. There they spent the night.
In the morning after sunrise they invaded Saint Sophia, broke down
the doors, and wrecked the choir with its silver ornaments and twelve
silver pillars, the priest standing by. They smashed four reredoses
against the wall, which were hung with icons, and the holy altar with
its twelve crosses, the best of which were carved like trees and taller
than a man. The sides of the altar near the pillars were of silver,
embossed, and they also stole a marvellous table set with precious
stones and a great gem, ignorant of the evil they were doing.

They seized forty chalices which were on the altar and the silver
candlesticks, too numerous for me to count, and the silver vases
which the Greeks use on major festivals. They took the Gospel used
in the celebration of the mysteries and the sacred crosses, all the
images, the altar cover, and forty censers of pure gold. As well as
priceless vases they carried away everything of gold and silver that
they could find in the cupboards, on the walls, or wherever they were
shut away; it would be impossible to count them.

Christianity in Russia

13.5   THE BOYHOOD OF THEODOSIUS

The conversion of Russia or at least of the Ukraine is best dated by the
baptism of Vladimir of Kiev a little before 990. An old legend tells how he was
visited by envoys of Orthodox and Catholic Christianity, of Islam, and of
Judaism and chose the first of these faiths. This is a late story which, however,
reflects a genuine range of choice. His grandmother had invited Catholic
missionaries; his neighbours, the Kazars, had strong Jewish sympathies; and
Islam was strong and near. He chose Orthodox Christianity, though he kept
his church free from Greek control.

Theodosius, who died in 1074, was the founder of the Caves monastery at Kiev. He was strongly influenced by Palestinian monasticism. He sought a balance between contemplative and active life. Thus he built a hospital for beggars and sick people, and sent food to the gaol for the prisoners.

When Theodosius was about thirteen years old his father died. From that time on he applied himself even more zealously to holy undertakings. That is, he now went into the fields with his serfs, where he did the humblest work. To prevent this his mother used to keep him indoors. She also tried to prevail upon him to put on good clothes and go out to play with boys of his own age, for she said that if he was so poorly dressed he would expose himself and his family to disgrace. But he would not obey her, and often she would beat him in her vexation. She was robust of body, and if you could not see her, but only hear her voice, you might well have mistaken her for a man.

The devout youth, meanwhile, was meditating and searching for the means of salvation. When he heard of the Holy Land, where our Lord had walked in the flesh, he longed to make a pilgrimage to this place. He prayed to God, saying, 'Holy Lord Jesus, listen to my prayer, and grant that I may go to the Holy Land.' After he had prayed in this manner for a long time some pilgrims came to the city. The holy youth rejoiced when he saw them. He went out to meet them, and greeted them affectionately, asking them whence they had come and whither they were going. And when they told him that they had come from the Holy Land and that, God permitting, they intended to return there, he begged to be taken with them. . . . During the night he left his home secretly, taking with him nothing except the poor clothes he had on. It was in this manner that he set out to join the pilgrims.

But God, in his mercy, would not permit the man whom he had predestined in his mother's womb to be the shepherd of the divinely enlightened sheep to leave this land lest, when the shepherd departed, the pastures that God had planted would lie desolate, overgrown with thorns, and haunted by wolves which would scatter the flock. After three days his mother learnt that he had gone with the pilgrims, and taking her other son (who was younger than Theodosius) with her, they set out to overtake him. After a long pursuit they caught up with him. Carried away by fury, she seized him by the hair, flung him to the ground, and trampled on him. Then, having rebuked the pilgrims, she returned home, leading the saint bound like a criminal. So greatly incensed was she, that when they had entered the house she beat her

12th Century Byzantine Church, 'The Intercession of the Virgin'
near Vladimar, Russia

son until she was exhausted. Then she flung him into a room, shackled him, and locked the door. The holy youth suffered all this joyfully, giving thanks to God in prayer.

After two days his mother returned, unfastened him, and placed food before him. But her anger was still unsatisfied, so she put chains on his feet, and ordered him to go about the house in them, and she watched him so that he might not run away from her again. He wore these chains for many weeks, but at last his mother relented. She began to beg him not to run away again, saying that she loved him more than all her other children, and could not live without him. . . .

Theodosius saw that often mass could not be celebrated for lack of altar bread so he worked as a baker to make it. His mother eventually became a nun.

13.6   SERGIUS AND THE PEASANT

Three centuries separate Sergius from Theodosius. Between them fall the Mongol invasions which devastated the lands north of the Caspian and the Black Seas. Sergius embarked on the religious life as a hermit, but was rapidly joined by others, each living in a separate cell. Eventually he was ordained priest and became abbot of the community. He practised mysticism, but also played a considerable part in public affairs. He encouraged the prince of Moscow to resist the Mongols. The prince won a great victory which he attributed to the prayers of Sergius. Sergius died in 1392. He was soon recognized as the patron saint of Russia. This story is from the life by Epiphanius.

One day a peasant came to the monastery who had never seen Sergius. At that hour the saint was working in the vegetable garden. The peasant looked about him, asking: 'Which of the monks is Sergius? Where is that wonderful and famous man?'

The brethren said to him: 'He is working alone in the kitchen-garden. Wait for a while, till he has finished his work.'

But the peasant, becoming impatient, looked through the chink in the fence and saw the saint, in his torn and patched old cassock, working in the sweat of his brow, and he could not believe that this was the abbot about whom he had heard such extraordinary accounts. When the saint came to join them, the brethren pointed to him, saying: 'Here is the man whom you wished to see.'

The peasant turned away, laughing. 'I have come to see a prophet,' he exclaimed, 'and you show me a beggar!'

The brethren related this to the abbot: 'We do not dare tell you all he says, venerable Father, but we would like to send this visitor away as a good for nothing, churlish fellow. He does not bow to you or render you the honours due to your rank. He rebukes us and will not listen to us.'

But the man of God, seeing the perplexity of the brethren, said: 'Do not do that, brothers, for he did not come to you, but to ask for me.' And not waiting to receive the peasant's obeisance, Sergius bowed low before him; when he had given the man his blessing, he praised him for the correctness of his judgment concerning himself. Taking the visitor's hand, the saint had him sit at his right hand, and persuaded him to taste of the food and drink. But the peasant went on protesting that he deplored the absence of abbot Sergius, whom he had come to see, but with whom he had been denied an interview.

The saint said to him: 'Do not be troubled; so great is the grace of God in this place that no one leaves here with a sad heart.'

And while he was speaking, a prince arrived at the monastery in great pomp and splendour, surrounded by a vast retinue of boyars and servants. The soldiers who went before the prince took the peasant by the shoulders and pushed him away from Sergius and the prince. The noble visitor bowed low before Sergius, even before he had approached him. The abbot blessed him and gave him the kiss of peace, after which they both sat down, while all the others remained standing.

Meanwhile the peasant had made his way back through the crowd, and inquired of one of the attendants: 'Tell me, who is this monk, sitting on the right hand of the prince?'

The man, looking at him in astonishment, exclaimed: 'Are you a stranger in these parts? Have you never heard of the blessed Sergius? It is he who is conversing with the prince.'

Hearing this, the peasant was shaken with fear and remorse. He fell at the saint's feet, crying: 'Oh, how greatly I have sinned, wretch that I am! Forgive me and help my unbelief.'

The saint forgave him, gave him his blessing, and having spoken words of comfort to him, let him return to his home.

Christians under Islam

These two extracts resume the story left off on p. 105. There were in North Africa and the Middle East numerous Christian communities content to live a quiet and often prosperous life, cut off from political power but enjoying religious toleration from their Moslem masters. The first of these two extracts concerns Catholic Christians in Algeria. It is notable for the way in which one of the most intransigent of popes could diplomatically go out of his way to stress common ground between Islam and Christianity. The second extract concerns Nestorian Christians in what is now Iraq. They tended to find life under Moslem rulers easier than it would have been for them under either Orthodox or Catholic masters.

13.7   A CHRISTIAN BISHOP BY MOSLEM REQUEST   *c.* 1076

Gregory . . . to Anazir, king of the province of Mauretania Sitifensis in Africa

Your highness asked us to ordain the priest Servandus as bishop according to the Christian order. This we have taken pains to do, as your request was proper and augurs well. You also sent us presents and freed some Christian captives and promised to release others; this was out of respect to St. Peter chief of the apostles and of friendship with us. This good action was inspired in your heart by God. . . . Who desires that all men should be saved and is most pleased when a man loves his fellow man next to his God and does nothing to him which he would not have others do to himself.

This affection we owe each other is peculiar to us and not to people of other races, because we worship the same God, though in different forms, daily praising and adoring him as the creator and ruler of the world. For in the words of the apostle, 'He is our peace who hath made both one' (Eph. 2, 14).

. . . God knows how earnestly we pray with our lips and with our heart that he himself, after the long journey of life, may lead you into the bosom of the most holy patriarch Abraham.

13.8   THE CALIPH AND THE PATRIARCH   1138

In 1138 the Caliph Muktafi II granted a charter to Abdishu III, the Nestorian Patriarch (Catholicos) of Bagdad. It shows Christianity as a tolerated, though supervised religion, and records that this had long been its status. The charter was preserved in a copybook of fine examples of Arabic style which was made before 1167. The editor of the book noted that it was 'composed by my brother (Abu Nasr, secretary of the Caliph, who died in 1150), may God have mercy on his soul.' The copy-book was published by Dr. Mingana in the Bulletin of John Rylands Library, Manchester in 1925.

. . . I brought your petition to the notice of the Commander of the Faithful and informed him that you were the worthiest of your people in devotion and the nearest of them all to goodness in saintliness and other accomplishments, and that you were possessed of qualities and merits which singled you out from all of them, and that you had contained in you all the pre-requisites, provisions, and qualifications of the Catholicate known to your people. With me there was a deputation of Christians well versed in the regulations affecting this high office, and they submitted that, after a careful and searching examination of your claim, they had come to the conclusion that they were in need of a Catholicos to look after their affairs and minister to their collective needs, and that by a spontaneous and unanimous decision they had acquiesced in your elevation to the headship of their religion for regulating their affairs, satisfying their needs, and rendering justice to the strongest and weakest among them. They asked for the confirmation of your election in the form of a charter which would place it on a solid basis and unassailable foundations.

The Commander of the Faithful ordered, therefore, that their request be granted and their wish be gratified ... [there follow provisions for punishing bishops and priests who disobeyed the new patriarch]...

Following the precedent sanctioned by the Imams, my predecessors, in their dealings with the Catholicoi, your predecessors, the Commander of the Faithful ... provided that your life and property, and those of your people, will be protected, great care will be taken in the promotion of your welfare, your ways of interring your dead will be respected, and your churches and monasteries will be protected. In all this we are in conformity with the method adopted by the Orthodox Caliphs with your predecessors, a method that has been followed by the high Imams, my predecessors—may God be pleased with them—in their interpretation of the terms of our convention with you; that we shall be satisfied by your payment of the capitation tax, levied upon the males of your community who have passed the age of minority, and who are rational and solvent; that all your females and your males in their minority shall be exempt from it, and that it shall be levied once a year in strict conformity with the kindly rules of the *Shar*.

The Commander of the Faithful was also gracious to be willing to mediate between the different Christian communities in their lawsuits in order to exact justice from the strong in favour of the weak, and to direct to the right path anyone who was straying from it, to look after them according to the requirements of their religion, and to follow it in its clear path and straight course.

Be worthy of all these favours granted to you, which fulfil the desires of your soul, and set up prayers and invocations for the Commander of the Faithful as a token of your gratitude and a sign of your allegiance....

Christians in Tartary

Central Asia was the heartland of the great Mongol confederacy which in the thirteenth century dominated a greater portion of the world's surface than any previous empire had done. It covered 'the whole land-mass of Eurasia, excluding only the four peninsulas of Indo-China (in part), India, Arabia, and Western Europe.' The Mongols had been following a decaying pagan religion, and were open to influences from all the major religions of mankind. The next four extracts illustrate the contact between Christianity and the Mongol rulers.

13.9   THE SECRET CHRISTIANS OF FOO-CHAU

Marco Polo and his uncle, Venetian merchants, spent over twenty years in business travels in the East, returning to Europe in 1295. The account of their travels was soon a 'best-seller', but not one of the numerous manuscripts can be regarded as complete. The following passage occurs in a source which was long known only in an eighteenth century transcript. More recently it has been traced back to a fifteenth century manuscript in Toledo.

Almost everywhere in his travels Marco Polo found established Christian communities, which were usually Nestorian. Most Christians were living openly and in good standing with their rulers. In Foo-chau, however, the Christian community had gone underground.

When Marco and his uncle Maffeo were in Foochow [now Minhow], a certain learned Saracen in their company said:

'In such-and-such a place there is a community of unknown religion. They are not idolaters for they keep no idols. They do not worship fire or follow Mohammed, and do not seem to follow Christianity. Why not go and talk to them? Perhaps you will recognise some of their customs.'

So they went there and talked to the people about their religious customs and creed. They were afraid that the questions were aimed at depriving them of their religion. When they realized this, Maffeo and Marco tried to quieten their fears with words of encouragement.

'Do not be alarmed. We have come not to harm you but help you and improve your condition.'

They were still afraid that the visitors had been sent by the Great Khan to get them into trouble. But Maffeo and Marco came day after day and got to know the people and their ways. They discovered that they were indeed Christians, for they had books which after careful translation were found to be psalters. How had they received their faith and their rule? From their forefathers, they said.

It transpired that there were three portraits in a certain temple of theirs representing three of the seventy apostles who went out into the world preaching [Cp. Luke 10, 1]. They asserted that these three had instructed their ancestors in the faith long ago. They had preserved it for 700 years, but had been without any instruction for so long that they were ignorant of fundamental doctrines.

'But we hold fast to what we have received from our forefathers. We worship according to our books and reverence these three apostles.'

'You are Christians and so are we,' said Maffeo and Marco. 'We advise you to explain your position to the Great Khan so that he can grant you recognition. Then you can keep your faith and your rule free of fear.'

They had not dared to practise their religion openly for fear of the idolaters, but they sent two men to the Great Khan . . . and he ordered that they should be recognised as Christians, with the privileges of that status for all who followed their rule. And this was found to apply to 700,000 families in the province of Manzi.

13.10   A MESSAGE FROM THE KING OF FRANCE   1253

In the latter half of the thirteenth century the Christian West was coming under renewed and intensified pressure from Islam. Beyond the lands of Islam lay the as yet unaligned power of the Great Khan. Not surprisingly for a time Karakoram was the diplomatic centre of the world. Louis IX, king of France, better known as Saint Louis, sent William of Rubruck there to arrange, if he could, for help against the Moslems. The episode described here took place on the Lower Volga at the court of Sartak, a subordinate ruler, who sent William on to Karakoram. William was a Franciscan.

Next day Coiak asked me to come to court, bringing the letters from King Louis, the vestments, church ornaments and books, as his master wished to see them. . . .

He asked us to explain all about the books and vestments, which we did while many Tartars and Christians and Saracens looked on, seated on their horses. After examining them he asked if I was going to give all these things to his master. I was shocked and displeased, but concealed it as I answered,

'My lord, we beg your lord to condescend to accept this bread, wine and fruit, not as a gift, for it is too trifling, but as a blessing, and so that we shall not come before him with empty hands. He shall see the letters of our lord the king and by them he shall know why we come to him and then we shall await his pleasure, we and all our belongings. As for these vestments, they are holy and only priests may touch them.'

Coiak told us to put them on before going into the presence of Sartak his lord and this we did. I put on the richest of the vestments, and held a beautiful gospel-cushion against my breast; and I took the Bible you had given me, and the beautiful Psalter with the very lovely pictures, presented to me by my lady the Queen. My companion took the missal and the cross, while the clerk put on a surplice and carried a censer. So we came to Sartak's residence and they lifted the felt which hung before the entry so that he could see us. Then they made the clerk and the interpreter bow the knee three times, but did not demand it of us. They strongly urged us to be careful not to touch the threshold of the house as we entered and left and also to chant some blessing for him. So we went in chanting *Salve regina....*

When this Coiak handed him the censer and incense, Sartak took it in his hand most carefully and examined it. When given the Psalter he took a close look at it and so did the wife who was seated beside him. When handed the Bible he asked if the Gospels were in it. I said it contained all the sacred writings. He also took the cross in his hand and asked if the image on it was of Christ. I said it was. (Nestorians ... never show the figure of Christ on their crosses, which seems to show that they have some doubts about the passion or are ashamed of it.) Then he ordered those standing by to withdraw so that he could see our ornaments better. Then I presented your letter to him, with translations in Arabic and Syriac, for I had got it translated and written in these languages at Acre.

All this took place on the feast of St. Peter in Chains (August 1st). *Source:* William of Rubruck, *Itinerary*.

13.11   CHRISTIAN RIVALS IN PEKING

Another Franciscan, John of Monte Corvino, a generation later spent thirty-five years at the court of the Great Khan at Peking. After twelve years he sent this report back.

Jan. 8 1305

I brother John of Monte Corvino of the Order of Minor Brothers came into Cathay, the realm of the Emperor of the Tartars who is called the great Khan. With the letter of the lord Pope moreover I invited the emperor himself to the catholic faith of our Lord Jesus Christ. But he has grown too old in idolatry. But he bestows many kindnesses on the Christians, and it is now the twelfth year that I am with him.

The Nestorians indeed, who bear the Christian name but deviate very far from the Christian religion, have grown so powerful in these parts that they have not allowed any Christian of another rite to have however small a chapel, nor to publish any other doctrine than the Nestorian. For to these lands there never came any Apostle or disciple of the Apostles. And so these Nestorians . . . have brought the gravest persecutions on me, declaring that I was not sent by the lord Pope but as a spy, magician, and deceiver of men. And after some time they produced other false witnesses to say that another messenger had been sent bringing the emperor a very great treasure, and that I killed him in India and took away what he was carrying. And this intriguing lasted about five years, so that I was often dragged to the Judgement Seat and threatened with death. At last by God's providence and the confession of certain persons the emperor came to know of my innocence and the malice of the rivals and sent them with wives and children into exile.

I indeed was alone in this pilgrimage without confession for eleven years, until brother Arnold a German of the province of Cologne came to me. I have built a church in the city of Khan-baliq (Peking), where is the chief residence of the king and I finished it six years ago. There I also made a bell-tower and put three bells. I have also baptized there, as I reckon, up to today about 6,000 persons. And if there had not been the above-named slanders I should have baptized more than 30,000; and I am often engaged in baptizing.

Also I have bought 40 boys one after another, the sons of pagans of an age of between seven and eleven years, who as yet were learning no religion. And I have baptized them and taught them Latin letters and our rite. And I have written for them 30 psalters with hymnaries and two breviaries. Some eleven boys now know our Office and maintain the choir services and weekly turns as we do in a convent whether I am present or not. And several of them are writing psalters and other necessary things. And the lord emperor is greatly delighted with their chanting. I strike the bells at all the hours and perform the divine Office with a congregation of babes and sucklings. But we sing by heart because we have no service-book with notes. . . .

I beg the Minister General of our Order for an antiphoner and a Legends of the Saints, a gradual and a psalter with musical notes, for I have nothing but a portable breviary with shortened lessons [for travelling friars] and a small missal. The aforesaid boys can copy them.

Now I am in the act of building another church with a view to distributing the boys among several places.

I am now old and am become white more from toils and troubles than from age; for I am 58. I have a competent knowledge of the Tartar language and script and have now translated in that language and script the whole New Testament and the Psalter, which I have written in their fairest writing. And I understand and read and preach openly in public in testimony of the law of Christ.

I arranged with king George, if he had lived, to translate the whole Latin Office, that it might be sung throughout the whole land in his dominion. And while he was alive Mass used to be celebrated in his Church according to the Latin rite in the Tartar script and tongue, both the words of the canon and the prefaces. And the son of the said king is called John because of my name. And I hope in God he will copy his father's steps.

In fact George's brother succeeded him and reverted to Nestorianism. Marco Polo called George a descendant of Prester John. He was a Nestorian who had gone over to Rome. It is interesting that the Jesuits were given leave to celebrate mass in Chinese in 1615.

13.12   MARCO POLO'S 'IF'

This passage occurs only in the edition of the Travels printed in Venice in 1553 and based, according to the editor, on a Latin manuscript 'of marvellous antiquity' now lost. This is true also of a number of other passages in the Travels which there is strong external evidence for regarding as 'genuine Marco Polo'.

Marco Polo was a business man, not a missionary. He was content to accept things as he found them, but he could see when an opportunity was missed. That was his verdict on the missions, more diplomatic than religious, which went to the Great Khan. No doubt he was over-optimistic about possibilities, but he leaves us with an uneasy conscience as we close this chapter. If only....

Kubla Khan stayed at Peking until March, the season of our Easter, and learning that this was one of our chief festivals, he summoned all the Christians and told them to bring with them the book of the four Gospels. This he caused to be incensed many times with great ceremony, then kissed it devoutly and desired all the barons and lords who were present to do the same. He always acts like this at the chief Christian festivals, such as Easter and Christmas. And he does the like at the chief feasts of the Saracens, Jews, and Idolaters. Asked why, he said:

'There are four prophets worshipped and revered by all the world. The Christians say their God is Jesus Christ, the Saracens Mahommed, the Jews Moses, and the Idolaters Buddha, the first god among idols. And I worship and reverence all four and pray that he among them who is truly the greatest in heaven may give me aid.'

But the Great Khan let it be seen that he held the Christian faith to be the truest and best, because it commands only what is perfectly good and holy. But he will not allow the Christians to carry the cross before them, because on it so great a man as Christ suffered and died.

Some may ask why, since he holds that the Christian faith is best, he does not become a Christian. Well this is the reason he gave to Masters Niccolo and Maffeo Polo when he sent them as envoys to the Pope....

'Why would you have me become a Christian? You see that the Christians of these parts are so ignorant that they cannot achieve anything, while the Idolaters can do anything they please.... They control storms, causing them to pass in whatever direction they please, and do many other marvels. Their idols speak and give them predictions on any subject they choose. If I were to become a Christian my barons and others who are not converted would ask what had induced me to be baptised and take the faith of Christ. What miracles of his had I seen? For they claim that their wonders are performed by the sanctity and power of their idols. I should not know how to answer them, so they would only be confirmed in their errors. And the Idolaters who are adepts in such surprising arts, would soon compass my death. But now go to your pope and pray him on my behalf to send me a hundred men skilled in your religion, who will be able to condemn the practices of the Idolaters to their faces and tell them that they too can do such things but will not, because they are done by the devil and evil spirits. They shall so control the Idolaters that these shall have no power to perform such things in their presence. When I see this I will denounce the Idolaters and their religion and receive baptism. Then all my barons and chiefs will be baptised also and their followers will do the same, and there will be more Christians here than in your part of the world.'

So if the pope had sent men fit to preach our religion, the Great Khan would have turned Christian; for it is an undoubted fact that he greatly desired to do so.

CHAPTER FOURTEEN

CHRISTENDOM

This chapter is about politics—struggles between popes and emperors, kings and archbishops, church and state. The differences were not trivial, but they were really only demarcation disputes about who did what and on whose authority, and not disputes about what had to be done. No one doubted that those who bore earthly rule did so by God's permission and as his duly appointed servants. Every Coronation service expressed this. In the same way no one except a few Albigensians had any doubt that God had given power to his church on earth to bind and loose in heaven; nor in the West did men doubt that in the church the primacy was Peter's and his successors'. What was at stake was whether in the last resort the emperor was dependant on the pope in something vaguely like the way that an archbishop was; or conversely, whether the emperor was the guardian of the church's purity, the man who could, if occasion demanded, call a council and see that a bad pope was removed. These stresses did not arise in the same way in the East where the emperors still ruled. In the West they were virtually powerless, leaving strong popes to give political as well as religious leadership. But in the Dark Ages one could no more count on a good pope than a strong emperor. Time and again the church had to be rescued from an evil pope, usually by the Holy Roman Emperor. But the Holy Roman Empire was as fragile as the Papacy. Moreover its base was north of the Alps in what is now Germany; in Italy the emperors were in effect only periodical visitors. The extracts in this chapter show the see-saw in operation. Sometimes the pope is on top; sometimes the emperor. It is convenient to call this dyarchy and the society of which it formed part by the name of Christendom.

The First Holy Roman Emperor

14.1

An exploration of Christendom must start with Charlemagne, the powerful ninth century Frankish king whose capital was at Aachen in the Rhineland. He was a ruler in church affairs as well as in secular. Round him he gathered a court of scholars and administrators among whom Alcuin, an Englishman born at York, was outstanding. A younger member of the circle was Einhard who came from the lower Main, a happily married man who was also abbot of monasteries at Ghent and Rouen—there was no scandal in the ninth century in the thought of a married abbot. Charlemagne's close-knit circle called each other by descriptive nicknames—Charles predictably was

David; Alcuin was Flaccus (i.e. Horace); and Einhard, a master craftsman as well as Charles's secretary, was Bezaleel, the worker 'in gold, and in silver, and in brass, and in cutting of stones, and in carving of timber' (Exodus 31, 4, 5). This is Einhard's description of his royal master:

Charles constantly went riding and hunting. This was a national habit of the Franks for there is hardly a people on earth to equal them in this respect. He enjoyed the steam that rises from hot springs, and constantly practised swimming. He swam so regularly and well that it is fair to say that no one swam better. It was partly for this reason that he built his palace at Aachen, and lived there continuously during the last years of his life up to the time of his death. It was his custom to invite his nobles and friends as well as his sons to swim in the bath, and sometimes he extended the invitation to many of his followers and body-guards.

In speech Charles was fluent and ready, able to express with clarity his thoughts on any subject. He was not merely content with his native tongue, but took the trouble to learn foreign languages. He learnt Latin so thoroughly that he could speak it as well as his mother tongue; but he could understand Greek better than he spoke it. He was so fluent that sometimes he even seemed a little garrulous.

Charles paid the greatest attention to all the liberal arts, and showed the greatest respect for those who taught them, giving them high honours. He took his lessons in Grammar from an old man, Peter of Pisa, a deacon. For all other subjects Albinus, called Alcuin, also a deacon, was his teacher. Alcuin came from Britain, was a Saxon by race, and the most learned man of his time. Charles spent much time and effort in learning Rhetoric and Dialectic, especially astronomy, from Alcuin. He learnt too the art of calculation and followed with greatest care and application the procession of the stars. He tried also to learn the scribe's art [literally 'to write'], and for this purpose used to carry with him, and keep under his pillow in bed, tablets and writing sheets so that, when he had a spare moment, he could practise the formation of letters. He made little headway, however, in this strange task, which he had taken up too late in life.

Charles was a most devout and pious Christian, the religion in which he had been brought up from infancy. It was because of his faith that he built the great and very beautiful church at Aachen, and decorated it with gold and silver and candelabras and with gates and doors of brass. He brought pillars from Rome and from Ravenna because he could not get marble columns elsewhere. As long as his health permitted, he regularly went to church for the morning, evening and night services and at the time of the Sacrifice [Mass]. . . . He carefully reformed the manner of reading and singing, in both of which he had been thoroughly trained, though he never read publicly himself nor sang, except in a low voice and with the rest of the congregation. He was most devout in relieving the poor and in making those charitable gifts which the Greeks call alms. He did this not only in his own land and in his own kingdom, but he also used to send money overseas to Syria, to Egypt, to Africa—to Jerusalem, Alexandria, and Carthage—when he heard of Christians living there in miserable poverty. It was for this reason chiefly that he cultivated the friendship of kings beyond the seas, hoping in this way to get some aid and relief to the Christians living under their rule.

14.2   'THE CHURCH DEPENDS ON YOU ALONE'   May 799

Pope Leo III was accused by the Romans of various crimes. They drove him from the city and tried to put out his eyes and cut off his tongue. He fled to Charles. Charles sent the news by messenger to Alcuin who was at Tours, where he was abbot. Alcuin replied in a letter which hinted that Charles had better take the imperial title to match his imperial power. The wording of the introductory paragraph has been much simplified.

Greetings from Flaccus Albinus to David the Peacemaker, Lord King: . . . Up to now there have been three world powers. One rules as vicar the see of blessed Peter, chief of the apostles. You have told me the things that have been done to the man who has been the present ruler of that see. The second world power has been the holder of the imperial dignity of the Second Rome [Constantinople]. It is becoming known throughout the world that he has been impiously deposed by his own people and fellow-citizens. The third power is the royal dignity with which our Lord Jesus Christ has invested you, who are more powerful than the other two, wiser and more august in your dominion. The whole safety of the churches of Christ has come to depend on you alone. You are the one who can punish crime, guide the erring, comfort the sorrowful, and reward the good.

Is it not in Rome itself, where once religion shone clear in brightest piety, that the worst examples of impiety have burst into view? Blind in their hearts, they have blinded their head. There is neither fear of God, nor wisdom, nor love there. What good can there be when all three are totally lacking? If the Romans had feared God, they would not have dared to do what they have done; if they had been wise, they would not have wished to do it; if they had been loving, they could not possibly have done it. These are the perilous times, foretold of old by him who is Truth itself, because the love of many grows cold....

14.3   CHARLES CROWNED EMPEROR

Christmas Day, 800

Charles reinstated Leo and then went to Rome himself. He explained in a public assembly that there were grave charges against Leo. Although no witness came forward to prove them, it was desirable that the pope should clear himself. Einhard recorded how 'in the presence of all the people, in the basilica of blessed Peter the Apostle, the pope, holding in his hands the gospels, went up into the pulpit and, invoking the name of the Holy Trinity, purged himself by oath.'

On Christmas Day Charles went to mass in St. Peter's. Leo took him by surprise and crowned him emperor. Einhard says that Charles was annoyed, fearing that this would worsen his relations with the eastern emperor at Constantinople. There may have been another reason for his annoyance. He had certainly been considering taking the title, but to appear to be given it by the pope was quite another matter. Three hundred years later it was frequently quoted as proof that the emperor depended on the pope, but it was so far from the realities of 800 that perhaps only a very far-sighted man could have foreseen the danger.

Charles loved the church of the holy apostle Peter at Rome more than any other holy place. He poured into its treasury silver, gold and jewels of great value.... But although he prized Rome so highly, he only went there four times in all the 47 years of his reign. He went to pay his vows and to pray, but his last visit had other purposes as well. The Romans had inflicted vile injuries on Pope Leo. They had torn out his eyes and cut off his tongue, and thus forced him to seek the king's protection. Charles, therefore, came to Rome to restore the condition of the Church, which was terribly disturbed. He spent the whole winter there. Then it was that he received the title of Emperor and Augustus. At first he disliked it so much that he declared he would not have entered the church that [Christmas] day if he could have foreseen what the Pope planned to do. But once he had taken the title, he bore very quietly the hostility it caused and the indignation of the Roman Emperors [at Constantinople]. He won them over by his magnanimity, a quality in which he doubtless far surpassed them. He sent frequent embassies to them, and called them his brothers.

14.4   The Donation of Constantine   *c.* 750

The realities of papal power in the eighth century were illustrated in the previous extracts. This did not inhibit papal dreams. Somewhere about the year 750 a clerk in the papal chancery forged the famous 'Donation of Constantine', the alleged gift of Rome and the West by the first Christian emperor to Pope Silvester in gratitude for his cure from leprosy and for baptism. This would have been a respectable and ancient title to the temporal power of the popes. About a hundred years after its production it was included in the False Decretals, a combination of genuine and spurious papal decisions, probably made in France. It was widely used by popes from the middle of the eleventh century onwards, and was accepted by everyone on both sides of the controversy. No one challenged its authenticity until the Renaissance. No one now considers it genuine. The key text is Matt. 16, 18, 19.

In the name of the holy and undivided Trinity, the Father, the Son and the Holy Spirit. The Emperor Caesar Flavius Constantinus in Christ Jesus ... to the most holy and blessed father of fathers, Silvester, Bishop of the Roman city and Pope; and to all his successors, the pontiffs, who shall sit in the chair of blessed Peter to the end of time; ...

The first day after my reception of the mystery of Holy Baptism and the cure of my body from the filthiness of leprosy I understood that there is no other God than the Father, the Son and the Holy Spirit, whom most blessed Silvester, the Pope, preaches, a Trinity in unity and Unity in trinity. For all the gods of the nations, whom I have hitherto worshipped, are shown to be demons, the works of men's hands. And the same venerable father told us clearly how great power in heaven and earth our Saviour gave to His Apostle, blessed Peter, when in answer to questioning He found him faithful and said: 'Thou art Peter, and upon this rock I will build My Church; and the gates of hell shall not prevail against it.' Attend, ye mighty, and incline the ear of your heart to what the good Lord and Master gave in addition to His disciple when He said: 'I will give unto thee the keys of the kingdom of heaven, and whatsoever thou shalt bind on earth shall be bound in heaven, and whatsoever thou shalt loose on earth shall be loosed in heaven.' And when I learned these things at the mouth of the blessed Silvester, and since I found that I was wholly restored to health by the beneficence of blessed Peter himself ... we therefore ordain and decree that he shall rule as well over the four principal sees, Antioch, Alexandria, Constantinople, and Jerusalem, as also over all the churches of God in all the world. And the Pontiff who for the time being presides over that most holy Roman Church shall be the highest and chief of all priests in the whole world, and according to his decision shall all matters be settled which shall be taken in hand for the service of God or the confirmation of the faith of Christians. . . .

Wherefore, that the pontifical crown . . . may be adorned with glory and influence even beyond the dignity of the earthly empire, we hand over and relinquish our palace, the city of Rome, and all the provinces, places, and cities of Italy and the Western regions to the most blessed Pontiff and Universal Pope, Silvester; and we ordain by our Pragmatic Constitution that they shall be governed by him and his successors, and we grant that they shall remain under the authority of the Holy Roman Church.

Wherefore we have thought it fitting that our empire and royal power be transferred to the Eastern regions, and that a city bearing our name be built in an excellent place in the province of Byzantia, and that there our empire be established since it is not fitting that the earthly Emperor should bear sway in the same place where the sovereign of priests and the head of the Christian religion has been placed by the Heavenly Emperor.

14.5   The Emperor Deposes the Pope   963

In the tenth century the condition of the church in Rome was so bad that it could only be reformed by outside intervention. Otto the Great had been king in Germany since 936. In 962 he came to Rome to be crowned Holy Roman Emperor by John XII, who had succeeded to the Papacy seven years before when he had been a mere boy of seventeen. Almost as soon as he had crowned Otto, and the new emperor had left Rome, the pope started a rebellion with the help of Moslems and Hungarians. Otto returned, drove out the pope and presided over a synod of Italian and German bishops. What happened there is described by bishop Liutprand of Cremona:

As the Romans could not understand his native Saxon tongue, the emperor bade Liutprand bishop of Cremona to deliver the following speech in the Latin language to all the Romans.

'I call upon you all by the Lord God, whom no one, even if he wishes, can deceive, and by his holy mother the pure virgin Mary, and by the most precious body of the chief of the apostles, in whose church this is now being read, cast no foul words against the lord pope nor accuse him of anything that he has not really done and that has not been witnessed by men on whom we can rely.'

Thereupon the bishops, the priests, the deacons, the rest of the clergy, and the whole Roman people cried out as one man:—'If Pope

John has not committed all the shameful crimes that the deacon Benedict read out to us and done things even worse and more disgusting than those, may the most blessed Peter, whose verdict closes the gates of heaven against the unworthy and opens them for the righteous, never free us from the chains of our sins.'

So the holy synod pronounced: 'If it please the holy emperor let a letter be sent to the lord pope that he come here and purge himself from all these charges.'

Thereupon a letter was sent to him as follows: '... Know then that you are charged, not by a few men but by all the clergy and laity alike, of homicide, perjury, sacrilege, and of the sin of unchastity with your own kinswoman and with two sisters. They tell me too something that makes me shudder, that you have drunk wine for love of the devil, and that in dice you have asked the help of Jupiter, Venus, and the other demons.'

When they arrived at Tivoli they could not find the pope. He had gone off into the country with bow and arrows and no one could tell them where he was. Not being able to find him they returned with the letter to Rome and the holy synod met for the third time.... To the emperor the Roman pontiffs and the other clergy and all the people replied:

'A mischief for which there is no precedent must be cauterized by methods equally novel. If the pope's moral corruption only hurt himself and not others, we should have to bear with him as best we could. But how many chaste youths by his example have become unchaste? How many worldly men by association with him have become reprobates? We therefore ask your imperial majesty that this monster, whom no virtue redeems from vice, shall be driven from the holy Roman Church and another be appointed in his place, who by the example of his goodly conversation may prove himself both ruler and benefactor, living rightly himself and setting us an example of like conduct.'

Then the emperor said: 'I agree with what you say; nothing will please me more than for you to find such a man and to give him control of the holy, universal see.'

At that all cried with one voice: 'We elect as our shepherd, Leo, the venerable chief notary of the holy Roman Church, a man of proved worth, deserving of the highest sacerdotal rank. He shall be the supreme and universal pope of the Holy Roman Church, and we hereby reprobate the apostate John because of his vicious life.' [At this time Leo was a layman.]

14.6　The Pope's Kingdoms

The change from the degraded and humiliated papacy of the previous extract to the powerful and reformed papacy illustrated in this and the following section is explicable only in the light of the Cluniac movement (see chapter 6). Hildebrand (*c.* 1020–1085) was pope as Gregory VII from 1073 and had been the most important figure at the papal court since 1050. The first extract shows the Donation of Constantine being put to practical use—'from ancient times subject to St. Peter in full sovereignty'. The second extract shows Gregory basing a claim on more recent and more authentic history. Hungary had been Christianized by Stephen who was crowned in 1001 with a crown specially sent by the pope. He took the title Apostolic King.

A　　　　　　　　　　　SPAIN　　　　　　　　　　　1073

Gregory, Roman pontiff-elect, to all the barons [in France] who intend to make an expedition into Spain, greeting for evermore in Jesus Christ.

We are certain that it is not a secret as far as you are concerned that the kingdom of Spain has from of old been subject to St. Peter in full sovereignty and still is, though it has now been occupied for a long time by pagans.... The Church may indeed lose the enjoyment of property that once was hers by God's will, but never so long as God lives can she forfeit her title to it unless by a lawful conveyance. Therefore Count Evulus of Roucy, whose reputation we believe is well known to you, plans to invade that country and rescue it from pagan hands. He has received a grant from the Apostolic See which provides that he shall hold in the name of St. Peter those lands from which he can drive the pagans by his own effort and the help of others on the terms agreed between us.

B　　　　　　　　　　　HUNGARY　　　　　　　　　　　1074

To King Solomon of Hungary.

As you may learn from the chief men of your country, king Stephen long ago devoutly gave the kingdom of Hungary to St. Peter as the absolute property of the Roman Church under its full jurisdiction and control. Moreover after the emperor Henry (III) of pious memory had conquered that kingdom he sent a spear and a crown to the shrine of St. Peter and celebrated his triumph by delivering the regalia to the seat from which he knew the royal authority derived.

In spite of this we hear that you, who in other ways too are far from behaving as a king should, have dishonoured St. Peter and denied him his right, as far as you could, by accepting his kingdom as a fief from the king of the Germans. If this is so, you realise how much of

St. Peter's favour or our good will you can expect. They will not be forthcoming; nor can you hope long to escape the apostolic censure unless you correct your fault and acknowledge that your sceptre is held as a fief of the apostolic and not of the royal majesty.

Christ crowning Emperor Henry II and the Empress, 1014
From Henry II's Gospel Book, Munich Staatsbibliothek, Lat. 4452

Who Makes a Bishop? The Investiture Contest

The pope's claim to be Caesar's heir was never more than shadowy, but his presence inside every state was a thoroughly practical matter, and an awkward one for kings and emperors. To some extent every bishop was bound to be the pope's man since the pope was the supreme bishop. In another way every bishop had to be the king's man since bishops were among the chief men of the realm without whose educated support government could hardly have functioned. They were as well among the principal landowners.

14.7   CIVIL WAR IN THE CHURCH   January 1076

Bishops were not necessarily on the pope's side in disputes between Rome and secular rulers. By no means all bishops were willing to recognize him as an absolute spiritual monarch to whom they owed unqualified obedience. The emperor Henry IV was able to muster very strong church support in his quarrel with Gregory VII as the Synod of Worms showed.

Siegfried, archbishop of Mainz (and 25 other bishops mainly from Germany) to brother Hildebrand.

You have spread to all the churches of Italy, Germany, Gaul, and Spain the quarrelsome flames with which you set the Roman church on fire in ruinous party strife. You have taken away from the bishops as much of their authority as you possibly could, authority which, as is well known, is divinely theirs by the grace of the Holy Spirit conveyed in their consecration. You have sacrificed ecclesiastical discipline to mob clamour. No one is now recognized to be a bishop or priest unless he has obtained his office by degrading subordination to your magnificence. You have reduced to miserable confusion the vigour of the apostolic order and the perfection by which, as the Teacher of the Gentiles commends to our attention, the various members of the Body of Christ ought to be joined together (Cp. 1 Cor. 12).

For this reason we renounce, now and for the future, all obedience to you, obedience which in fact we never promised you. And since you have publicly announced that not one of us is a bishop in your eyes, so from henceforth you shall be no Pope to us.

14.8   THE POPE DEPOSES THE EMPEROR   February, 1076
Gregory not only excommunicated Henry (deprived him of the sacraments), but at once deposed him.

God has given me through blessed Peter, chief of the apostles, ... the power of binding and loosing in heaven and on earth. Relying on this article of belief ... I prohibit Henry the king, son of Henry the emperor, who has risen up against your Church with unexampled arrogance, from ruling in Germany and Italy. And I release all Christians from the oaths which they have sworn or shall swear to him; I forbid all men to serve him as king ... and I bind him with the bonds of anathema.

14.9   HENRY GOES TO CANOSSA   January 21, 1077
Gregory's risky ruthlessness worked at least for a time. Henry was forced literally to his knees. Gregory described the astonishing scene in a letter he wrote to the German princes, Henry's subordinates but Gregory's allies. In the same way that many bishops had reservations about a papal autocrat's power over them, so many lay princes had misgivings about the imperial power. This was the material basis of Gregory's success.

Gregory VII to the German Princes

Because for the love of justice you have made common cause with us and run the same risks in fighting in Christ's service, we have taken special trouble to send you this accurate account of the king's humble penance and absolution, and of everything that has happened from the day he entered Italy to the present time.

We came to Lombardy, as arranged with your envoys, about twenty days before the date at which some of your leaders were to meet us at the pass. We waited there for their arrival which would have made it possible for us to cross over into that region. But when that time had come and gone, and we were told that because of the present troubles—as indeed we can well believe—no escort could be provided for us, we were in considerable anxiety about the best course for us to take since we had no alternative method of reaching you.

Meanwhile we received reliable information that the king was on the way to us. Before he entered Italy he sent us word that he would make satisfaction to God and St. Peter. He offered to amend his way of life and to be and remain obedient to us, provided only that we gave him absolution and the apostolic blessing. We held back our reply for a long time while we took advice. We sent messengers back and forth reproaching him bitterly for his outrageous conduct. Finally, of his own free-will and without any sign of hostility or defiance, he came with a few followers to the castle of Canossa where we were staying. Standing there before the castle gate, barefoot and coarsely clothed, on three successive days he begged ceaselessly and with many tears for our apostolic help and comfort. At last all who were present or who heard the story were so moved by pity and compassion that they supported his request with their own tearful prayers. They were all astonished by our unaccustomed severity. Some even protested that, so far from confronting him with apostolic authority in all its gravity, we were behaving like a cruel and savage tyrant.

At last, overcome by the persistent demonstration of his penitence and the insistence of everyone around us, we released him from the bonds of anathema and received him back into the grace of Holy Mother Church, accepting from him the guarantees described below which were witnessed and confirmed by the abbot of Cluny; our [spiritual] daughters, the Countess Matilda and the Countess Adelaide; and other princes, bishops, and laymen. . . .

Henry soon recovered his strength and the struggle with the Papacy went on. In a letter to the Bishop of Metz, Gregory puts clearly the nature of the psychological hold which the church had over the minds of all men—the pope's opponents as well as his supporters.

Every Christian king on his death-bed seeks as a pitiful suppliant the help of a priest so that he may escape hell's prison, pass from darkness into light, and stand at God's judgment seat absolved from the bondage of his sins. What layman, to say nothing of priests, has ever in his last hour asked an earthly king's help for the salvation of his soul? And what king or emperor can, by reason of his office, save a Christian from the power of the devil by holy baptism, number him

Pope Paschal II confers the Imperial Regalia
on Henry V in Rome, 1111
Ekkehard of Aura, *Chronicon Universale,*
C.C.C. Camb. MS 373

among the sons of God, strengthen him with holy unction? Can any king by his own words make the body and blood of our Lord—the greatest act in our Christian religion? Which of them has the power to bind and loose in heaven and on earth? These considerations make it clear how far the priestly office excels.

What king can ordain a single clerk in holy church, much less depose him for any fault?—for in the church a higher rank is needed to depose than to ordain. Bishops may consecrate bishops, but cannot depose them without the authority of the apostolic see. What man, therefore, of even moderate intelligence can hesitate to give priests precedence over kings?

14.11   PEACE AT LAST   September 1122

The investiture contest was finally settled in the next generation by an agreement between the emperor Henry V and Pope Calixtus II. The concordat of Worms recognized the dual nature of a bishop's position in medieval society by separating homage from canonical obedience and providing separate civil and religious ceremonies. Plate 8 in which Otto III (d. 1002) gives a bishop his crozier or pastoral staff shows the old practice which the emperors now gave up.

I, Calixtus, bishop, servant of the servants of God, do grant to you, my beloved son, Henry ... that bishops and abbots of the German kingdom shall be elected in your presence, without simony or violence. If there is any dispute, you shall, with the advice or judgment of the archbishop and bishops of the province, determine which claimant has the better right and give him support. The bishop or abbot-elect shall receive from you the sceptre, the token of his secular authority, and shall perform his lawful duty to you in respect of it.

In the name of the holy and indivisible Trinity, I, Henry, by the grace of God, Emperor of the Romans, Augustus, for the love of God and the holy Roman Church ... do surrender to God ... all investiture by ring and pastoral staff. I grant that in all the churches in my kingdom or empire there shall be canonical election and free consecration. All the possessions ... of St. Peter which ... have been seized, and which I hold, I restore to that same holy Roman Church.

14.12 The Murder of Thomas Becket   29 December 1170

There were two separate legal systems in the middle ages operating on different principles. Church law governed all men some of the time and claimed to govern some men all of the time (clerks in holy orders). What then

should happen to a clerk who was a criminal? Henry II maintained, to quote
F. W. Maitland, that 'A clerk who is suspected of a crime is to be brought
before the temporal court and accused there ... this done, he will be sent to
the ecclesiastical court for trial; if found guilty he is to be deposed from his
orders and brought back to the temporal court; he will then—perhaps
without any further trial, but this is not clear—be sentenced to the layman's
punishment, death or mutilation.' Becket disagreed. No one should be
punished twice for the same offence, a view he based on Nahum 1.9. This is
the most important element in the quarrel between king and archbishop
which led to Becket's murder, to his being made a saint two years later, and to
the king's virtual capitulation on the most important matters in dispute. As
Maitland said, 'the result was lamentable ... for centuries yet to come the
benefit of clergy will breed crime and impede the course of reasonable and
impartial justice.'

The account of Becket's murder given here is by Edward Grim who had
only lately come to Canterbury to see the archbishop. All four knights had
come from Henry's court in Normandy, prompted by his incautious words,
'Will no man rid me of this turbulent priest?' The second knight was William
de Tracy.

Before long the butchers were back in full armour, with swords, axes,
and hatchets, and other weapons fit for the crime they had conceived.
Finding the doors bolted and not opened to their knocking, they
turned aside by a private path through an orchard till they came to a
wooden partition which they hacked until they had broken it down.
At this dreadful noise the terrified clerks and servants were scattered
hither and thither like sheep before wolves. Those who remained
cried out to the archbishop that he should flee to the church; but he,
true to his promise that he would not flee for fear of death from those
who kill the body, refused to go....

The monks urged him, declaring that he ought not to be absent
from vespers, which were then being said in the church ... and when
they failed to persuade him by argument and entreaties, they seized
hold of him in spite of his resistance and pulled, dragged, and pushed
him into the church, not heeding his shouts to let him go.

The four knights came hard on their heels with rapid strides. A
certain sub-deacon came with them, armed with malice like their
own. This Hugh, suitably called Mauclerc, evil clerk, showed no
reverence to God or his saints, as he proved by what he did.
Immediately the archbishop entered the church the monks stopped
vespers and ran to meet him, praising God that they saw their father
alive and safe when they had heard he was dead. They also hurried to
bar the foe from the slaughter of their shepherd by bolting the folding

doors leading into the church. But Christ's wonderful champion ('athlete') ordered the doors to be thrown open:

'It is not right to make a fortress of the house of prayer. The church of Christ, even if it is not closed, gives protection enough to her children. By suffering, not by fighting, shall we triumph over the foe, for we came to suffer, not resist.'

And immediately these sacrilegious men entered the house of peace and reconciliation, with drawn swords, striking terror into the beholders by the very sight of them and the clanging of their armour....

In mad anger the knights shouted, 'Where is Thomas Becket, traitor to the King and the realm?'

When he did not answer they cried out even louder, repeatedly, 'Where is the archbishop?'

At this, fearlessly—as it is written, the righteous are bold as a lion (Prov. 28, 1)—he descended the steps whither the monks had dragged him in fear of the knights, and answered, in a perfectly clear voice,

'Lo! here am I, no traitor to the king, but a priest. What do you seek from me?'

'... Absolve and restore to communion those you have excommunicated and give back their offices to those you have suspended.'

'They have made no satisfaction and I will not absolve them.'

'Then you shall die now and get what you deserve.'

'I am ready to die for my Lord, that through my blood the Church may gain peace and liberty. But in the name of Almighty God I forbid you to harm any of my men, whether clerks or laymen'...

Then they rushed at him, laid sacrilegious hands on him, violently striving to drag him out of the church and kill him outside or carry him off in bonds, as they afterwards confessed. But as they could not force him from the pillar, one (Fitzurse) seized hold of him and clung to him more closely. The archbishop shook him off, saying,

'Pander! Touch me not, Reginald; you owe me faith and allegiance. You are behaving like madmen, you and your accomplices.'

Aflame with a terrible fury at this repulse, the knight brandished his sword about that sacred head.

'No faith nor allegiance do I owe you against my fealty to my lord the king.'

Then the unconquered martyr, knowing the hour had come which should release him from the miseries of this mortal life and bring him the crown of immortality, prepared and promised by the Lord, bent his head in prayer and joined his hands together, and raised them, and commended his cause and that of the Church to God, to St. Mary, and the blessed martyr St. Denys.

Scarcely had he spoken when the wicked knight, fearing that he would be rescued by the people and escape alive, leapt upon him and wounded the sacrificial lamb of God in the head, slicing off the top of the skull, where the sacred chrism had dedicated him to God, and by the same stroke he almost severed the arm of him who tells this story. For he, when other monks and clerks had fled, stood by the saintly archbishop and held his arms around him till the one he interposed was nearly severed. . . .

Becket received a second blow on the head, but still he staunchly stood. At the third blow he fell on knees and elbows, offering himself a living sacrifice and murmuring,

'For the Name of Jesus and the protection of the Church I am ready to embrace death.'

But the third knight (Richard Brito) inflicted a terrible wound on him as he lay prostrate, dashing the sword against the pavement. The whole crown of the head was hacked off, so that blood white with the brain and the brain red with the blood dyed the cathedral floor with the white of the lily and the red of the rose, the colours of the Virgin Mother and of the martyrs and confessors.

The fourth knight (Hugh of Morville) beat back any who tried to intervene, giving the others freedom and licence to commit the crime. But the fifth, no knight, but that clerk who had entered with the knights (that a fifth wound might not be lacking to him who in other things had imitated Christ) put his foot on the neck of the holy priest and precious martyr and, horrible to describe, strewed the blood and brains over the pavement, calling out to the others,

'Let us be off, knights. This fellow will rise no more.'

14.13　Paying for the Papacy　　　　　　　　　　　　　　1244–45

Someone, clerical or lay, or some body of people owned the right to appoint or elect to every ecclesiastical position from the smallest parish to the archbishopric of Canterbury. But it was possible for these rights to be over-ridden by the pope, who needed vacancies which he could fill with his officials, who would usually draw the income but leave someone else to do the duty. This was the cause of endless disputes. These were not quarrels between English churchmen and English laymen, but between Englishmen, clerical and lay, and the papacy. The writer of the following account, Matthew Paris, was a monk of St. Albans (and see picture on p. 171).

The new pope (Innocent IV) sent to England a new extortioner. Master Martin brought with him a papal commission which gave him power to excommunicate, suspend, and punish in a variety of ways those who set themselves against what he wanted to do. Armed with this authority he stopped the English prelates from filling vacant benefices until the pope's wishes had been met, for the pope demanded the income from them for the support of his own clergy and relatives. However Master Martin thought it beneath him to take the income of any benefice worth less than thirty marks, for fear that so great a man as he should seem to be collecting trifles. So Master Martin began in a hectoring way to exact from prelates, especially monastic prelates, gifts, preferably of good, sound saddle-horses. He used to write to an abbot or prior enjoining him strictly to send him horses fit for the lord pope's special clerk to sit upon. He severely punished those who refused or excused themselves even if, like the abbot of Malmesbury or the prior of Merton, they had good reasons for doing this. He suspended them till they had given complete satisfaction.

He was most careful to get wind of vacant livings and prebends in order to offer them to the capacious maw of papal destitution. When, for instance, the richest prebend of Salisbury, usually held by the precentor, fell vacant, Master Martin at once laid his greedy hands upon it, against the bishop's wish and to his great sorrow and that of the whole chapter. By papal authority he gave it to a very young relative of his, causing in this way general bitterness and astonishment. Many had hoped and believed that the Roman Curia, scourged by God's hand with so many blows, would curb its avarice.

The 'magnates and commonality' of England appealed to the pope. They set out the many subsidies, especially 'Peter's Pence', given by England to Rome, and continued:

We cannot be silent about our own burden. . . . We refer to the fact that Martin, without the permission of our lord the king, and with fuller powers than ever we have seen a legate hold, even when invited by our lord the king, has lately come to this realm. Although he does not wear a legate's dress, yet he multiplies a legate's functions. Daily he claims fresh, unheard-of powers so that he surpasses even himself in excesses. He has conferred on Italians certain benefices worth thirty marks or more, which happened to be vacant. When they die others are brought in without the knowledge of the patrons who are thus defrauded of their right of presentation. Moreover Master Martin tries to make future provision of a similar kind for other Italians by reserving to the Apostolic See the right of presentation to benefices, which now have incumbents, when next they become vacant. He also exacts over-large 'pensions' from monastic communities, excommunicating or placing under an interdict those who contradict or oppose him, to the great peril of their souls.

Since, therefore, this Master Martin, to the great disturbance of the whole realm, exercises these powers, which we cannot think you have knowingly given him, seeing that in many matters his functions are more extensive than we have ever known a legate's to be . . . we now, in all possible humility and devotion, pray your fatherly goodness to relieve us by a timely remedy from the burdens we have here set out. . . .

[As the appeal failed, the 'magnates and commonality' took direct action.]

On the morrow of the feast of Saints Peter and Paul [June 30] . . . Fulk Fitzwarin was sent on behalf of the community of the realm to Master Martin, who was then living in London at the New Temple. Fulk, frowning, thus addressed him:

'Begone, and leave England at once.'

Martin replied: 'Who bids me do so? Is it you, on your own authority?'

Fulk answered: 'I am the mouthpiece of all those who lately appeared in arms at Luton and Dunstable; it is they who bid you do this. And if you will listen to good advice, do not delay more than two days, lest you and all your people be torn to pieces.'

So Fulk went away in anger, after backing his threats with a terrible oath. Martin in alarm and terror went straight to our lord the king.

'My lord,' he said, 'this is what I have just heard. Is this done on your authority, or by the presumption of your followers?'

'I am not responsible for this,' the king answered, 'but my barons can scarce be kept from revolting against me, because I have so long allowed you to practise on them in my realm robbery and wrong that passes all bounds; and I could hardly restrain them in their rage from rushing upon you and tearing you limb from limb.'

Martin replied humbly in frightened tones: 'Then I crave, for the love of God and out of respect for our lord the pope, free passage and a safe departure from your land under your safe-conduct.'

But the king answered in a terrible rage: 'May the devil take you to hell and give you a conduct through it!'

And when his attendants had with difficulty pacified him, the king ordered Robert Norris, his chamberlain, to conduct Martin in safety as far as the sea. Martin started on his journey at once, keeping close to the side of his escort Robert; and whenever he happened to catch sight of any riders or wayfarers he was seized with such fear and trembling that if the earth had opened up he would have hidden under the turf. And on their way they came to the edge of a wood, which had been put up for sale by the archbishop-elect of Canterbury, and the countrymen had come to buy and choose the trees. Catching sight of them, Martin is terrified, and says to his escort Robert:

'Alas, alas! what I feared has happened. Look they are going to attack us! My good lord Robert, have you son, nephew, relative or friend for whom you desire preferment in the Church? I am ready to get you all you ask. See how they lie in ambush for my life; protect me under the shadow of your wings.'

Robert replied: 'God forbid that any friend of mine should by any means light upon such a step to an ecclesiastical benefice. Who those are yonder I do not know; but I will go to them at once, if you will await me here, and, by showing them the king's warrant, check their presumption in case they be ill-disposed.'

And when, on coming up to them, he learnt the facts of the case, he quickly returned to Martin, and, to deceive him, said:

'It was only with difficulty that I restrained them in their rage from cutting you to pieces. But now let us proceed, stealthily and cautiously, lest a worse thing come upon you. Take ship, and, if you are wise, depart to return no more, lest, unfortunately, you fall into the snares of those who seek your life.'

From that time, therefore, Martin spared not his horse's flanks, but chided his escort's delay and hastened to the sea. And when he arrived at Dover, he embarked on St. Swithin's Day [July 15] and gladdened the hearts of many by his departure.

14.14 The Zenith of Papal Claims 1302

Papal claims reached their culmination under Boniface VIII and their most complete expression in the Bull (papal edict) *Unam Sanctam*. In the first paragraph Boniface put outside the Church, and that meant outside salvation, all those Orthodox Christians who looked to Constantinople rather than to Rome. The second paragraph asserted that secular rulers are subordinate to spiritual, and that, while the pope might depose the emperor, he himself was subject to correction only by God.

The Bull infuriated Philip the Fair of France whose men raided Alagna, the modern Anagni, where Boniface was staying, and held him prisoner for three days. Boniface died only a month later. All that he had built up crumbled away. Six years after his death came the 'Babylonish Captivity' when the popes lived at Avignon under French tutelage. This was followed by the 'Great Schism' when three rival popes competed for the allegiance of the western world.

There is a case for considering Boniface the arch-villain of the *Divine Comedy*; but, though the Imperialist Dante put Boniface deep in hell, he remembered that even an unworthy pope was still God's vicar. An Imperialist's conscience would only let him use one hand to fight the Papacy.

> To put crimes past and future in the shade,
> I see the Lily storm Alagna's paling
> And in Christ's Vicar, Christ a captive made.

(Purgatorio 20.85. The lily is the Fleur de lys of France.)

We are obliged by the Faith to believe and hold ... that there is one Holy Catholic and Apostolic Church. Outside this Church there is neither salvation nor pardon for sins.... In the Church there is one Lord, one faith, one baptism ... one Body and one Head, Christ—not two heads like a monster. And Christ's Vicar is Peter and Peter's successor, for the Lord said to Peter 'Feed my sheep' (John 21, 15–17). My sheep, he said, in general, not some particular sheep. This means that he committed all his sheep to Peter. And so, when the Greeks and others claim that they were not committed to Peter, they automatically admit that they are not among Christ's sheep, for the Lord says in John (10, 16), 'There is one fold and one shepherd.'

And we learn from the words of the Gospel that in this Church and under her authority there are two swords, the spiritual and the temporal. For when the apostles said, 'Look, Lord, here are two swords'—that is here in the Church, for it was apostles who were speaking; the Lord's answer was not, 'It is too much,' but 'It is enough' (Luke 22, 38). There is no doubt that a man who denies that the temporal sword is under the authority of Peter misunderstands what the Lord says, to Peter, 'Put your sword into its sheath' (John 18, 11). Both swords are held by the authority of the Church; but the temporal sword is to be used for the Church, the spiritual by her; the spiritual by the priest, the temporal by kings and captains but at the will and by the permission of the priest.

If, therefore, a temporal power goes wrong it is to be judged by the spiritual power; and similarly a lower power by a higher. But if the supreme power goes wrong, it can only be judged by God, not by man: as the Apostle says, 'The spiritual man judges all things, but is himself to be judged by no man' (1 Cor. 2, 15).

Though a man has received and exercised this power, yet it is not a human power but divine. It is given to Peter and established on a rock for him and his successor in Christ in the words, 'Whatever you bind on earth shall be bound in heaven' (Matt. 16, 19). These words were spoken by the mouth of Him whom Peter acknowledged to be the Christ, the Son of the Living God. He who resists this power, resists the order established by God.... Furthermore we declare, state, define, and pronounce that it is altogether necessary for every human being to be subject to the Roman pontiff.

Man's Double Goal

Both Aquinas and Dante thought deeply about the nature of human society. Both saw man in the light of eternity and both therefore saw him in a different way from most modern thinkers. There is little in the extract from Aquinas except the last paragraph, with which Dante would have disagreed, and little in the two extracts from Dante which Aquinas would not have accepted. At the time their disagreement (clearly stated at the end of the extracts) seemed more important than their agreement.

14.15   AS SEEN BY AQUINAS

To govern is to lead the thing governed to its right destination in a suitable way. Thus a ship is said to be governed when, by the mariner's skill, it is brought by a direct route unharmed to harbour. So if anything is bound to an end outside itself, like a ship to a harbour, the governor's duty is not only to preserve it unharmed, but further to bring it to its end. But if on the contrary there is something whose end is not outside itself, then the governor's efforts would only tend to preserve the thing itself undamaged....

The ship's carpenter has to repair anything broken in the ship, but the mariner bears the responsibility for bringing the ship to port. It is the same with man. A doctor preserves his life in health, the tradesman supplies the necessities of his life, the teacher takes care to teach him the truth, and the tutor sees that he acts according to reason. If a man were not destined for any other end outside himself, these cares would be enough for him....

But man's destiny is the possession of God, and he cannot fulfil it by human power, but by divine power. Therefore the task of leading him to that end belongs not to human government but to divine.... So the ministry of this realm has been entrusted not to earthly kings but to priests and very specially to the chief priest, the successor of St. Peter, the Vicar of Christ, the Roman Pontiff, to whom all the kings of Christendom are to be subject, as to our Lord Jesus Christ himself.

Pagan priests were subjects to kings quite rightly, because they and the worship of their gods were only aimed at good fortune on this earth, where the common good was the responsibility of kings. Similarly, under the law of the Old Testament, prosperity was promised (by the true God, not by the pagan demons) to the people of the Covenant. So their priests, we read, were also subject to the kings. But under New Testament law there is a higher priesthood to guide people to heavenly bliss. Consequently by the law of Christ kings must be subject to priests.

Source: Aquinas, *On the Governance of Rulers.*

14.16　　　　　　　　AS SEEN BY DANTE　　　　　　　*c.* 1310

A.

Man is the only being who holds a place midway between the corruptible and the incorruptible, and is therefore compared by philosophers to the horizon between the two hemispheres. For man is corruptible only if he is considered as a body, but as a soul he is incorruptible. Since every nature exists to fulfil a certain purpose it follows that man with his two natures has a two-fold goal—as a corruptible being and as an incorruptible.

Divine Providence has therefore set two ends for man to follow. They are the blessedness of this life, which consists in the exercise of his own natural humanity and is expressed in the earthly paradise; and the blessedness of eternal life, which consists in the enjoyment of God. His humanity cannot reach this eternal blessedness unless it is assisted by the light of God. This is the blessedness which is given us in the heavenly paradise. These different goals and kinds of blessedness must be reached by different means. To the first we come by the teachings of philosophy—provided we carry them out—and by practising the moral and intellectual virtues. To the second we attain through spiritual doctrines which transcend human reason by carrying them out with the help of the theological virtues—faith, hope and charity.

These ends and means are made clear to us in one case by human reason which shines in all its purity in the philosophers, in the other by the Holy Spirit who has revealed to us what we need to know through the prophets and sacred writers, by the mouth of the Son of God, Jesus Christ, his co-equal, and by the Apostles. But human greed would make men shy away if they were not forced, like horses, by bit and rein to follow the right way. So, because of his two goals, man needs two pilots ('directing powers'): the Sovereign Pontiff who by the light of revelation brings man to eternal life; and the Emperor who by the light of philosophy brings him to temporal felicity. None can reach this latter port—or at least very few only and with extreme difficulty—in the absence of peace among men set free from deceiving passions. This then is the object that the Protector of the Universe, that is to say the Roman Prince, should above all set himself—that men should live on earth in freedom and in peace.

(Dante: De Monarchia III. 16 simplified.)

B.

In one of his letters Dante took the same line of argument and went on to give historical reasons for believing that the emperor got his authority directly from God and not at one remove through the pope. He argued that the Incarnation did not take place until God had slowly established the Roman Empire which gave the world those twelve years of universal peace during which Jesus was born. He then turned to the New Testament and wrote:

When the Son of God had become man to reveal the Spirit, and was preaching the Gospel upon earth, he said, as though dividing the universe between himself and Caesar—'Render unto Caesar the things that are Caesar's and unto God the things that are God's' (Mark 12, 17). But if a stubborn mind still wants more proof before agreeing, let him look carefully at what Christ said when he was already a prisoner in chains. When Pilate pointed out that he had power [to release Jesus], our Light replied that this authority of which Pilate, Caesar's deputy, boasted, came from above (John 19, 10, 11). Open your eyes and see that the Lord of heaven and earth has given us a king. He it is whom Peter, the vicar of God, bids us honour (1 Peter 2, 17).

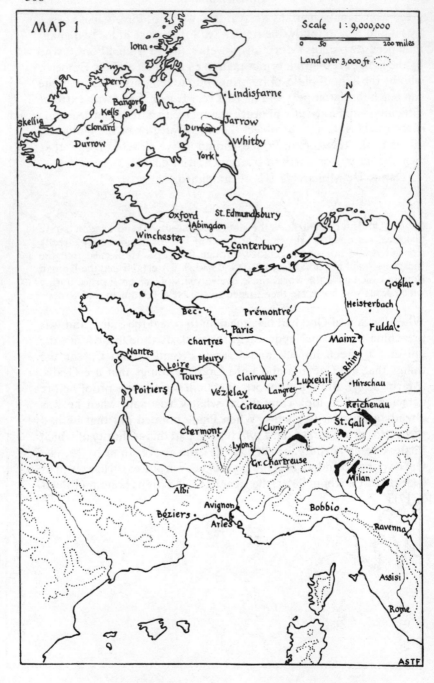

MAP 1

Scale 1 : 9,000,000

Land over 3,000 ft

N

309

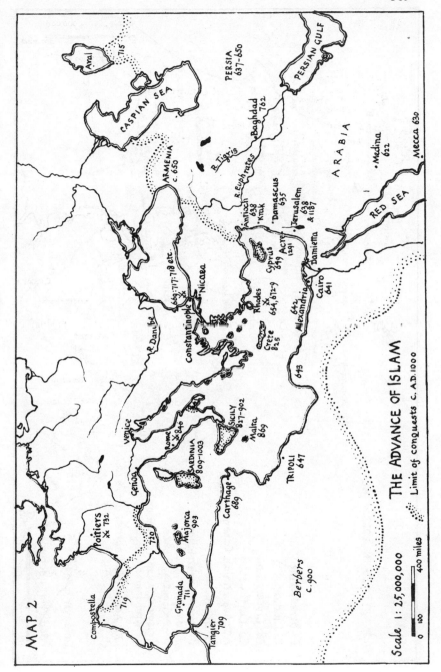

MAP 2

THE ADVANCE OF ISLAM

Limit of conquests c. A.D. 1000

Scale 1: 25,000,000

0   100   400 miles

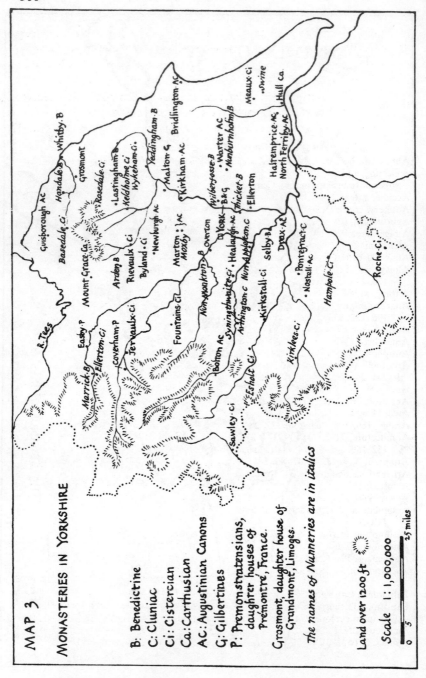

MAP 3

MONASTERIES IN YORKSHIRE

B: Benedictine
C: Cluniac
Ci: Cistercian
Ca: Carthusian
AC: Augustinian Canons
G: Gilbertines
P: Premonstratensians, daughter houses of Prémontré, France.

Grosmont, daughter house of Grandmont, Limoges.

The names of Nunneries are in italics

Land over 1200 ft

Scale 1:1,000,000

0 5   25 miles

INDEX OF SUBJECTS

INDEX OF PERSONS

Abbreviations: abp—archbishop, bp—bishop, K—king. The date in brackets is either the date of death or 'floruit'. The names of writers of extracts are in capitals, and the numbers of the extracts are in italics before the page references.

INDEX TO PLACES

The numbers in italics refer to the three maps